FROM THE MAKER OF THE TEST

The Official
SAT
Subject Test
Study Guide

Mathematics 1

The College Board
New York, N.Y.

About the College Board

The College Board is a mission-driven not-for-profit organization that connects students to college success and opportunity. Founded in 1900, the College Board was created to expand access to higher education. Today, the membership association is made up of over 6,000 of the world's leading educational institutions and is dedicated to promoting excellence and equity in education. Each year, the College Board helps more than seven million students prepare for a successful transition to college through programs and services in college readiness and college success—including the SAT® and the Advanced Placement Program®. The organization also serves the education community through research and advocacy on behalf of students, educators, and schools.

For further information, visit collegeboard.org

Copies of this book are available from your bookseller or may be ordered from College Board Publications at store.collegeboard.org or by calling 800-323-7155.

Editorial inquiries concerning this book should be addressed to the College Board, SAT Program, 250 Vesey Street, New York, New York 10281.

ISBN 13: 978-1-4573-0930-4

Printed in the United States of America

1 2 3 4 5 6 7 8 9   23 22 21 20 19 18 17

Distributed by Macmillan

Contents

The SAT Subject Tests

About SAT Subject Tests

SAT Subject Tests™ are a valuable way to help you show colleges a more complete picture of your academic background and interests. Each year, nearly one million Subject Tests are taken by students throughout the country and around the world to gain admission to the leading colleges and universities in the U.S.

SAT Subject Tests are one-hour exams that give you the opportunity to demonstrate knowledge and showcase achievement in specific subjects. They provide a fair and reliable measure of your achievement in high school—information that can help enhance your college admission portfolio. The Mathematics Level 1 Subject Test is a great way to highlight your understanding, skills, and strengths in mathematics.

This book provides information and guidance to help you study for and familiarize yourself with the Mathematics Level 1 Subject Test. It contains actual, previously administered tests and official answer sheets that will help you get comfortable with the tests' format, so you feel better prepared on test day.

The Benefits of SAT Subject Tests

SAT Subject Tests let you put your best foot forward, allowing you to focus on subjects that you know well and enjoy. They can help you differentiate yourself in a competitive admission environment by providing additional information about your skills and knowledge of particular subjects. Many colleges also use Subject Tests for course placement and selection; some schools allow you to place out of introductory courses by taking certain Subject Tests.

Subject Tests are flexible and can be tailored to your strengths and areas of interest. These are the **only** national admission tests where **you** choose the tests that best showcase your achievements and interests. You select the Subject Test(s) and can take up to three tests in one sitting. With the exception of listening tests, you can even decide to change the subject or number of tests you want to take on the day of the test. This flexibility can help you be more relaxed on test day.

REMEMBER

Subject Tests are a valuable way to help you show colleges a more complete picture of your academic achievements.

Who Should Consider Subject Tests?

Anyone can take an SAT Subject Test to highlight their knowledge of a specific subject. SAT Subject Tests may be especially beneficial for certain students:

- Students applying to colleges that require or recommend Subject Tests—be aware that some schools have additional Subject Test requirements for certain students, majors, or programs of study

- Students who wish to demonstrate strength in specific subject areas

- Students who wish to demonstrate knowledge obtained outside a traditional classroom environment (e.g., summer enrichment, distance learning, weekend study, etc.)

- Students looking to place out of certain classes in college

- Students enrolled in dual-enrollment programs

- Homeschooled students or students taking courses online

- Students who feel that their course grade may not be a true reflection of their knowledge of the subject matter

The SAT Subject Tests in Mathematics are particularly useful for students interested in majors with a quantitative focus, including Economics and STEM (Science, Technology, Engineering and Math) majors.

Who Requires the SAT Subject Tests?

Most college websites and catalogs include information about admission requirements, including which Subject Tests are needed or recommended for admission. Schools have varying policies regarding Subject Tests, but they generally fall into one or more of the following categories:

- Required for admission

- Recommended for admission

- Required or recommended for certain majors or programs of study (e.g., engineering, honors, etc.)

- Required or recommended for certain groups of students (e.g., homeschooled students)

- Required, recommended, or accepted for course placement

- Accepted for course credit

- Accepted as an alternative to fulfill certain college admission requirements

- Accepted as an alternative to fulfill certain high school subject competencies

- Accepted and considered, especially if Subject Tests improve or enhance a student's application

In addition, the College Board provides a number of resources where you can search for information about Subject Test requirements at specific colleges.

- Visit the websites of the colleges and universities that interest you.
- Visit College Search at www.collegeboard.org.
- Purchase a copy of *The College Board College Handbook*.

Some colleges require specific tests, such as mathematics or science, so it's important to make sure you understand the policies prior to choosing which Subject Test(s) to take. If you have questions or concerns about admission policies, contact college admission officers at individual schools. They are usually pleased to meet with students interested in their schools.

Subject Tests Offered

SAT Subject Tests measure how well you know a particular subject area and your ability to apply that knowledge. SAT Subject Tests aren't connected to specific textbooks or teaching methods. The content of each test evolves to reflect the latest trends in what is taught in typical high school courses in the corresponding subject.

The tests fall into five general subject areas:

English	History	Mathematics	Science	Languages	
				Reading Only	**with Listening**
Literature	United States History	Mathematics Level 1	Biology E/M	French	Chinese
	World History	Mathematics Level 2	Chemistry	German	French
			Physics	Italian	German
				Latin	Japanese
				Modern Hebrew	Korean
				Spanish	Spanish

Who Develops the Tests

The SAT Subject Tests are part of the SAT® Program of the College Board, a not-for-profit membership association of over 6,000 schools, colleges, universities, and other educational associations. Every year, the College Board serves seven million students and their parents, 24,000 high schools, and 3,800 colleges through major programs and services in college readiness, college admission, guidance, assessment, financial aid, and enrollment.

Each subject has its own test development committee, typically composed of teachers and college professors appointed for the different Subject Tests. The test questions are written and reviewed by each Subject Test Committee, under the guidance of professional test developers. The tests are rigorously developed, highly reliable assessments of knowledge and skills taught in high school classrooms.

Deciding to Take an SAT Subject Test

Which Tests Should You Take?

The SAT Subject Test(s) that you take should be based on your interests and academic strengths. The tests are a great way to indicate interest in specific majors or programs of study (e.g., engineering, pre-med, cultural studies).

You should also consider whether the colleges that you're interested in require or recommend Subject Tests. Some colleges will grant an exemption from or credit for a freshman course requirement if a student does well on a particular SAT Subject Test. Below are some things for you to consider as you decide which test(s) to take.

Think through your strengths and interests

- List the subjects in which you do well and that truly interest you.

- Think through what you might like to study in college.

- Consider whether your current admission credentials (high school grades, SAT scores, etc.) highlight your strengths.

Consider the colleges that you're interested in

- Make a list of the colleges you're considering.

- Take some time to look into what these colleges require or what may help you stand out in the admission process.

- Use College Search to look up colleges' test requirements.

- If the colleges you're interested in require or recommend SAT Subject Tests, find out how many tests are required or recommended and in which subjects.

Take a look at your current and recent course load

- Have you completed the required coursework? The best time to take SAT Subject Tests is at the end of the course, when the material is still fresh in your mind.

- Check the recommended preparation guidelines for the Subject Tests that interest you to see if you've completed the recommended coursework.

- Try your hand at some SAT Subject Test practice questions on collegeboard.org or in this book.

Don't forget, regardless of admission requirements, you can enhance your college portfolio by taking Subject Tests in subject areas that you know very well.

If you're still unsure about which SAT Subject Test(s) to take, talk to your teacher or counselor about your specific situation. You can also find more information about SAT Subject Tests on collegeboard.org.

When to Take the Tests

We generally recommend that you take the Mathematics Level 1 Subject Test after you complete three years of college-preparatory mathematics, prior to your senior year of high school, if possible. This way, you will already have your Subject Test credentials complete, allowing you to focus on your college applications in the fall of your senior year. Try to take the test soon after your courses end, when the content is still fresh in your mind.

Since not all Subject Tests are offered on every test date, be sure to check when the Subject Tests that you're interested in are offered and plan accordingly.

You should also balance this with college application deadlines. If you're interested in applying early decision or early action to any college, many colleges advise that you take the SAT Subject Tests by October or November of your senior year. For regular decision applications, some colleges will accept SAT Subject Test scores through the December administration. Use College Search to look up policies for specific colleges.

This book suggests ways you can prepare for the Subject Test in Mathematics Level 1. Before taking a test in a subject you haven't studied recently, ask your teacher for advice about the best time to take the test. Then review the course material thoroughly over several weeks.

How to Register for the Tests

There are several ways to register for the SAT Subject Tests.

- Visit the College Board's website at collegeboard.org. Most students choose to register for Subject Tests on the College Board website.

- Register by telephone (for a fee) if you have registered previously for the SAT or an SAT Subject Test. Call, toll free from anywhere in the United States, 866-756-7346. From outside the United States, call 212-713-7789.

- If you do not have access to the internet, find registration forms in *The Paper Registration Guide for the SAT and SAT Subject Tests*. You can find the booklet in a guidance office at any high school or by writing to:

  The College Board
  SAT Program
  P.O. Box 025505
  Miami, FL 33102

When you register for the SAT Subject Tests, you will have to indicate the specific Subject Tests you plan to take on the test date you select. You may take one, two, or three tests on any given test date; your testing fee will vary accordingly. Except for the Language Tests with Listening, you may change your mind on the day of the test and instead select from any of the other Subject Tests offered that day.

Student Search Service

The Student Search Service® helps colleges find prospective students. If you take the PSAT/NMSQT®, the SAT, an SAT Subject Test, or any AP® Exam, you can be included in this free service.

Here's how it works: During SAT or SAT Subject Test registration, indicate that you want to be part of the Student Search. Your name is put in a database along with other information such as your address, high school grade point average, date of birth, grade level, high school, email address, intended college major, and extracurricular activities.

Colleges and scholarship programs then use the Student Search to help them locate and recruit students with characteristics that might be a good match with their schools.

Here are some points to keep in mind about the Student Search Service:

- Being part of Student Search is voluntary. You may take the test even if you don't join Student Search.

- Colleges participating in Student Search do not receive your exam scores. Colleges can ask for the names of students within certain score ranges, but your exact score is not reported.

- Being contacted by a college doesn't mean you have been admitted. You can be admitted only after you apply. The Student Search Service is simply a way for colleges to reach prospective students.

- Student Search Service will share your contact information only with approved colleges and scholarship programs that are recruiting students like you. Your name will never be sold to a private company or mailing list.

Keep the Tests in Perspective

Colleges that require Subject Test scores do so because the scores are useful in making admission or placement decisions. Schools that don't have specific Subject Test policies generally review them during the application process because the scores can give a fuller picture of your academic achievement. The Subject Tests are a particularly helpful tool for admission and placement programs because the tests aren't tied to specific textbooks, grading procedures, or instruction methods but are still tied to curricula. The tests provide level ground on which colleges can compare your scores with those of students who come from schools and backgrounds that may be far different from yours.

It's important to remember that test scores are just one of several factors that colleges consider in the admission process. Admission officers also look at your high school grades, letters of recommendation, extracurricular activities, essays, and other criteria. Try to keep this in mind when you're preparing for and taking Subject Tests.

Fee Waivers

Students who face financial barriers to taking the SAT Subject Tests can be granted College Board fee waivers through schools and authorized community-based organizations to cover the cost of testing. Seniors who use a fee waiver to take the SAT will automatically receive four college application fee waivers to use in applying to colleges and universities that accept the waivers. You can learn about eligibility and other benefits offered to help you in the college application process at sat.org/fee-waivers.

Score Choice

In March 2009, the College Board introduced Score Choice™, a feature that gives you the option to choose the scores you send to colleges by test date for the SAT and by individual test for the SAT Subject Tests—at no additional cost. Designed to reduce your test day stress, Score Choice gives you an opportunity to show colleges the scores you feel best represent your abilities. Score Choice is optional, so if you don't actively choose to use it, all of your scores will be sent automatically with your score report. Since most colleges only consider your best scores, you should still feel comfortable reporting scores from all of your tests.

REMEMBER
Score Choice gives you an opportunity to show colleges the scores you feel best represent your abilities.

About collegeboard.org

The College Board website collegeboard.org is a comprehensive tool that can help you be prepared, connected, and informed throughout the college planning and admission process. In addition to registering for the SAT and SAT Subject Tests, you can find information about other tests and services, browse the College Board Store (where you can order *The Official Study Guide for all SAT Subject Tests* and other guides specific to mathematics, science and history), and send emails with your questions and concerns. You can also find free practice questions for each of the 20 SAT Subject Tests. These are an excellent supplement to this Study Guide and can help you be even more prepared on test day.

Once you create a free online account, you can print your SAT admission ticket, see your scores, and send them to schools.

More college planning resources The College Board offers free, comprehensive resources at Big Future™ to help you with your college planing. Visit **bigfuture.org** to put together a step-by-step plan for the entire process, from finding the right college, exploring majors and careers, and calculating costs, to applying for scholarships and financial aid.

How to Do Your Best on the SAT Subject Test

Get Ready

Give yourself plenty of time to review the material in this book before test day. The rules for the SAT Subject Tests may be different than the rules for most of the tests you've taken in high school. You're probably used to answering questions in order, spending more time answering the hard questions and, in the hopes of getting at least partial credit, showing all your work.

When you take the SAT Subject Tests, it's OK to move around within the test section and to answer questions in any order you wish. Keep in mind that the questions go from easier to harder. You receive one point for each question answered correctly. No partial credit is given, and only those answers entered on the answer sheet are scored. For each question that you try, but answer incorrectly, a fraction of a point is subtracted from the total number of correct answers. No points are added or subtracted for unanswered questions. If your final raw score includes a fraction, the score is rounded to the nearest whole number.

Avoid Surprises

Know what to expect. Become familiar with the test and test day procedures. You'll boost your confidence and feel a lot more relaxed.

- **Know how the tests are set up.** All SAT Subject Tests are one-hour multiple-choice tests. The first page of each Subject Test includes a background questionnaire. You will be asked to fill it out before taking the test. The information is for statistical purposes only. It will not influence your test score. Your answers to the questionnaire will assist us in developing future versions of the test. You can see a sample of the background questionnaire at the start of each test in this book.

- **Learn the test directions.** The directions for answering the questions in this book are the same as those on the actual test. If you become familiar with the directions now, you'll leave yourself more time to answer the questions when you take the test.

- **Study the sample questions.** The more familiar you are with question formats, the more comfortable you'll feel when you see similar questions on the actual test.

- **Get to know the answer sheet.** At the back of this book, you'll find a set of sample answer sheets. The appearance of the answer sheets in this book may differ from the answer sheets you see on test day.

- **Understand how the tests are scored.** You get one point for each right answer and lose a fraction of a point for each wrong answer. You neither gain nor lose points for omitting an answer. Hard questions count the same amount as easier questions.

A Practice Test Can Help

Find out where your strengths lie and which areas you need to work on. Do a run-through of a Subject Test under conditions that are close to what they will be on test day.

- **Set aside an hour so you can take the test without interruption.** You will be given one hour to take each SAT Subject Test.

- **Prepare a desk or table that has no books or papers on it.** No books, including dictionaries, are allowed in the test room.

- **Read the instructions that precede the practice test.** On test day, you will be asked to do this before you answer the questions.

- **Remove and fill in an answer sheet from the back of this book.** You can use one answer sheet for up to three Subject Tests.

- **For the mathematics tests,** use the calculator that you plan to use on test day.

- **Use a clock or kitchen timer to time yourself.** This will help you to pace yourself and to get used to taking a test in 60 minutes.

The Day Before the Test

It's natural to be nervous. A bit of a nervous edge can keep you sharp and focused. Below are a few suggestions to help you be more relaxed as the test approaches.

Do a brief review on the day before the test. Look through the sample questions, answer explanations, and test directions in this book, or on the College Board website. Keep the review brief; cramming the night before the test is unlikely to help your performance and might even make you more anxious.

The night before test day, prepare everything you need to take with you. You will need:

- Your admission ticket.

- An acceptable photo ID. (see page 10)

- Two No. 2 pencils with soft erasers. Do not bring pens or mechanical pencils.

- A watch without an audible alarm.

- An approved calculator with fresh batteries.

- A snack.

Know the route to the test center and any instructions for finding the entrance.

Check the time your admission ticket specifies for arrival. Arrive a little early to give yourself time to settle in.

REMEMBER
You are in control.
Come prepared.
Pace yourself.
Guess wisely.

Get a good night's sleep.

Acceptable Photo IDs

- Driver's license (with your photo)

- State-issued ID

- Valid passport

- School ID card

- Student ID form that has been prepared by your school on school stationery and includes a recognizable photo and the school seal, which overlaps the photo (go to www.collegeboard.org for more information)

The most up-to-date information about acceptable photo IDs can be found on collegeboard.org.

REMINDER   What I Need on Test Day
Make a copy of this box and post it somewhere noticeable.

I Need   **I Have**

Appropriate photo ID   _____

Admission ticket   _____

Two No. 2 pencils with clean soft erasers   _____

Watch (without an audible alarm)   _____

Snack   _____

Bottled water   _____

Directions to the test center   _____

Instructions for finding the entrance on weekends   _____

I am leaving the house at _____ a.m.

Be on time or you can't take the test.

On Test Day

You have good reason to feel confident. You're thoroughly prepared. You're familiar with what this day will bring. You are in control.

Keep in Mind

You must be on time or you can't take the test. Leave yourself plenty of time for mishaps and emergencies.

Think positively. If you are worrying about not doing well, then your mind isn't on the test. Be as positive as possible.

Stay focused. Think only about the question in front of you. Letting your mind wander will cost you time.

Concentrate on your own test. The first thing some students do when they get stuck on a question is to look around to see how everyone else is doing. What they usually see is that others seem busy filling in their answer sheets. Instead of being concerned that you are not doing as well as everyone else, keep in mind that everyone works at a different pace. Your neighbors may not be working on the question that puzzled you. They may not even be taking the same test. Thinking about what others are doing takes you away from working on your own test.

Making an Educated Guess

Educated guesses are helpful when it comes to taking tests with multiple-choice questions; however, making random guesses is not a good idea. To correct for random guessing, a fraction of a point is subtracted for each incorrect answer. That means random guessing—guessing with no idea of an answer that might be correct—could lower your score. The best approach is to eliminate all the choices that you know are wrong. Make an educated guess from the remaining choices. If you can't eliminate any choice, move on.

REMEMBER
All correct answers are worth one point, regardless of the question's difficulty level.

IMPORTANT

Cell phones are not allowed to be used in the test center or the testing room. If your cell phone is on, your scores will be canceled.

10 Tips
FOR TAKING THE TEST

1. **Read carefully.** Consider all the choices in each question. Avoid careless mistakes that will cause you to lose points.

2. **Answer the easier questions first.** Work on less time-consuming questions before moving on to the more difficult ones.

3. **Eliminate choices that you know are wrong.** Cross them out in your test book so that you can clearly see which choices are left.

4. **Make educated guesses or skip the question.** If you have eliminated the choices that you know are wrong, guessing is your best strategy. However, if you cannot eliminate any of the answer choices, it is best to skip the question.

5. **Keep your answer sheet neat.** The answer sheet is scored by a machine, which can't tell the difference between an answer and a doodle. If the machine mistakenly reads two answers for one question, it will consider the question unanswered.

6. **Use your test booklet as scrap paper.** Use it to make notes or write down ideas. No one else will look at what you write.

7. **Check off questions as you work on them.** This will save time and help you to know which questions you've skipped.

8. **Check your answer sheet regularly.** Make sure you are in the right place. Check the number of the question and the number on the answer sheet every few questions. This is especially important when you skip a question. Losing your place on the answer sheet will cost you time and may cost you points.

9. **Work at an even, steady pace and keep moving.** Each question on the test takes a certain amount of time to read and answer. Good test-takers develop a sense of timing to help them complete the test. Your goal is to spend time on the questions that you are most likely to answer correctly.

10. **Keep track of time.** During the hour that each Subject Test takes, check your progress occasionally so that you know how much of the test you have completed and how much time is left. Leave a few minutes for review toward the end of the testing period.

If you erase all your answers to a Subject Test, that's the same as a request to cancel the test. All Subject Tests taken with the erased test will also be canceled.

7 Ways
TO PACE YOURSELF

1. Set up a schedule. Know when you should be one-quarter of the way through and halfway through. Every now and then, check your progress against your schedule.

2. Begin to work as soon as the testing time begins. Reading the instructions and getting to know the test directions in this book ahead of time will allow you to do that.

3. Work at an even, steady pace. After you answer the questions you are sure of, move on to those for which you'll need more time.

4. Skip questions you can't answer. You might have time to return to them. Remember to mark them in your test booklet, so you'll be able to find them later.

5. As you work on a question, cross out the answers you can eliminate in your test book.

6. Go back to the questions you skipped. If you can, eliminate some of the answer choices, then make an educated guess.

7. Leave time in the last few minutes to check your answers to avoid mistakes.

After the Tests

Most, but not all, scores will be reported online several weeks after the test date. A few days later, a full score report will be available to you online. Your score report will also be mailed to your high school, and to the colleges, universities, and scholarship programs that you indicated on your registration form or on the correction form attached to your admission ticket. The score report includes your scores, percentiles, and interpretive information. You will only receive a paper score report if you indicate that you would like one.

What's Your Score?

Scores are available for free at www.collegeboard.org several weeks after each SAT is given. You can also get your scores—for a fee—by telephone. Call Customer Service at 866 756-7346 in the U.S. From outside the U.S., dial 212 713-7789.

Some scores may take longer to report. If your score report is not available online when expected, check back the following week. If you have not received your mailed score report by eight weeks after the test date (by five weeks for online reports), contact Customer Service by phone at 866 756-7346 or by e-mail at sat@info.collegeboard.org.

Should You Take the Tests Again?

Before you decide whether or not to retest, you need to evaluate your scores. The best way to evaluate how you really did on a Subject Test is to compare your scores to the admissions or placement requirements, or average scores, of the colleges to which you are applying. You may decide that with additional work you could do better taking the test again.

Contacting the College Board

If you have comments or questions about the tests, please write to us at the College Board SAT Program, P.O. Box 025505, Miami, FL 33102, or e-mail us at sat@info.collegeboard.org.

The Mathematics Subject Tests

Purpose

There are two, one-hour SAT Subject Tests in Mathematics: Mathematics Level 1 and Mathematics Level 2. The purpose of these tests is to measure your knowledge of mathematics through the first three years of college-preparatory mathematics for Level 1 and through precalculus for Level 2.

Mathematics Level 1 Subject Test

Format

Mathematics Level 1 is a one-hour broad survey test that consists of 50 multiple-choice questions. The test has questions in the following areas:

- Number and Operations
- Algebra and Functions
- Geometry and Measurement (plane Euclidean/measurement, coordinate, three-dimensional, and trigonometry)
- Data Analysis, Statistics, and Probability

How to Prepare

The Mathematics Level 1 Subject Test is intended for students who have taken three years of college-preparatory mathematics, including two years of algebra and one year of geometry. You are not expected to have studied every topic on the test. Familiarize yourself with the test directions in advance. The directions in this book are identical to those that appear on the test.

Calculator Use

It is NOT necessary to use a calculator to solve every question on the Level 1 test, but it is important to know when and how to use one. **Students who take the test without a calculator will be at a disadvantage.** For about 50 to 60 percent of the questions, there is no advantage, perhaps even a disadvantage, to using a calculator. For about 40 to 50 percent of the questions, a calculator may be useful or necessary.

A graphing calculator may provide an advantage over a scientific calculator on some questions. However, you should bring the calculator with which you are most familiar. If you are comfortable with both a scientific calculator and a graphing calculator, you should bring the graphing calculator.

Mathematics Level 2 Subject Test

Format

Mathematics Level 2 is also a one-hour test that contains 50 multiple-choice questions that cover the following areas:

- Number and Operations
- Algebra and Functions
- Geometry and Measurement (coordinate geometry, three-dimensional geometry, and trigonometry)
- Data Analysis, Statistics, and Probability

How to Prepare

The Mathematics Level 2 Subject Test is intended for students who have taken college-preparatory mathematics for more than three years, including two years of algebra, one year of geometry, and elementary functions (precalculus) and/or trigonometry. You are not expected to have studied every topic on the test.

Choosing Between Mathematics Levels 1 and 2

If you have taken trigonometry and/or elementary functions (pre-calculus), received grades of B or better in these courses, and are comfortable knowing when and how to use a scientific or a graphing calculator, you should select the Level 2 test. If you are sufficiently prepared to take Level 2, but elect to take Level 1 in hopes of receiving a higher score, you may not do as well as you expect. You may want to consider taking the test that covers the topics you learned most recently, since the material will be fresh in your mind. You should also consider the requirements of the colleges and/or programs you are interested in.

Pages 19 and 20 explain in greater detail the similarities and differences between the two Mathematics tests. Take the time to review this information prior to deciding which Mathematics test to take. Seek advice from your high school math teacher if you are still unsure of which test to take. Keep in mind you can choose to take either test on test day, regardless of what test you registered for.

Calculator Use

It is NOT necessary to use a calculator to solve every question on the Level 2 test, but it is important to know when and how to use one. For about 35 to 45 percent of the questions, there is no advantage, and perhaps even a disadvantage, to using a calculator. For about 55 to 65 percent of the questions, a calculator may be useful or necessary.

As with the Level 1 test, a graphing calculator may provide an advantage over a scientific calculator on some questions. However, you should bring the calculator with which you are most familiar. If you are comfortable with both a scientific calculator and a graphing calculator, you should bring the graphing calculator.

Calculator Policy: You may NOT use a calculator on any Subject Test other than the Mathematics Level 1 and Level 2 Tests.

What Calculator to Bring

- Bring a calculator that you are used to using. If you're comfortable with both a scientific calculator and a graphing calculator, bring the graphing calculator.

- Before you take the test, make sure that your calculator is in good working order. You may bring batteries and a backup calculator to the test center.

- The test center will not have substitute calculators or batteries on hand. Students may not share calculators.

- If your calculator malfunctions during one of the Mathematics Level 1 or Level 2 Tests and you do not have a backup calculator, you must tell your test supervisor when the malfunction occurs. The supervisor will then cancel the scores on that test only, if you desire to do so.

What Is NOT Permitted

- Laptops or other computers, tablets, cell phones, or smartphones, smartwatches, or wearable technology

- Models that can access the internet, have wireless, Bluetooth, cellular, audio/video recording and playing, camera, or any smartphone-type feature

- Models that have typewriter-like keypad, pen-input, or stylus

- Models that use electrical outlets, make noise, or have a paper tape (unless approved by the College Board as an accommodation)

- In addition, the use of hardware peripherals such as a stylus with an approved calculator is not permitted. Some models with touch-screen capability are not permitted (e.g., Casio ClassPad)

Additional information about calculator usage can be found on collegeboard.org.

Using Your Calculator

- Only some questions on these tests require the use of a calculator. First decide how you will solve a problem, then determine if you need a calculator. For many of the questions, there's more than one way to solve the problem. **Don't pick up a calculator if you don't need to**—you might waste time.

- **The answer choices are often rounded,** so the answer you get might not match the answer in the test book. Since the choices are rounded, plugging the choices into the problem might not produce an exact answer.

- **Don't round any intermediate calculations.** For example, if you get a result from your calculator for the first step of a solution, keep the result in the calculator and use it for the second step. If you round the result from the first step and the answer choices are close to each other, you might choose the wrong answer.

- **Read the question carefully** so that you know what you are being asked to do. Sometimes a result that you may get from your calculator is NOT the final answer. If an answer you get is not one of the choices in the question, it may be that you didn't answer the question being asked. You should read the question again. It may also be that you rounded at an intermediate step in solving the problem, and that's why your answer doesn't match any of the choices in the question.

- **Think about how you are going to solve the question** before picking up your calculator. It may be that you only need the calculator for the final step or two and can do the rest in your test book or in your head. Don't waste time by using the calculator more than necessary.

- If you are taking the **Level 1 test, make sure your calculator is in degree mode** ahead of time so you won't have to worry about it during the test. If you're taking the Level 2 test, make sure your calculator is in the correct mode (degree or radian) for the question being asked.

- For some questions on these tests, a **graphing calculator** may provide an advantage. If you use a graphing calculator, you should know how to perform calculations (e.g., exponents, roots, trigonometric values, logarithms), graph functions and analyze the graphs, find zeros of functions, find points of intersection of graphs of functions, find minima/maxima of functions, find numerical solutions to equations, generate a table of values for a function, and perform data analysis features, including finding a regression equation.

- **You will not be allowed to share calculators.** You will be dismissed and your scores canceled if you use your calculator to share information during the test, or to remove test questions or answers from the test room.

Comparing the Two Tests

Although there is some overlap between Mathematics Levels 1 and 2, the emphasis for Level 2 is on more advanced content. Here are the differences in the two tests.

Topics Covered*	Approximate Percentage of Test	
	Level 1	Level 2
Number and Operations	10–14	10–14
Operations, ratio and proportion, complex numbers, counting, elementary number theory, matrices, sequences, *series*, *vectors*		
Algebra and Functions	38–42	48–52
Expressions, equations, inequalities, representation and modeling, properties of functions (linear, polynomial, rational, exponential, *logarithmic*, *trigonometric*, *inverse trigonometric*, *periodic*, *piecewise*, *recursive*, *parametric*)		
Geometry and Measurement	38–42	28–32
Plane Euclidean/Measurement	18–22	—
Coordinate	8–12	10–14
Lines, parabolas, circles, *ellipses*, *hyperbolas*, symmetry, transformations, *polar coordinates*		
Three-dimensional	4–6	4–6
Solids, surface area and volume (cylinders, cones, pyramids, spheres, prisms), *coordinates in three dimensions*		
Trigonometry	6–8	12–16
Right triangles, identities, *radian measure*, *law of cosines*, *law of sines*, *equations*, *double angle formulas*		
Data Analysis, Statistics, and Probability	8–12	8–12
Mean, median, mode, range, interquartile range, *standard deviation*, graphs and plots, least-squares regression (linear, *quadratic*, *exponential*), probability		

* Topics in italics are tested on Level 2 only. The content of Level 1 overlaps somewhat with that on Level 2, but the emphasis on 2 is on more advanced content. Plane Euclidean Geometry is not tested directly on Level 2.

Areas of Overlap

The content of Level 1 has some overlap with Level 2, especially in the following areas:

- elementary algebra
- three-dimensional geometry
- coordinate geometry
- statistics
- basic trigonometry

How Test Content Differs

Although some questions may be appropriate for both tests, the emphasis for Level 2 is on more advanced content. The tests differ significantly in the following areas:

Number and Operations. Level 1 measures a more basic understanding of the topics than Level 2. For example, Level 1 covers the *arithmetic of complex numbers, but Level 2 also covers graphical and other properties of complex numbers.* Level 2 also includes *series and vectors.*

Algebra and Functions. Level 1 contains mainly *algebraic* equations and functions, whereas Level 2 also contains more advanced equations and functions, such as *exponential, logarithmic, and trigonometric.*

Geometry and Measurement. A significant percentage of the questions on Level 1 is devoted to *plane Euclidean geometry and measurement*, which is not tested directly on Level 2. On Level 2, the concepts learned in plane geometry are applied in the questions on *coordinate geometry* and *three-dimensional geometry.*

The trigonometry questions on Level 1 are primarily limited to *right triangle trigonometry (sine, cosine, tangent)* and *the fundamental relationships among the trigonometric ratios.* Level 2 includes questions about *ellipses, hyperbolas, polar coordinates,* and *coordinates in three dimensions.* The trigonometry questions on Level 2 place more emphasis on *the properties and graphs of trigonometric functions, the inverse trigonometric functions, trigonometric equations and identities, and the laws of sines and cosines.*

Data Analysis, Statistics, and Probability. Both Level 1 and Level 2 include *mean, median, mode, range, interquartile range, data interpretation,* and *probability.* Level 2 also includes *standard deviation.* Both include *least-squares linear regression,* but Level 2 also includes *quadratic and exponential regression.*

Scores

The total score for each test is reported on the 200 to 800 point scale. Because the content measured by Level 1 and Level 2 differs considerably, you should not use your score on one test to predict your score on the other.

Note: Geometric Figures

Figures that accompany problems are intended to provide information useful in solving the problems. They are drawn as accurately as possible EXCEPT when it is stated in a particular problem that the figure is not drawn to scale. Even when figures are not drawn to scale, the relative positions of points and angles may be assumed to be in the order shown. Also, line segments that extend through points and appear to lie on the same line *may be assumed* to be on the same line.

When "Note: Figure not drawn to scale," appears below a figure in a question, it means that degree measures may not be accurately shown and specific lengths may not be drawn proportionately.

Mathematics Level 1
Sample Questions

All questions in the Mathematics Level 1 Test are multiple-choice questions in which you must choose the BEST response from the five choices offered. The directions that follow are the same as those on the Mathematics Level 1 Test.

Directions: For each of the following problems, decide which is the BEST of the choices given. If the exact numerical value is not one of the choices, select the choice that best approximates this value. Then fill in the corresponding circle on the answer sheet.

Notes: (1) A scientific or graphing calculator will be necessary for answering some (but not all) of the questions in this test. For each question you will have to decide whether or not you should use a calculator.

(2) The only angle measure used on this test is degree measure. Make sure your calculator is in the degree mode.

(3) Figures that accompany problems in this test are intended to provide information useful in solving the problems. They are drawn as accurately as possible EXCEPT when it is stated in a specific problem that its figure is not drawn to scale. All figures lie in a plane unless otherwise indicated.

(4) Unless otherwise specified, the domain of any function f is assumed to be the set of all real numbers x for which $f(x)$ is a real number. The range of f is assumed to be the set of all real numbers $f(x)$, where x is in the domain of f.

(5) Reference information that may be useful in answering the questions in this test can be found on the following page.

Reference Information: The following information is for your reference in answering some of the questions in this test.

Volume of a right circular cone with radius r and height h: $V = \frac{1}{3}\pi r^2 h$

Volume of a sphere with radius r: $V = \frac{4}{3}\pi r^3$

Volume of a pyramid with base area B and height h: $V = \frac{1}{3}Bh$

Surface Area of a sphere with radius r: $S = 4\pi r^2$

Number and Operations

1

How many of the first 200 positive integers are multiples of neither 6 nor 15?

A) 154

B) 156

C) 160

D) 164

E) 166

Choice (C) is the correct answer. Of the first 200 positive integers, the integers 6, 12, 18, ..., 198, or (1)(6), (2)(6), (3)(6), ..., (33)(6), are the multiples of 6. Thus, there are 33 multiples of 6. Of the first 200 positive integers, the integers 15, 30, 45, ..., 195, or (1)(15), (2)(15), (3)(15), ..., (13)(15) are the multiples of 15. Thus, there are 13 multiples of 15.

An integer is a multiple of 6 and 15 if and only if it is a multiple of 30. Of the first 200 positive integers, the integers 30, 60, 90, 120, 150, and 180 are the multiples of 30. Thus, there are 6 multiples of 30.

Therefore, of the first 200 positive integers, $33 + 13 - 6 = 40$ are multiples of 6 or 15 or both 6 and 15. In choice (C), $200 - 40 = 160$ of these integers are multiples of neither 6 nor 15, making it the correct answer.

2

The 3rd term of an arithmetic sequence is 14 and the 17th term is 63. What is the sum of the first 10 terms of the sequence?

A) 227.5

B) 245

C) 262.5

D) 297.5

E) 385

Choice (A) is the correct answer. In an arithmetic sequence, the difference between consecutive terms is constant. Since the 3rd term of the sequence is 14 and the 17th term is 63, the common difference is $\dfrac{63-14}{17-3} = 3.5$.

If the 3rd term of the sequence is 14, the 2nd term is $14 - 3.5 = 10.5$, and the 1st term is 7. Likewise, the 10th term is equal to $7 + 9(3.5) = 38.5$. The sum of the first 10 terms of the sequence is given by $S_{10} = \dfrac{10(7 + 38.5)}{2} = 227.5$.

Algebra and Functions

3

For a school trip to the circus, each bus costs b dollars and holds 30 passengers. Two of the passengers on each bus must be adults. If each child and each adult must pay x dollars for admission to the circus, what is the minimum total cost, in dollars, for 75 children to go on the trip?

A) $69x + 2b$

B) $75x + 3b$

C) $75x + 9b$

D) $81x + 3b$

E) $81x + 30b$

Choice (D) is the correct answer. Since each bus holds 30 passengers and 2 of these passengers must be adults, each bus can take a maximum of 28 children. Therefore, a minimum of 3 buses are required, at a total cost of $3b$ dollars. On the 3 buses, a total of at least 6 adults must accompany the 75 children. Therefore, there will be a total of at least 81 people on the trip, and the total cost for admission to the circus will be at least $81x$ dollars. Thus, the minimum total cost, in dollars, for 75 children to go on the trip is $81x + 3b$.

4

If $\log_a x^2 = 5$, what is the value of $\log_a x$?

A) $\dfrac{5}{2}$

B) 7

C) 10

D) 25

E) 32

Choice (A) is the correct answer. By the properties of logarithms, $\log_a x^2 = 2 (\log_a x)$. Thus, $\log_a x = \dfrac{\log_a x^2}{2} = \dfrac{5}{2}$.

5

$$y > x^2 + 1$$
$$y < x + 3$$

If $(1, t)$ is a solution to the system of inequalities above, which of the following could be the value of t?

A) 0.1

B) 1.1

C) 1.9

D) 3.9

E) 4.6

Choice (D) is the correct answer. One way to solve the problem is to substitute 1 for x and t for y in the given inequalities. This gives $t > 2$ and $t < 4$. Only the value of t in choice (D) satisfies both of these inequalities.

Another way to solve this problem is to use a graphing calculator to graph or make tables for $Y1 = x^2 + 1$ and $Y2 = x + 3$. Since $(1, t)$ is a solution to the system, look at the graph or table for the value of $Y1$ and $Y2$ when $x = 1$. You can see that when $x = 1$, $Y1 = 2$ and $Y2 = 4$. Thus, we need $Y1 > 2$ and $Y2 < 4$. Therefore, t could be any value between 2 and 4. Of the given choices, only choice (D) could be the value of t.

6

If $f(g(x)) = x$ and $f(x) = 3x + 1$, which of the following is $g(x)$?

A) $g(x) = \dfrac{1}{3}x - \dfrac{1}{9}$

B) $g(x) = \dfrac{1}{3}x - \dfrac{1}{3}$

C) $g(x) = \dfrac{1}{3}x + 1$

D) $g(x) = \dfrac{1}{3}x - 1$

E) $g(x) = 3x - 1$

Choice (B) is the correct answer. If $f(g(x)) = x$ and $f(x) = 3x + 1$, then $f(g(x)) = 3g(x) + 1 = x$. Solving this equation for $g(x)$ yields $x - 1 = 3g(x)$ and $g(x) = \dfrac{x-1}{3}$ or $\dfrac{1}{3}x - \dfrac{1}{3}$.

7

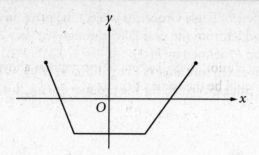

The graph of the function $y = f(x)$ is shown in the figure above. Which of the following could be the graph of $y = |f(x)|$?

(A)
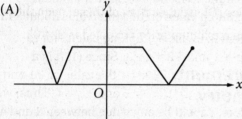

(B)
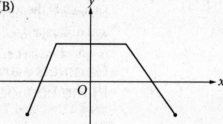

(C)
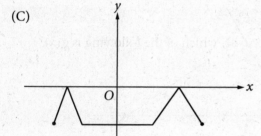

(D)
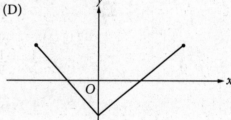

(E)
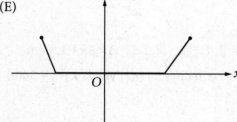

Choice (A) is the correct answer. The graph of $|y|$ is equal to the graph of y for $y \geq 0$ and to the graph of $-y$ for $y < 0$. The graph of $y = |f(x)|$ is the same as the graph of $y = f(x)$ for all values of x where $y \geq 0$ (points on or above the x-axis; those in quadrants I and II). For values of x where $y < 0$ (points below the x-axis; those in quadrants III and IV), the graph of $y = |f(x)|$ consists of the reflection of the graph of $y = f(x)$ about the x-axis.

8

The managers of Eagle Groceries project the price, in dollars, of a certain product from the year 2005 through the year 2013 by using the function P, defined by $P(t) = -0.11t^3 + 0.71t^2 + 2.1t + 9.3$, where t is the number of years after the beginning of 2005. What is the maximum price projected for the product during this period?

A) $5.47

B) $15.22

C) $24.03

D) $69.30

E) $211.30

Choice (C) is the correct answer. One way to solve this is to use a graphing calculator to graph the function, and look for a maximum between $t = 0$ and $t = 8$. The maximum value on this interval is about 24.03 and occurs at $t \approx 5.47$. Thus, the maximum price projected is $24.03.

Geometry and Measurement: Plane Euclidean Geometry

9

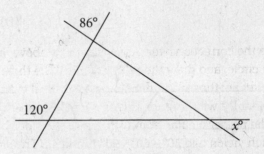

In the figure above, three lines intersect as shown. What is the value of x?

A) 33

B) 34

C) 35

D) 36

E) 37

Choice (B) is the correct answer. The interior angles of the triangle in the figure have measures 60° (supplementary angle to the angle marked 120°), 86° (vertical angle to the angle marked 86°), and $x°$ (vertical angle to the angle marked $x°$). Thus, $60 + 86 + x = 180$, and $x = 34$.

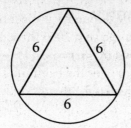

In the figure above, the equilateral triangle is inscribed in the circle. What is the area of the circle?

A) 6π

B) 9π

C) 10π

D) 12π

E) $6\sqrt{3}\pi$

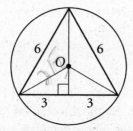

Choice (D) is the correct answer. As in the figure above, let O be the center of the circle, and draw the radii from O to the three vertices of the equilateral triangle; these radii divide the equilateral triangle into three congruent triangles with interior angles of measures 30°, 30°, and 120°. Then draw the perpendicular from O to one of the sides of the equilateral triangle, which yields two 30° – 60° – 90° triangles. The side opposite the 60° angle is half of one side of the equilateral triangle and, thus, has length 3. Thus, the hypotenuse of each 30° – 60° – 90° triangle has length $2\sqrt{3}$. Since each hypotenuse is a radius of the circle, the area of the circle is $\pi(2\sqrt{3})^2 = 12\pi$.

Geometry and Measurement: Coordinate Geometry

11

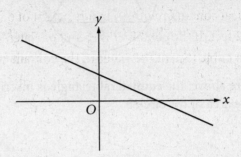

The line with equation $y = mx + b$ is graphed above. Which of the following <u>must</u> be true?

A) $m + b = 0$

B) $m + b < 0$

C) $m - b = 0$

D) $m - b > 0$

E) $m - b < 0$

Choice (E) is the correct answer. The slope of the line is m, and the y-intercept of the line is b. By the direction of the line in the figure, you can tell that the slope of the line is negative. Also, from the figure you can tell that the y-intercept is positive. Thus, $m < 0$ and $b > 0$. You can use this information to evaluate each option. Choice (A) does not have to be true since we cannot conclude that $m = -b$. Choice (B) does not have to be true since the value of $m + b$ could be positive, negative, or zero. Choice (C) is not true since $m \neq b$. The value of $m - b$ must be negative since m is negative and b is positive. Choice (D) cannot be true.

Geometry and Measurement:
Three-Dimensional Geometry

12

A cylindrical container with an inside height of 6 feet has an inside radius of 2 feet. If the container is $\frac{2}{3}$ full of water, what is the volume, in cubic feet, of the water in the container?

A) 25.1

B) 37.7

C) 50.3

D) 62.3

E) 75.4

Choice (C) is the correct answer. The volume V of a cylinder with radius r and height h is given by $V = \pi r^2 h$. Thus, the volume, in cubic feet, of the container is $\pi \cdot 2^2 \cdot 6 = 24\pi$. Since the container is $\frac{2}{3}$ full of water, the volume of the water in the container is $\frac{2}{3} \cdot 24\pi \approx 50.3$.

Geometry and Measurement: Trigonometry

13

In the xy-plane, points $D(1,0)$, $E(1,6)$, and $F(r, s)$ are the vertices of a right triangle. If $\overline{DE}$ is the hypotenuse of the triangle, which of the following CANNOT be the area of the triangle?

A) 0.6

B) 4.7

C) 7.5

D) 8.8

E) 9.2

Choice (E) is the correct answer. Since $\overline{DE}$ is the hypotenuse of the right triangle DEF, this triangle can be inscribed in the circle with diameter $\overline{DE}$, as shown in the figure on the following page. The area of the triangle is $A = \dfrac{1}{2}bh$, where $b = 6$, and h could be any value greater than 0 and less than or equal to the radius of the circle. That is, $0 < h \le 3$. Therefore, the area A of $\triangle DEF$ could be any value that satisfies $0 < A \le 9$. Of the choices, only 9.2 *cannot* be the value of A.

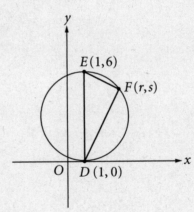

14

In triangle ABC, the measure of $\angle B$ is 90°. Which of the following must be true?

I) $\sin A < \sin C$

II) $\sin A = \cos C$

III) $\sin^2 A + \cos^2 C = 1$

A) None

B) II only

C) I and II

D) I and III

E) II and III

Choice (B) is the correct answer. Statement I need not be true. For example, if the measure of $\angle A$ is 60°, then the measure of $\angle C$ is 30°. Then $\sin A = \sin 60° = \dfrac{\sqrt{3}}{2}$ and $\sin C = \sin 30° = \dfrac{1}{2}$, so $\sin A > \sin C$. Statement II must be true. Since $m\angle B = 90°$, it follows that $m\angle A + m\angle C = 90°$, which implies that $\sin A = \cos C$. Statement III need not be true. For example, if the measure of $\angle A$ is 60°, then the measure of $\angle C$ is 30°. Then $\sin^2 A + \cos^2 C = \dfrac{3}{4} + \dfrac{3}{4} \neq 1$. Since only statement II must be true, the correct answer is (B).

Data Analysis, Statistics, and Probability

15

At a small design company, each of the 89 employees received a 4 percent salary increase from 2004 to 2005. Which of the following must be true about the salaries of the 89 employees from 2004 to 2005?

    I) The mean of the salaries increased by 4 percent.

    II) The median of the salaries increased by 4 percent.

    III) The range of the salaries increased by 4 percent.

A) None

B) II only

C) I and II only

D) II and III only

E) I, II, and III

Choice (E) is the correct answer. Since each 2004 salary is increased by 4 percent to get the corresponding 2005 salary, the total of all 89 salaries also increased by 4 percent. Thus, the average salary, which is the total divided by 89, also increased by 4 percent. Therefore, statement I must be true.

If the 89 salaries for 2004 are listed in order from lowest to highest, the middle (45th) number in the list is the median salary for 2004. If each salary is increased by 4 percent, and the new salaries are listed in order from lowest to highest, the median salary for 2005 will again be the middle (45th) number, which is 4 percent greater than the median number for 2004. Therefore, statement II must be true.

The range of salaries for 2004 is $H-L$, where H is the highest salary among the 89 employees and L is the lowest salary. Since each salary increased by 4 percent, the highest salary for 2005 is $(1.04)H$ and the lowest salary is $(1.04)L$. Thus, the range of salaries for 2005 is $1.04(H-L)$. Therefore, statement III must be true.

Since statements I, II, and III must all be true, the correct answer is choice (E).

Mathematics Level 1 – Practice Test 1

Practice Helps

The test that follows is an actual, previously administered SAT Subject Test in Mathematics Level 1. To get an idea of what it's like to take this test, practice under conditions that are much like those of an actual test administration.

- Set aside an hour when you can take the test uninterrupted.

- Sit at a desk or table with no other books or papers. Dictionaries, other books, or notes are not allowed in the test room.

- Remember to have a scientific or graphing calculator with you.

- Tear out an answer sheet from the back of this book and fill it in just as you would on the day of the test. One answer sheet can be used for up to three Subject Tests.

- Read the instructions that precede the practice test. During the actual administration you will be asked to read them before answering test questions.

- Use a clock or kitchen timer to time yourself.

- After you finish the practice test, read the sections "How to Score the SAT Subject Test in Mathematics Level 1" and "How Did You Do on the Subject Test in Mathematics Level 1?"

- The appearance of the answer sheet in this book may differ from the answer sheet you see on test day.

- The Reference Information at the start of the practice test is slightly different from what appeared on the original test. It has been modified to reflect the language included on tests administered at the time of this book's printing. These changes are minor and will not affect how you answer the questions.

MATHEMATICS LEVEL 1 TEST

The top portion of the page of the answer sheet that you will use to take the Mathematics Level 1 Test must be filled in exactly as illustrated below. When your supervisor tells you to fill in the circle next to the name of the test you are about to take, mark your answer sheet as shown.

○ Literature	● Mathematics Level 1	○ German	○ Chinese Listening	○ Japanese Listening
○ Biology E	○ Mathematics Level 2	○ Italian	○ French Listening	○ Korean Listening
○ Biology M	○ U.S. History	○ Latin	○ German Listening	○ Spanish Listening
○ Chemistry	○ World History	○ Modern Hebrew		
○ Physics	○ French	○ Spanish	Background Questions: ① ② ③ ④ ⑤ ⑥ ⑦ ⑧ ⑨	

After filling in the circle next to the name of the test you are taking, locate the Background Questions section, which also appears at the top of your answer sheet (as shown above). This is where you will answer the following Background Questions on your answer sheet.

BACKGROUND QUESTIONS

Please answer Part I and Part II below by filling in the appropriate circle in the Background Questions box on your answer sheet. The information you provide is for statistical purposes only and will not affect your test score.

Part I. Which of the following describes a mathematics course you have taken or are currently taking? (FILL IN **ALL** CIRCLES THAT APPLY.)

- Algebra I or Elementary Algebra **OR** Course I of a college preparatory mathematics sequence —Fill in circle 1.

- Geometry **OR** Course II of a college preparatory mathematics sequence —Fill in circle 2.

- Algebra II or Intermediate Algebra **OR** Course III of a college preparatory mathematics sequence —Fill in circle 3.

- Elementary Functions (Precalculus) and/or Trigonometry **OR** beyond Course III of a college preparatory mathematics sequence —Fill in circle 4.

- Advanced Placement Mathematics (Calculus AB or Calculus BC) —Fill in circle 5.

Part II. What type of calculator did you bring to use for this test? (FILL IN THE **ONE** CIRCLE THAT APPLIES. If you did not bring a scientific or graphing calculator, do not fill in any of circles 6-9.)

- Scientific —Fill in circle 6.

- Graphing (Fill in the circle corresponding to the model you used.)

    Casio 9700, Casio 9750, Casio 9800, Casio 9850, Casio 9860, Casio FX 1.0, Casio CG-10, Sharp 9200, Sharp 9300, Sharp 9600, Sharp 9900, TI-82, TI-83, TI-83 Plus, TI-83 Plus Silver, TI-84 Plus, TI-84 Plus CE, TI-84 Plus Silver, TI-84 Plus C Silver, TI-85, TI-86, TI-Nspire, or TI-Nspire CX —Fill in circle 7.

    Casio 9970, Casio Algebra FX 2.0, HP 38G, HP 39 series, HP 40 series, HP 48 series, HP 49 series, HP 50 series, HP Prime, TI-89, TI-89 Titanium, TI-Nspire CAS, or TI-Nspire CX CAS —Fill in circle 8.

    Some other graphing calculator —Fill in circle 9.

When the supervisor gives the signal, turn the page and begin the Mathematics Level 1 Test. There are 100 numbered circles on the answer sheet and 50 questions in the Mathematics Level 1 Test. Therefore, use only circles 1 to 50 for recording your answers.

MATHEMATICS LEVEL 1 TEST

REFERENCE INFORMATION

THE FOLLOWING INFORMATION IS FOR YOUR REFERENCE IN ANSWERING SOME OF THE QUESTIONS IN THIS TEST.

Volume of a right circular cone with radius r and height h: $V = \frac{1}{3}\pi r^2 h$

Volume of a sphere with radius r: $V = \frac{4}{3}\pi r^3$

Volume of a pyramid with base area B and height h: $V = \frac{1}{3}Bh$

Surface Area of a sphere with radius r: $S = 4\pi r^2$

DO NOT DETACH FROM BOOK.

GO ON TO THE NEXT PAGE

MATHEMATICS LEVEL 1 TEST

For each of the following problems, decide which is the BEST of the choices given. If the exact numerical value is not one of the choices, select the choice that best approximates this value. Then fill in the corresponding circle on the answer sheet.

<u>Notes:</u> (1) A scientific or graphing calculator will be necessary for answering some (but not all) of the questions in this test. For each question you will have to decide whether or not you should use a calculator.

(2) The only angle measure used on this test is degree measure. Make sure your calculator is in the degree mode.

(3) Figures that accompany problems in this test are intended to provide information useful in solving the problems. They are drawn as accurately as possible EXCEPT when it is stated in a specific problem that its figure is not drawn to scale. All figures lie in a plane unless otherwise indicated.

(4) Unless otherwise specified, the domain of any function f is assumed to be the set of all real numbers x for which $f(x)$ is a real number. The range of f is assumed to be the set of all real numbers $f(x)$, where x is in the domain of f.

(5) Reference information that may be useful in answering the questions in this test can be found on the page preceding Question 1.

USE THIS SPACE FOR SCRATCH WORK.

1. If $3^{\sqrt{x}} = 81$, then $x =$

    (A) 729   (B) 27   (C) 16   (D) 9   (E) 4

MATHEMATICS LEVEL 1 TEST—*Continued*

USE THIS SPACE FOR SCRATCH WORK.

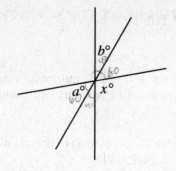

Note: Figure not drawn to scale.

2. In the figure above, the three lines intersect at a point. If $a = 60$ and $b = 40$, what is the value of x?

(A) 20
(B) 40
(C) 60
(D) 80
(E) 100

3. A sequence of integers begins with 3 and ends with 21. Each term after the first is 3 more than the preceding term. What is the middle term of the sequence?

(A) 9   (B) 11   (C) 12   (D) 13   (E) 15

GO ON TO THE NEXT PAGE

MATHEMATICS LEVEL 1 TEST—*Continued*

4. If $a = -2$, $b = -3$, and $c = 4$, what is the value
   of $|a| + b - |c|$?

   (A) −9
   (B) −5
   (C) −3
   (D) −1
   (E)   1

USE THIS SPACE FOR SCRATCH WORK.

5. A company that manufactures tennis racquets has
   total daily expenses of $11,760. If these expenses
   consist of daily operating expenses of $3,360 and
   a cost per racquet of $21, how many racquets are
   manufactured each day?

   (A) 160
   (B) 400
   (C) 420
   (D) 560
   (E) 720

6. Which of the following ordered pairs (x, y) is
   NOT a solution to $2x + 3y < 12$?

   (A) $(3, 2)$
   (B) $(1, 3)$
   (C) $(-1, 4)$
   (D) $(-2, 5)$
   (E) $(-3, 1)$

GO ON TO THE NEXT PAGE

MATHEMATICS LEVEL 1 TEST—*Continued*

$$h = 1.5 + 1.25c$$

7. The equation above expresses the relationship between a car's average gas mileage, in miles per gallon, for highway driving (h), and its average gas mileage for city driving (c). If a car averages 37 miles per gallon for highway driving, what is its average gas mileage for city driving?

(A) 28.1 miles per gallon

(B) 28.4 miles per gallon

(C) 30.8 miles per gallon

(D) 44.4 miles per gallon

(E) 47.8 miles per gallon

8. If y varies directly with x and if $y = 20$ when $x = 6$, what is the value of y when $x = 9$?

(A) $\dfrac{10}{3}$

(B) $\dfrac{40}{3}$

(C) 23

(D) 27

(E) 30

9. If $x + y = 10$ and $x - y = 6$, then $x^2 + y^2 =$

(A) 20
(B) 52
(C) 68
(D) 80
(E) 136

GO ON TO THE NEXT PAGE

1   1   1   1   1   1   1   1

USE THIS SPACE FOR SCRATCH WORK.

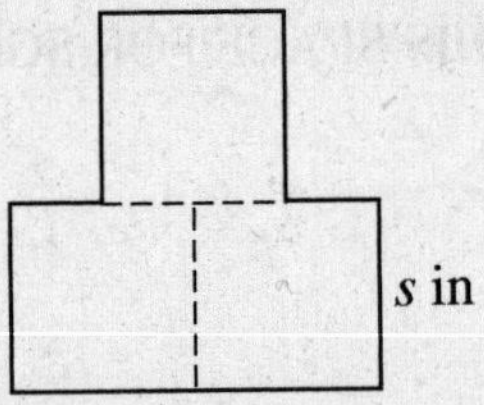

s in

10. The polygon in the figure above can be divided
    into three squares, each with side of length
    s inches. If the area of the polygon is 36 square
    inches, what is the value of *s* ?

    (A) 2.12
    (B) 2.45
    (C) 3.00
    (D) 3.46
    (E) 4.50

11. A student may select a wooden object in the shape
    of a cube, a sphere, or a cylinder and paint it
    either red or blue. How many choices of shape
    and color are possible?

    (A) Five
    (B) Six
    (C) Seven
    (D) Eight
    (E) Nine

GO ON TO THE NEXT PAGE

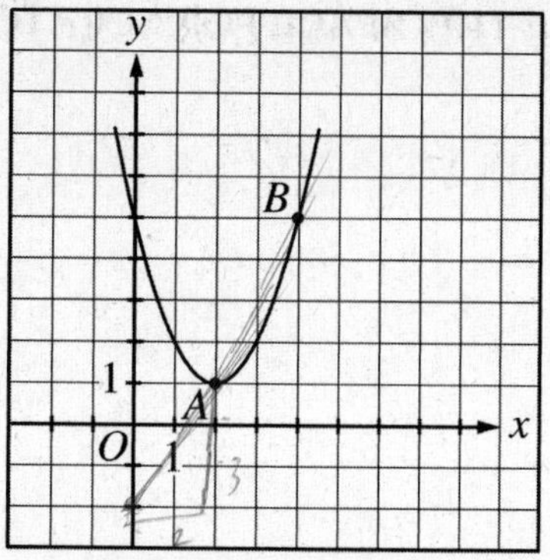

12. In the figure above, what is the slope of the line that contains points A and B ?

(A) $\frac{1}{2}$ (B) $\frac{3}{2}$ (C) 2 (D) 3 (E) 4

13. In the xy-plane, the lines $y = 2x - 1$ and $y = -x + 2$ intersect at which of the following points?

(A) $(-1, 1)$

(B) $(0, -1)$

(C) $(0, 2)$

(D) $(1, 1)$

(E) $(1, 3)$

GO ON TO THE NEXT PAGE

MATHEMATICS LEVEL 1 TEST—*Continued*

USE THIS SPACE FOR SCRATCH WORK.

14. If $f(x) = x + \dfrac{1}{x+1}$, what is the value of

$f(4) - f(3)$?

(A) 0.75
(B) 0.95
(C) 1.05
(D) 1.45
(E) 1.50

15. Which of the following pairs of numbers are farthest apart on the number line?

(A) π^2 and 9

(B) π and 3

(C) π^0 and 1

(D) $\dfrac{1}{\pi}$ and $\dfrac{1}{3}$

(E) $\dfrac{1}{\pi^2}$ and $\dfrac{1}{9}$

16. A container holds x beads, only one of which is blue. If one of the beads is selected at random, what is the probability that the bead is NOT blue?

(A) $\dfrac{1}{x}$

(B) $\dfrac{x-1}{x}$

(C) $\dfrac{x}{x-1}$

(D) $\dfrac{1}{x-1}$

(E) $\dfrac{1}{x+1}$

GO ON TO THE NEXT PAGE

MATHEMATICS LEVEL 1 TEST—*Continued*

17. If $x - y$ is 2 more than x, then $y =$

    (A) $x - 2$
    (B) 2
    (C) -2
    (D) $2x$
    (E) $-2x$

USE THIS SPACE FOR SCRATCH WORK.

18. What is the least positive integer that is divisible by 3, 4, and 7 and that has a remainder of 1 when divided by 5 ?

    (A) 21
    (B) 56
    (C) 84
    (D) 336
    (E) 420

HEIGHTS OF PLANTS
(centimeters)

Stem	Leaf
3	6
4	4 7
5	1 8
6	3 6 7 7
7	1 1 4 4 5 7
8	3 3 3
9	1 9

6 | 3 represents 63.

19. The stem-and-leaf plot above displays the heights, in centimeters, of various plants in a particular garden. What is the mode of these heights?

    (A) 63 cm
    (B) 69 cm
    (C) 71 cm
    (D) 77 cm
    (E) 83 cm

GO ON TO THE NEXT PAGE

MATHEMATICS LEVEL 1 TEST—*Continued*

20. In the figure above, *ABCD* and *EFGH* are squares. What is the area of square *EFGH*, in square centimeters?

    (A) 3.16
    (B) 8
    (C) 10
    (D) 12
    (E) 12.65

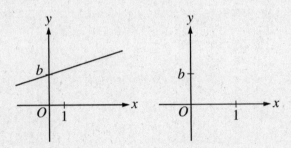

Figure I   Figure II

21. Figure I above shows the graph of the line
    $y = ax + b$. This line is also to be graphed in
    Figure II above, in which the scale of the *x*-axis
    is enlarged but the scale of the *y*-axis is kept the
    same. How would the line in Figure II look,
    compared with the line in Figure I ?

    (A) It would be steeper.
    (B) It would be less steep.
    (C) Its *y*-intercept would be higher.
    (D) Its *y*-intercept would be lower.
    (E) It would be the same as the line in Figure I.

GO ON TO THE NEXT PAGE

MATHEMATICS LEVEL 1 TEST—*Continued*

22. Jan needs an average (arithmetic mean) test score of at least 90 to have an A average in geometry. His average score for his first 4 tests is 91.5. What is the lowest score Jan can earn on the fifth test and still have an A average?

(A) 84.0
(B) 88.5
(C) 90.0
(D) 91.5
(E) 96.0

USE THIS SPACE FOR SCRATCH WORK.

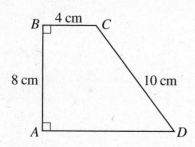

23. What is the area of quadrilateral *ABCD* in the figure above?

(A) 35 sq cm
(B) 40 sq cm
(C) 56 sq cm
(D) 70 sq cm
(E) 80 sq cm

GO ON TO THE NEXT PAGE

MATHEMATICS LEVEL 1 TEST—*Continued*

Questions 24-25 refer to the following table.

USE THIS SPACE FOR SCRATCH WORK.

MAXIMUM LEVEL OF EDUCATION COMPLETED
FOR RESIDENTS OF OAKTOWN
(by percent)

Age (in years)	Less than 4 Years High School	4 Years High School	1-3 Years College	4 Years College or More
18-24	21.8	45.1	26.4	6.7
25-34	13.5	40.9	21.3	24.3
35-44	16.7	39.4	18.6	25.3
45-54	26.0	42.4	14.0	17.6
55-64	34.5	39.9	11.5	14.1
65+	52.4	28.7	9.5	9.4

24. There are 1,000 residents of Oaktown in the 45-54 age group. How many of these residents have less than 4 years of high school education?

(A) 740
(B) 684
(C) 424
(D) 260
(E) 164

25. Which age group has the greatest percent of its members having completed at least 1 year of college?

(A) 18-24
(B) 25-34
(C) 35-44
(D) 45-54
(E) 55-64

GO ON TO THE NEXT PAGE ⟩

MATHEMATICS LEVEL 1 TEST—*Continued*

26. If $f(x) = (x - k)^2$ for all x, and if $f(6) = 16$, what are the possible values for k ?

    (A) −4 or 4
    (B) 2 or 10
    (C) 4 or 5
    (D) 6 or 10
    (E) 8 or 20

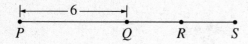

Note: Figure not drawn to scale.

27. In the figure above, R is the midpoint of segment QS, and Q is $\frac{3}{4}$ of the way from P to R. What is the length of segment PS ?

    (A) 18   (B) 16   (C) 12   (D) 10   (E) 8

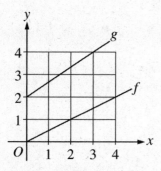

28. The figure above shows the graphs of linear functions f and g. What is the value of $f(3) + g(3)$?

    (A) 1.5   (B) 2   (C) 3   (D) 4   (E) 5.5

GO ON TO THE NEXT PAGE

MATHEMATICS LEVEL 1 TEST—*Continued*

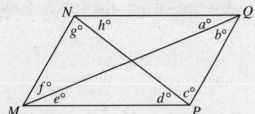

USE THIS SPACE FOR SCRATCH WORK.

29. In the figure above, which of the following conditions is sufficient to prove that $\overline{MP}$ is parallel to $\overline{NQ}$?

   (A) $b = f$
   (B) $h = a$
   (C) $h = c$
   (D) $a = e$
   (E) $c = g$

30. The amount of water in a storage tank is 93 cubic feet. A pump operates at a constant rate to pump water out of the tank. After 8 minutes, 87 cubic feet are left in the tank. At this rate, how many <u>more</u> minutes will it take for the amount of water in the tank to be reduced to 72 cubic feet?

   (A) 14   (B) 16   (C) 17   (D) 20   (E) 28

31. The population $P(t)$ of a certain bacterium is growing over a 24-hour period according to the model $P(t) = 100(1.06)^{t^2}$, where t is the number of hours that elapse. How many hours will it take for the population to first exceed 1,000 ?

   (A)   1.22
   (B)   3.07
   (C)   6.29
   (D) 10
   (E) 10.89

GO ON TO THE NEXT PAGE

MATHEMATICS LEVEL 1 TEST—*Continued*

32. If $f(x) = 3x + 4$ and $f(g(x)) = 6x + 7$, then $g(x) =$

    (A) $2x + 1$

    (B) $3x + 3$

    (C) $3x + 4$

    (D) $4x + 3$

    (E) $\dfrac{6x + 7}{3x + 4}$

USE THIS SPACE FOR SCRATCH WORK.

33. A hotel calculates the rental fee for a rectangular banquet room by charging by the square foot. If a 150-foot by 200-foot banquet room rents for $2,400, what is the cost per square foot?

    (A) $ 0.08
    (B) $ 0.29
    (C) $ 3.43
    (D) $ 6.86
    (E) $12.50

34. If $\angle A$ is an acute angle, then $\dfrac{\cos A}{\sin A} =$

    (A) $-\tan A$

    (B) $1 - \tan A$

    (C) $\tan A$

    (D) $1 + \tan A$

    (E) $\dfrac{1}{\tan A}$

GO ON TO THE NEXT PAGE

MATHEMATICS LEVEL 1 TEST—*Continued*

USE THIS SPACE FOR SCRATCH WORK.

35. In the xy-plane, the points $(-2, -2)$, $(2, -2)$, $(1, 3)$, and $(3, 2)$ are the vertices of a quadrilateral. What is the length of its longer diagonal?

(A) 6.40
(B) 5.83
(C) 5.10
(D) 4.12
(E) 4.00

36. Jenna bought college textbooks on Monday, Tuesday, and Wednesday. On Monday she spent $165. On Tuesday she spent y dollars more than on Monday. On Wednesday she spent x dollars less than on Tuesday. Which of the following expressions represents the total amount, in dollars, she spent all three days?

(A) $165 + y - x$
(B) $330 + y - x$
(C) $330 + 2y - x$
(D) $495 + y - x$
(E) $495 + 2y - x$

37. The graph of $y = x^2$ is transformed in the xy-plane. Of the following, which transformation produces a graph with the greatest y-intercept?

(A) $y = -x^2 + 10$
(B) $y = x^2 - 8$
(C) $y = x^2 + 5$
(D) $y = (x + 3)^2$
(E) $y = (x - 5)^2$

GO ON TO THE NEXT PAGE

USE THIS SPACE FOR SCRATCH WORK.

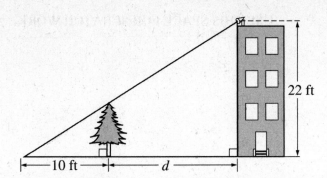

22 ft

|—10 ft—|—— d ——|

Note: Figure not drawn to scale.

38. A light on top of a building shines down on the
ground so that a 7-foot tall tree casts a 10-foot
shadow, as shown in the figure above. What is
the distance d from the tree to the building?

(A) 15.4 ft
(B) 21.4 ft
(C) 30 ft
(D) 31.4 ft
(E) 150 ft

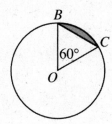

39. In the circle above, radius OB has length 6. What
is the area of the shaded region?

(A) 0.42
(B) 0.85
(C) 0.97
(D) 3.26
(E) 12.85

GO ON TO THE NEXT PAGE

MATHEMATICS LEVEL 1 TEST—*Continued*

40. A book club is offering a novel at a sale price of 45 percent off the list price. As a new member of the club, Sarah can buy the novel at 45 percent off the <u>sale</u> price. If Sarah bought the novel for $6.05, what was the <u>list</u> price?

(A) $6.72

(B) $9.38

(C) $11.00

(D) $20.00

(E) $29.88

USE THIS SPACE FOR SCRATCH WORK.

41. If f and f^{-1} are inverse functions and the domain of both functions is all real numbers, which of the following must be equal to $f^{-1}(f(x))$?

(A) -1 (B) 0   (C) 1   (D) $-x$ (E) x

GO ON TO THE NEXT PAGE

MATHEMATICS LEVEL 1 TEST—*Continued*

USE THIS SPACE FOR SCRATCH WORK.

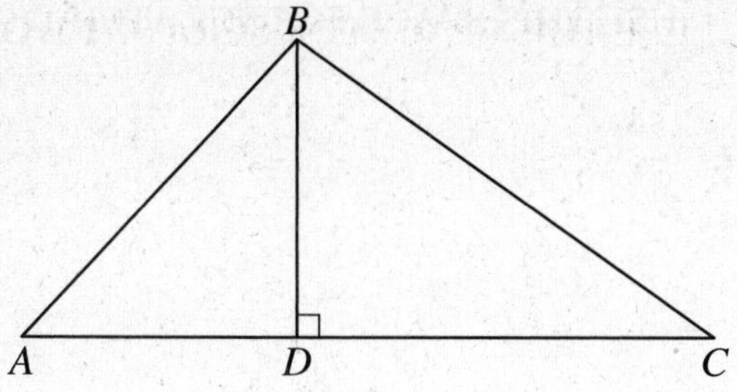

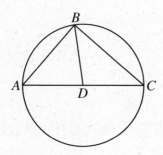

42. In triangle ABC above, if $AB = DC$, which of
the following must be equal to $\sin \angle A$?

   (A) $\cos \angle A$
   (B) $\tan \angle A$
   (C) $\sin \angle C$
   (D) $\cos \angle C$
   (E) $\tan \angle C$

43. In the figure above, $\overline{AC}$ is a diameter of the circle
with center D. If $AB = 3$ and $BC = 4$, what is
the area of $\triangle BCD$?

   (A) 3   (B) 5   (C) 6   (D) 12   (E) 18

GO ON TO THE NEXT PAGE

MATHEMATICS LEVEL 1 TEST—*Continued*

USE THIS SPACE FOR SCRATCH WORK.

$$\begin{cases} 2x - 5y = 8 \\ 4x + ky = 17 \end{cases}$$

44. For which of the following values of k will the system of equations above have no solution?

(A) −10 (B) −5 (C) 0 (D) 5 (E) 10

45. If $2x + 2y = 0$, then $x - y =$

(A) 0 (B) 1 (C) 2 (D) $2y$ (E) $2x$

46. The volume of a cube is 100 cubic inches. What is the surface area of the cube?

(A) 28 square inches
(B) 60 square inches
(C) 129 square inches
(D) 259 square inches
(E) 600 square inches

GO ON TO THE NEXT PAGE

MATHEMATICS LEVEL 1 TEST—*Continued*

USE THIS SPACE FOR SCRATCH WORK.

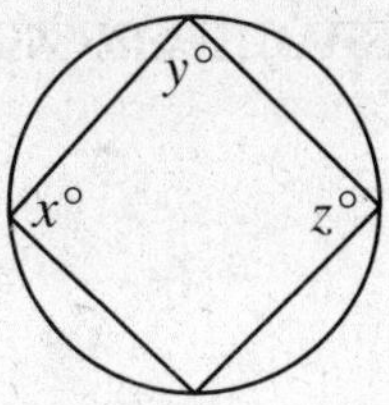

Note: Figure not drawn to scale.

47. In the figure above, a quadrilateral is inscribed in a circle. Which of the following must be true?

(A) $x + z = 180$
(B) $x + y = 180$
(C) $x = z$
(D) $x = y$
(E) $x = 90$

48. The function f defined by $f(x) = mx$, where m is a constant greater than 1, has which of the following properties?

I. $f(mx) = mf(x)$
II. $f(x_1 + x_2) = f(x_1) + f(x_2)$
III. $f(x_1 \cdot x_2) = f(x_1) \cdot f(x_2)$

(A) I only
(B) II only
(C) I and II
(D) I and III
(E) II and III

GO ON TO THE NEXT PAGE

MATHEMATICS LEVEL 1 TEST—*Continued*

49. Let T be a pyramid with a triangular base. If the intersection of a plane and the pyramid T is a figure with n sides, what is the greatest possible value of n ?

    (A) Zero
    (B) One
    (C) Two
    (D) Three
    (E) Four

USE THIS SPACE FOR SCRATCH WORK.

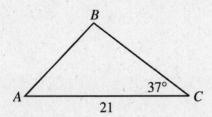

Note: Figure not drawn to scale.

50. In isosceles triangle ABC above, $AB = BC$. What is the perimeter of the triangle?

    (A) 34.2
    (B) 47.3
    (C) 55.9
    (D) 73.6
    (E) 90.8

STOP

IF YOU FINISH BEFORE TIME IS CALLED, YOU MAY CHECK YOUR WORK ON THIS TEST ONLY. DO NOT TURN TO ANY OTHER TEST IN THIS BOOK.

How to Score the SAT Subject Test in Mathematics Level 1

When you take an actual SAT Subject Test in Mathematics Level 1, your answer sheet will be "read" by a scanning machine that will record your response to each question. Then a computer will compare your answers with the correct answers and produce your raw score. You get one point for each correct answer. For each wrong answer, you lose one-fourth of a point. Questions you omit (and any for which you mark more than one answer) are not counted. This raw score is converted to a scaled score that is reported to you and to the colleges you specify.

Worksheet 1. Finding Your Raw Test Score

STEP 1: Table A on the following page lists the correct answers for all the questions on the Subject Test in Mathematics Level 1 that is reproduced in this book. It also serves as a worksheet for you to calculate your raw score.

- Compare your answers with those given in the table.

- Put a check in the column marked "Right" if your answer is correct.

- Put a check in the column marked "Wrong" if your answer is incorrect.

- Leave both columns blank if you omitted the question.

STEP 2: Count the number of right answers.

Enter the total here: _____

STEP 3: Count the number of wrong answers.

Enter the total here: _____

STEP 4: Multiply the number of wrong answers by .250.

Enter the product here: _____

STEP 5: Subtract the result obtained in Step 4 from the total you obtained in Step 2.

Enter the result here: _____

STEP 6: Round the number obtained in Step 5 to the nearest whole number.

Enter the result here: _____

The number you obtained in Step 6 is your raw score.

Answers to Practice Test 1 for Mathematics Level 1

Table A
Answers to the Subject Test in Mathematics Level 1 - Practice Test 1 and Percentage of Students Answering
Each Question Correctly

Question Number	Correct Answer	Right	Wrong	Percent Answering Correctly*	Question Number	Correct Answer	Right	Wrong	Percent Answering Correctly*
1	C			86	26	B			81
2	D			91	27	D			64
3	C			91	28	E			79
4	B			91	29	D			58
5	B			85	30	D			58
6	A			91	31	C			74
7	B			86	32	A			60
8	E			79	33	A			51
9	C			85	34	E			66
10	D			75	35	A			36
11	B			86	36	E			56
12	C			81	37	E			50
13	D			86	38	B			53
14	B			86	39	D			38
15	A			79	40	D			35
16	B			72	41	E			34
17	C			75	42	E			50
18	D			65	43	A			20
19	E			74	44	A			34
20	C			74	45	E			39
21	B			59	46	C			51
22	A			60	47	A			26
23	C			77	48	C			30
24	D			88	49	E			31
25	B			39	50	B			60

* These percentages are based on an analysis of the answer sheets for a random sample of 8,168 students who took the original administration of this test and whose mean score was 595. They may be used as an indication of the relative difficulty of a particular question. Each percentage may also be used to predict the likelihood that a typical Subject Test in Mathematics Level 1 candidate will answer correctly that question on this edition of this test.

Finding Your Scaled Score

When you take SAT Subject Tests, the scores sent to the colleges you specify are reported on the College Board scale, which ranges from 200–800. You can convert your practice test score to a scaled score by using Table B. To find your scaled score, locate your raw score in the left-hand column of Table B; the corresponding score in the right-hand column is your scaled score. For example, a raw score of 25 on this particular edition of the Subject Test in Mathematics Level 1 corresponds to a scaled score of 560.

Raw scores are converted to scaled scores to ensure that a score earned on any one edition of a particular Subject Test is comparable to the same scaled score earned on any other edition of the same Subject Test. Because some editions of the tests may be slightly easier or more difficult than others, College Board scaled scores are adjusted so that they indicate the same level of performance regardless of the edition of the test taken and the ability of the group that takes it. Thus, for example, a score of 500 on one edition of a test taken at a particular administration indicates the same level of achievement as a score of 500 on a different edition of the test taken at a different administration.

When you take the SAT Subject Tests during a national administration, your scores are likely to differ somewhat from the scores you obtain on the tests in this book. People perform at different levels at different times for reasons unrelated to the tests themselves. The precision of any test is also limited because it represents only a sample of all the possible questions that could be asked.

Table B
Scaled Score Conversion Table
Subject Test in Mathematics Level 1 - Practice Test 1

Raw Score	Reported Score	Raw Score	Reported Score	Raw Score	Reported Score
50	800	29	590	8	420
49	800	28	580	7	410
48	790	27	570	6	410
47	780	26	560	5	400
46	770	25	560	4	390
45	760	24	550	3	380
44	750	23	540	2	370
43	740	22	530	1	360
42	730	21	520	0	350
41	720	20	510	−1	340
40	710	19	510	−2	340
39	700	18	500	−3	330
38	690	17	490	−4	320
37	670	16	480	−5	310
36	660	15	480	−6	300
35	650	14	470	−7	300
34	640	13	460	−8	290
33	630	12	450	−9	280
32	620	11	450	−10	270
31	610	10	440	−11	260
30	600	9	430	−12	250

How Did You Do on the Subject Test in Mathematics Level 1?

After you score your test and analyze your performance, think about the following questions:

Did you run out of time before reaching the end of the test?

If so, you may need to pace yourself better. For example, maybe you spent too much time on one or two hard questions. A better approach might be to skip the ones you can't answer right away and try answering all the questions that remain on the test. Then if there's time, go back to the questions you skipped.

Did you take a long time reading the directions?

You will save time when you take the test by learning the directions to the Subject Test in Mathematics Level 1 ahead of time. Each minute you spend reading directions during the test is a minute that you could use to answer questions.

How did you handle questions you were unsure of?

If you were able to eliminate one or more of the answer choices as wrong and guess from the remaining ones, your approach probably worked to your advantage. On the other hand, making haphazard guesses or omitting questions without trying to eliminate choices could cost you valuable points.

How difficult were the questions for you compared with other students who took the test?

Table A shows you how difficult the multiple-choice questions were for the group of students who took this test during its national administration. The right-hand column gives the percentage of students that answered each question correctly.

A question answered correctly by almost everyone in the group is obviously an easier question. For example, 86 percent of the students answered question 7 correctly. But only 26 percent answered question 47 correctly.

Keep in mind that these percentages are based on just one group of students. They would probably be different with another group of students taking the test.

If you missed several easier questions, go back and try to find out why: Did the questions cover material you haven't yet reviewed? Did you misunderstand the directions?

Answer Explanations

For Practice Test 1

The solutions presented here provide one method for solving each of the problems on this test. Other mathematically correct approaches are possible.

Question 1

Choice (C) is the correct answer. Since $3^{\sqrt{x}} = 81$ and $81 = 3^4$, it follows that $3^{\sqrt{x}} = 3^4$. Thus, $\sqrt{x} = 4$, which gives you $x = 16$.

Choice (E) is incorrect. This is the value of $\sqrt{x}$. If $x = 4$, then $3^{\sqrt{4}} = 3^2 = 9$.

Question 2

Choice (D) is the correct answer. Using the fact that vertical angles are congruent, the measure of the angle in between the angles labeled $a°$ and $x°$ is also $b°$. Thus, $a + b + x = 180$. Since $a = 60$ and $b = 40$, it follows that $60 + 40 + x = 180$ and $x = 80$.

Choice (E) is incorrect. The angle labeled $x°$ is supplementary to rather than congruent to the angle with measure $(a + b)° = 100°$.

Question 3

Choice (C) is the correct answer. Since the sequence begins with 3 and ends with 21, and each successive term of the sequence is increased by 3, the sequence is 3, 6, 9, 12, 15, 18, 21. Therefore, the fourth term is the middle term, which is 12.

Choice (A) is incorrect. This is an error in determining the middle term. There are two terms before 9 in the sequence and four terms after 9, so 9 is not the middle term.

Question 4

Choice (B) is the correct answer. Substituting the values of a, b, and c into the expression gives you $|-2| + (-3) - |4| = 2 - 3 - 4 = -5$.

Choice (A) is incorrect. This is the result of incorrectly evaluating $|-2|$ as -2.

Question 5

Choice (B) is the correct answer. Since each racquet costs $21, it costs $21n$ dollars to manufacture n racquets each day. Since the total daily expenses of $11,760 consist of the cost of manufacturing n racquets and $3,360 in operating expenses, $11,760 = 3,360 + 21n$.

Thus, $11{,}760 = 3{,}360 + 21n$

$\qquad 8{,}400 = 21n$

$\qquad\quad 400 = n.$

Choice (E) is incorrect. This is the result of incorrectly adding 3,360 to 11,760, producing the equation $15{,}120 = 21n$.

Question 6

Choice (A) is the correct answer. Each of the five choices must be examined to determine the ordered pair that is NOT a solution. Substituting $x = 3$ and $y = 2$ in the inequality produces $2(3) + 3(2) < 12$. This can be simplified to $12 < 12$, which is a false statement. Thus, $(3, 2)$ is NOT a solution to the inequality.

Choice (B) is incorrect. This ordered pair produces $11 < 12$, which is a true statement. Thus, $(1, 3)$ is a solution to the inequality.

Choice (C) is incorrect. This ordered pair produces $10 < 12$, which is a true statement. Thus2, $(-1, 4)$ is a solution to the inequality.

Choice (D) is incorrect. This ordered pair produces $11 < 12$, which is a true statement. Thus, $(-2, 5)$ is a solution to the inequality.

Choice (E) is incorrect. This ordered pair produces $-3 < 12$, which is a true statement. Thus, $(-3, 1)$ is a solution to the inequality.

Question 7

Choice (B) is the correct answer. The given gas mileage for highway driving is 37 miles per gallon. By substituting 37 for h in the equation provided, you produce $37 = 1.5 + 1.25c$. This simplifies to $35.5 = 1.25c$. Solving for c gives you 28.4 miles per gallon.

Choice (E) is incorrect. This is the value for h obtained by incorrectly substituting 37 for c in the equation provided.

Question 8

Choice (E) is the correct answer. Since y varies directly with x, it follows that $y = kx$ for some constant k. Substituting the given values in this equation produces $20 = k(6)$, and so $k = \dfrac{10}{3}$. Thus, when $x = 9$, $y = \dfrac{10}{3}(9) = 30$.

Choice (A) is incorrect. This is the value of k in the proportional relationship $y = kx$.

Choice (C) is incorrect. This is the result when the difference between the x-values of 6 and 9 is added to the y-value of 20. This is not the relationship between x and y stated in the problem.

Question 9

Choice (C) is the correct answer. Taking the square of both sides of the equations and adding, you produce

$$(x + y)^2 = x^2 + 2xy + y^2 = 100$$
$$(x - y)^2 = x^2 - 2xy + y^2 = 36$$
$$\overline{2x^2 + 2y^2 = 136}$$

and thus, $x^2 + y^2 = 68$. Alternately, adding the right-hand sides of the equations and the left-hand sides of the equations, you obtain $2x = 16$. Thus, $x = 8$. By substituting this in the first equation, you produce $8 + y = 10$, and thus $y = 2$. Substituting these values into the expression $x^2 + y^2$ produces $(8)^2 + (2)^2 = 64 + 4 = 68$.

Choice (E) is incorrect. This is the result obtained by substituting $x = 10$ and $y = 6$ in the expression $x^2 + y^2$. It is also the value of $2x^2 + 2y^2$ when using the first method above.

Question 10

Choice (D) is the correct answer. Since the area of the polygon is 36 square inches, each of the three squares has an area of 12 square inches. Since the length of a side of each square is s inches, $s^2 = 12$ and $s = \sqrt{12} \approx 3.4641$, which rounds to 3.46.

Choice (C) is incorrect. This results from incorrectly using 12 as the perimeter of each square instead of the area. If the perimeter of a square is 12, then each side has length 3. If the length was 3 inches, then the area of each square would be 3^2 or 9 square inches. Since the polygon consists of three squares, the area of the polygon would be 27 square inches.

Question 11

Choice (B) is the correct answer. The student must make two choices independent of one another: selecting 1 of 3 objects and selecting 1 of 2 colors of paint. There are 3 ways to choose the object and 2 ways to choose the color of paint. Therefore, by the multiplication counting principle, there are $(3)(2) = 6$ total choices.

Choice (E) is incorrect. This results from thinking that the number of choices are 3^2 rather than $(3)(2)$.

Question 12

Choice (C) is the correct answer. The slope of the line that contains two points can be calculated by $\frac{\triangle y}{\triangle x} = \frac{\text{change (difference) in the } y\text{-coordinates}}{\text{change (difference) in the } x\text{-coordinates}}$. The coordinates of point A are $(2, 1)$, and the coordinates of point B are $(4, 5)$. Thus, the slope of the line that contains A and B is $\frac{5-1}{4-2} = \frac{4}{2} = 2$.

Choice (A) is incorrect. This results from an incorrect understanding of slope as $\frac{\triangle x}{\triangle y} = \frac{\text{change (difference) in the } x\text{-coordinates}}{\text{change (difference) in the } y\text{-coordinates}} = \frac{4-2}{5-1} = \frac{2}{4} = \frac{1}{2}$.

Question 13

Choice (D) is the correct answer. Use the graphing calculator to find the point of intersection of the graphs of $y = 2x - 1$ and $y = -x + 2$. The lines intersect at the point $(1, 1)$. Alternately, you can set up and solve the equation $2x - 1 = -x + 2$, which simplifies to $3x = 3$ and thus, $x = 1$. Substituting $x = 1$ in one of the given equations results in $y = 1$.

Choice (C) is incorrect. This results from focusing on $y = -x + 2$ and finding the point of intersection with the y-axis, which is $(0, 2)$.

Question 14

Choice (B) is the correct answer. Since $f(x) = x + \frac{1}{x+1}$, it follows that

$$f(4) - f(3) = \left[(4) + \frac{1}{(4)+1}\right] - \left[(3) + \frac{1}{(3)+1}\right]$$

$$= 4 + \frac{1}{5} - 3 - \frac{1}{4} = 1 + 0.2 - 0.25 = 0.95.$$

Alternately, the graphing calculator can be used to define the function f and evaluate $f(4) - f(3)$ or define f as Y1 and evaluate Y1(4) − Y1(3).

Choice (D) is incorrect. This is the answer obtained by not distributing the negative sign in the evaluation of $f(3)$, thus incorrectly computing

$$f(4) - f(3) = \left[(4) + \frac{1}{(4)+1}\right] - \left[(3) + \frac{1}{(3)+1}\right] \Rightarrow 4 + \frac{1}{5} - 3 + \frac{1}{4}$$

$$= 1 + 0.2 + 0.25 = 1.45.$$

Question 15

Choice (A) is the correct answer. Each of the five choices must be examined. The approximate distance between π^2 and 9 on the number line is 0.8696, which is the greatest distance between any of the pairs of numbers.

Choice (B) is incorrect. The approximate distance between π and 3 on the number line is 0.1416.

Choice (C) is incorrect. Since $\pi^0 = 1$, the distance between π^0 and 1 on the number line is 0.

Choice (D) is incorrect. The approximate distance between $\frac{1}{\pi}$ and $\frac{1}{3}$ on the number line is 0.0150.

Choice (E) is incorrect. The approximate distance between $\frac{1}{\pi^2}$ and $\frac{1}{9}$ on the number line is 0.0098.

Question 16

Choice (B) is the correct answer. The probability of selecting at random a bead from the container that is NOT blue is

$\frac{\text{the number of beads that are NOT blue}}{\text{the total number of beads}}$. Since there are x total beads and only 1 bead that is blue, there are $x - 1$ beads that are NOT blue. Thus, the probability of selecting a bead that is NOT blue is $\frac{x-1}{x}$.

Choice (A) is incorrect. This is the probability of selecting the blue bead from the container, $\frac{\text{the number of beads that are blue}}{\text{the total number of beads}}$.

Question 17

Choice (C) is the correct answer. The given information can be translated into the equation $x - y = x + 2$. Solving for y gives you $y = -2$.

Choice (B) is incorrect. This results from a sign error in solving $x - y = x + 2$. It is the value of $-y$.

Question 18

Choice (D) is the correct answer. The integers 3, 4, and 7 do not share any positive common factors except for 1, so the least positive integer that is divisible by all three is their product $(3)(4)(7) = 84$. Thus, all multiples of 84 will be divisible by 3, 4, and 7. The calculator is helpful in calculating multiples of 84. The least multiple of 84 that has a remainder of 1 when divided by 5 is 336.

Choice (C) is incorrect. This is the least positive integer that is divisible by 3, 4, and 7, but it has a remainder of 4 when divided by 5.

Question 19

Choice (E) is the correct answer. The mode of a list of numbers is a number that occurs most often in the list. The height of 83 cm appears three times, which is the most for any height in the stem-and-leaf plot.

Choice (C) is incorrect. 71 cm is the median of the heights and only appears two times in the plot.

Question 20

Choice (C) is the correct answer. It is helpful to use the given figure to solve the problem.

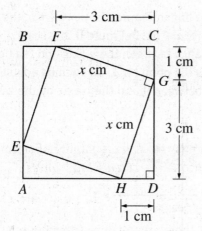

The Pythagorean Theorem can be used to find the value of x. Using $\triangle GHD$, $1^2 + 3^2 = x^2$. Thus, $1 + 9 = x^2$ and $\sqrt{10} = x$. $\triangle FGC$ can also be used, since $\triangle GHD \cong \triangle FGC$. Since the area of square *EFGH* is x^2, the area is $\left(\sqrt{10}\right)^2 = 10$ square centimeters.

Choice (A) is incorrect. This is the value of x, $\sqrt{10}$, which is the length of a side of square *EFGH*.

Question 21

Choice (B) is the correct answer. It is helpful to use the given figures to solve the problem.

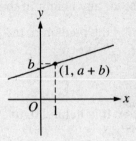

Since the equation of the line in Figure I is $y = ax + b$, the coordinates of the point at $x = 1$ are $(1, a + b)$. In Figure II, the scale of the x-axis is adjusted so that the distance between the y-axis and the tick mark at $x = 1$ is increased. This means the point $(1, a + b)$ will be adjusted similarly, increasing the distance between it and the y-axis by the same amount.

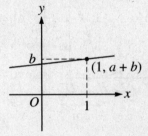

This adjustment to the scale of the x-axis makes the graph of the line look less steep in Figure II. Since the scale of the y-axis is kept the same in Figure II, the position of the y-intercept does not change.

Choice (A) is incorrect. The graph would look steeper if the scale of the x-axis was adjusted such that the tick mark representing $x = 1$ moved closer to the y-axis.

Question 22

Choice (A) is the correct answer. Let the lowest score Jan can earn on the fifth test and still have an average of at least 90 be n. Since the average of the first 4 test scores is 91.5, the sum of the first 4 test scores is $4(91.5) = 366$. The average of the 5 tests will be the sum of all 5 test scores divided by 5. Thus,

$$\frac{366 + n}{5} = 90$$
$$366 + n = 450$$
$$n = 84.$$

Choice (B) is incorrect. This results from an incorrect calculation that forgets to count the 91.5 four times, which results in

$$\frac{91.5 + n}{2} = 90$$
$$91.5 + n = 180$$
$$n = 88.5.$$

Question 23

Choice (C) is the correct answer. It is helpful to use the given figure to solve the problem.

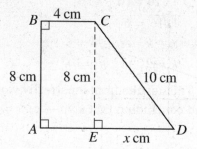

The quadrilateral can be broken up into rectangle *ABCE* and right triangle *ECD*. The area of rectangle *ABCE* is $(8)(4) = 32$. If $ED = x$ cm, then by the Pythagorean Theorem, $x^2 + 8^2 = 10^2$. Thus, $x^2 + 64 = 100$ and $x = 6$. The area of right triangle *ECD* is $\frac{1}{2}(6)(8) = 24$. Therefore, the area of quadrilateral *ABCD* is $32 + 24 = 56$. Alternately, quadrilateral *ABCD* is a trapezoid, and the area is given by $\frac{1}{2}(4 + 10)(8) = 56$.

Choice (E) is incorrect. This is the result obtained if the area of right triangle *ECD* is incorrectly computed as $(6)(8) = 48$. $32 + 48 = 80$.

Question 24

Choice (D) is the correct answer. The table states that 26.0% of Oaktown residents in the 45–54 age group have less than 4 years of high school education. Since there are 1,000 residents in this age group, $0.26(1,000) = 260$ residents in the 45–54 age group have less than 4 years of high school education.

Choice (E) is incorrect. This results from incorrectly reasoning that the percent of residents who have less than 4 years of high school education is found taking the difference $42.4 - 26.0$, using the values in the table for the 45–54 age group.

Question 25

Choice (B) is the correct answer. The age group that has the greatest percent of its members having completed at least 1 year of college is found by examining the sum of the last two columns of the table. You are looking for the greatest total percent at the 1–3 years of college <u>and</u> 4 years of college or more education levels. The 25–34 age group has the greatest, at $21.3\% + 24.3\% = 45.6\%$.

Choice (A) is incorrect. This results from incorrectly using only the percent at the 1–3 years of college. The 18–24 age group has $26.4\% + 6.7\% = 33.1\%$ of its members having completed at least 1 year of college, which is less than that of the 25–34 age group.

Question 26

Choice (B) is the correct answer. Since $f(6) = 16$, it follows that

$$16 = (6 - k)^2$$
$$\pm\sqrt{16} = 6 - k$$
$$4 = 6 - k \quad \text{or} \quad -4 = 6 - k$$
$$k = 2 \quad \text{or} \quad k = 10.$$

Choice (A) is incorrect. This results from incorrectly working with the equation $0 = 16 - k^2$ and concluding that $k = -4$ or $k = 4$.

Question 27

Choice (D) is the correct answer. Since $PQ = 6$ and $PQ = \frac{3}{4}PR$, $PR = 8$. Thus, $QR = 2$. Since R is the midpoint of $\overline{QS}$, $QR = RS = 2$. Thus, $PS = 10$.

Choice (C) is incorrect. This is the result obtained by incorrectly assuming Q is the midpoint of $\overline{PS}$. Note that the figure is not drawn to scale.

Question 28

Choice (E) is the correct answer. The slope and y-intercept for each linear function can be determined from the graph. Since f has a slope of $\frac{1}{2}$ and intersects the origin, $f(x) = \frac{1}{2}x$. Since g has a slope of $\frac{2}{3}$ and a y-intercept of 2, $g(x) = \frac{2}{3}x + 2$. Thus, $f(3) = 1.5$ and $g(3) = 4$, so that $f(3) + g(3) = 1.5 + 4 = 5.5$.

Choice (C) is incorrect. This is the value of $g(f(3))$.

Question 29

Choice (D) is the correct answer. Each of the five choices must be examined. For $\overline{MP}$ and $\overline{NQ}$ and transversal $\overline{MQ}$, $\angle NQM$ and $\angle PMQ$ are alternate interior angles. If the alternate interior angles are congruent, then the line segments are parallel. Thus, if $a = e$, this is sufficient to prove that $\overline{MP}$ and $\overline{NQ}$ are parallel.

Choice (E) is incorrect. If $c = g$, this is sufficient to prove that $\overline{MN}$ is parallel to $\overline{PQ}$. $\angle NPQ$ and $\angle PNM$ are alternate interior angles with respect to $\overline{MN}$ and $\overline{PQ}$ with transversal $\overline{NP}$.

Question 30

Choice (D) is the correct answer. Since the pump removed 6 cubic feet of water from the tank in 8 minutes, and the pump is working at a constant rate, the pump's rate is $\frac{6}{8}$ cubic feet of water per minute. Thus, the equation $\frac{6}{8}x = 15$ can be used to calculate how much time is needed to remove 15 more cubic feet of water. The result is 20 minutes.

Choice (E) is incorrect. This results from calculating the <u>total</u> amount of time needed to remove 21 cubic feet of water and ending with 72 cubic feet. Using $\frac{6}{8}x = 21$ gives $x = 28$.

Question 31

Choice (C) is the correct answer. To solve this problem, you must solve $P(t) = 1,000$ for t. Graph $Y1 = 100(1.06)^{x^2}$ and $Y2 = 1000$ using the graphing calculator. The point of intersection of the two graphs provides the information needed. A suitable viewing window is $[0, 12]$ for x-values and $[0, 1250]$ for y-values. The graphs intersect at $(6.2862, 1000)$. Thus, it will take approximately 6.29 hours for the population to first exceed 1,000.

Choice (B) is incorrect. This results from incorrect simplification of $P(t)$ as $P(t) = 106t^2$. Solving $1000 = 106t^2$ gives $t \approx 3.0715$.

Question 32

Choice (A) is the correct answer. Since $f(g(x)) = 3(g(x)) + 4$,

$$3g(x) + 4 = 6x + 7$$
$$3g(x) = 6x + 3$$
$$g(x) = 2x + 1.$$

Choice (E) is incorrect. This results from an incorrect thinking that $g(x) = \dfrac{f(g(x))}{f(x)} = \dfrac{6x + 7}{3x + 4}$.

Question 33

Choice (A) is the correct answer. The total area of the room is $(150)(200) = 30,000$ square feet. Since the cost to rent the room is $2,400, the cost per square foot is $\dfrac{\$2,400}{30,000} = \$0.08$.

Choice (E) is incorrect. This results from incorrectly thinking that the cost per square foot is $\dfrac{30,000}{\$2,400} = \$12.50$.

Question 34

Choice (E) is the correct answer. It is helpful to draw a figure to solve the problem.

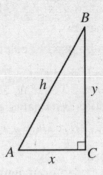

Since $\cos A = \frac{x}{h}$ and $\sin A = \frac{y}{h}$, $\dfrac{\cos A}{\sin A} = \dfrac{\frac{x}{h}}{\frac{y}{h}} = \left(\dfrac{x}{h}\right)\left(\dfrac{h}{y}\right) = \dfrac{x}{y}$. Also,

$\tan A = \dfrac{y}{x}$. Thus, $\dfrac{1}{\tan A} = \dfrac{x}{y}$ and $\dfrac{\cos A}{\sin A} = \dfrac{1}{\tan A}$.

Choice (C) is incorrect. By definition, $\tan A = \dfrac{\sin A}{\cos A}$.

Question 35

Choice (A) is the correct answer. It is helpful to draw a figure to solve the problem.

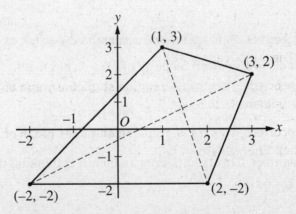

You can find the lengths of the diagonals by using the distance formula. For the diagonal connecting $(1, 3)$ and $(2, -2)$, the length is $\sqrt{(2-1)^2 + (-2-3)^2} = \sqrt{1+25} \approx 5.0990$. For the diagonal connecting $(-2, -2)$ and $(3, 2)$, the length is $\sqrt{(3-(-2))^2 + (2-(-2))^2} = \sqrt{25+16} = \sqrt{41} \approx 6.4031$. The length of the longer diagonal is 6.40.

Choice (C) is incorrect. This is the length of the shorter diagonal.

Choice (B) is incorrect. This is the result of incorrect thinking that the longer diagonal connects $(1, 3)$ and $(-2, -2)$, with length $\sqrt{(-2-1)^2 + (-2-3)^2} = \sqrt{9+25} = \sqrt{34} \approx 5.8310$. This is the length of the longest side of the quadrilateral.

Question 36

Choice (E) is the correct answer. On Tuesday, Jenna spent $165 + y$ dollars. On Wednesday, she spent $165 + y - x$ dollars. Thus, Jenna spent a total of $(165) + (165 + y) + (165 + y - x)$ or $495 + 2y - x$ dollars all three days.

Choice (A) is incorrect. This is the amount Jenna spent on Wednesday only.

Question 37

Choice (E) is the correct answer. Each of the five choices must be examined to determine which transformation produces a graph with the greatest y-intercept. The y-intercept is the point where the graph intersects the y-axis; its x-coordinate is 0. A graphing calculator is helpful here. The graph of $y = x^2$ is a parabola that opens up with a y-intercept of 0. This transformation shifts the graph of $y = x^2$ to the right 5 units. The y-intercept is 25.

Choice (A) is incorrect. This transformation reflects the graph of $y = x^2$ about the x-axis and then shifts the graph up 10 units. The y-intercept is 10.

Choice (B) is incorrect. This transformation shifts the graph of $y = x^2$ down 8 units. The y-intercept is -8.

Choice (C) is incorrect. This transformation shifts the graph of $y = x^2$ up 5 units. The y-intercept is 5.

Choice (D) is incorrect. This transformation shifts the graph of $y = x^2$ to the left 3 units. The y-intercept is 9.

Question 38

Choice (B) is the correct answer. It is helpful to draw a figure to solve the problem.

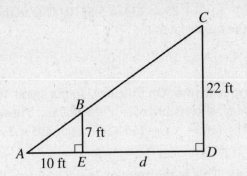

Since $\triangle ABE$ and $\triangle ACD$ are right triangles that both share $\angle A$, the two triangles are similar. Thus,

$$\frac{7}{22} = \frac{10}{10 + d}$$
$$7(10 + d) = 22(10)$$
$$70 + 7d = 220$$
$$7d = 150$$
$$d \approx 21.4286,$$

which rounds to 21.4.

Choice (D) is incorrect. This is AD, which represents the distance from the tree to the building <u>plus</u> the length of the tree's shadow.

Question 39

Choice (D) is the correct answer. You can solve this problem by finding the area of the sector containing the shaded region and subtracting the area of $\triangle OBC$. Since the radius of the circle is 6 and the central angle is 60°, the area of the sector is $\frac{60}{360}(\pi)(6)^2 = 6\pi$. Since $OB = OC$, you know that $m\angle OBC = m\angle OCB = 60°$ and thus $\triangle OBC$ is equilateral.

The area of $\triangle OBC$ is $\frac{1}{2}(6)\left(\frac{6}{2}\sqrt{3}\right) = 9\sqrt{3}$. Thus, the area of the shaded region is $6\pi - 9\sqrt{3} \approx 3.2611$, which rounds to 3.26.

Choice (B) is incorrect. This results from the incorrect assumption that both the base and the height of $\triangle OBC$ have length 6, so the area of the shaded region is $6\pi - 18 \approx 0.8496$. Note that the height of an equilateral triangle is $\frac{\sqrt{3}}{2}$ times the side length.

Question 40

Choice (D) is the correct answer. Since the sale price is 45 percent off the list price, the sale price of the novel is $(1-0.45)n = 0.55n$, where n is the list price. Since Sarah is purchasing the novel for 45 percent off the <u>sale</u> price, the price she pays for the novel is $(1-0.45)(0.55n) = (0.55)^2 n$. Thus,

$$(0.55)^2 n = 6.05$$
$$0.3025n = 6.05$$
$$n = 20.$$

The list price is $20.

Choice (E) is incorrect. This results from incorrectly thinking that the sale price is $0.45n$ and that $(0.45)^2 n$ is the price that Sarah pays. Solving $(0.45)^2 n = 6.05$ gives $n \approx 29.8765$.

Question 41

Choice (E) is the correct answer. Since f and f^{-1} are inverse functions with domain all real numbers, by definition, $f\left(f^{-1}(x)\right) = x$ and $f^{-1}(f(x)) = x$.

Choice (C) is incorrect. A way to show that this is incorrect is with a counterexample. Take $f(x) = 3x + 1$. Let $y = f(x)$. Then,

$y = 3x + 1$

$x = 3y + 1$

$\dfrac{x-1}{3} = y = f^{-1}(x).$

Therefore, $f^{-1}(f(x)) = \dfrac{f(x)-1}{3} = \dfrac{(3x+1)-1}{3} = x$, which is only equal to 1 when $x = 1$.

Question 42

Choice (E) is the correct answer. It is helpful to use the given figure to solve the problem. Each of the five choices must be examined.

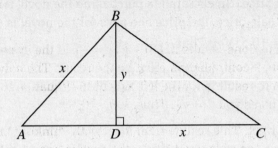

Using the definition, $\sin \angle A = \dfrac{y}{x}$, and thus $\tan \angle C = \dfrac{y}{x}$.

Choice (A) is incorrect. $\cos \angle A = \dfrac{AD}{x}$. Since no information about AD is given, this is not necessarily equal to $\sin \angle A$.

Choice (B) is incorrect. $\tan \angle A = \dfrac{y}{AD}$. Since no information about AD is given, this is not necessarily equal to $\sin \angle A$.

Choice (C) is incorrect. $\sin \angle C = \dfrac{y}{BC}$. Since no information about BC is given, this is not necessarily equal to $\sin \angle A$.

Choice (D) is incorrect. $\cos \angle C = \dfrac{x}{BC}$. Since no information about BC is given, this is not necessarily equal to $\sin \angle A$.

Question 43

Choice (A) is the correct answer. Since D is the midpoint of diameter $\overline{AC}$, $\overline{BD}$ splits the area of inscribed right triangle ABC in half. Note that a triangle inscribed in a semicircle is a right triangle. Thus, half the area of $\triangle ABC$ is the area of $\triangle BCD$. $\triangle ABC$ has area $\dfrac{1}{2}(4)(3) = 6$, making the area of $\triangle BCD$ equal to 3.

Choice (C) is incorrect. This is the area of $\triangle ABC$. It is also the result from incorrectly calculating the area of $\triangle ABC$ as 12 and then taking half of that for the area of $\triangle BCD$.

Question 44

Choice (A) is the correct answer. To solve the system of equations by the addition method, you multiply both sides of the first equation by -2. This results in $-4x + 10y = -16$

$$4x + ky = 17.$$

Adding the two equations results in $(10 + k)y = -1$. If the system is to have no solution, a contradiction must be the result. The only way for a contradiction to result is for the left side of the equation to be equal to 0, which gives you $0 = -1$. Thus, $k = -10$.

Choice (C) is incorrect. This results from incorrectly thinking that if there is no y term in the second equation, the system has no solution. When $k = 0$, the ordered pair $\left(\dfrac{17}{4}, \dfrac{1}{10}\right)$ is a solution to the system of equations.

Question 45

Choice (E) is the correct answer. From the equation,

$$2x + 2y = 0$$
$$2y = -2x$$
$$y = -x.$$

Substituting this into the expression $x - y$ produces $x - (-x) = 2x$.

Choice (A) is incorrect. This is the value of $x + y$. If $x - y = 0$, then $x = y$. From the previous result, $y = -x$, you have $-x = x$, which is only true if $x = 0$.

Question 46

Choice (C) is the correct answer. If the length of a side of the cube is x inches, then $V = x^3 = 100$ and $x = \sqrt[3]{100}$. The surface area of the cube is $6x^2$, since each of the 6 faces of the cube has area x^2. Thus, the surface area is $6\left(\sqrt[3]{100}\right)^2 \approx 129.2661$, which rounds to 129.27 square inches.

Choice (E) is incorrect. This is the result of incorrectly using $V = x^2$ for the volume of the cube to get $x = 10$. Thus, this gives a surface area of $6(10)^2 = 600$ square inches.

Question 47

Choice (A) is the correct answer. Each of the five choices must be examined. Since the quadrilateral is inscribed in the circle, the opposite angles are supplementary. Thus, $x + z = 180$. The arcs intercepted by the inscribed angles with measures $x°$ and $z°$ cover the entire circle, and so measure a combined 360°. Since inscribed angles have a measure of half the measure of their intercepted arcs,

$$x + z = \frac{360}{2} = 180.$$

Choice (B) is incorrect. The arcs intercepted by the inscribed angles with measures $x°$ and $y°$ overlap on a portion of the circle, and so the combined measure is not known. Therefore, the value of $x + y$ is not known.

Choice (C) is incorrect. There is not enough information given to determine the relationship between x and z.

Choice (D) is incorrect. There is not enough information given to determine the relationship between x and y.

Choice (E) is incorrect. There is not enough information to determine the value of x.

Question 48

Choice (C) is the correct answer. Each of the three statements must be analyzed separately using the given function f and the fact that m is a constant greater than 1. Consider statement I. Since $f(x) = mx$, $f(mx) = m(mx) = m^2x$ and $mf(x) = m(mx) = m^2x$. Thus, $f(mx) = mf(x)$, and statement I is true. Consider statement II. Since $f(x) = mx$, $f(x_1 + x_2) = m(x_1 + x_2) = mx_1 + mx_2$ and $f(x_1) + f(x_2) = mx_1 + mx_2$. Thus, $f(x_1 + x_2) = f(x_1) + f(x_2)$, and statement II is true. Consider statement III. Since $f(x) = mx$, $f(x_1 \cdot x_2) = m(x_1 \cdot x_2) = mx_1x_2$ and $f(x_1) \cdot f(x_2) = mx_1 \cdot mx_2 = m^2x_1x_2$. Thus, $f(x_1 \cdot x_2) \neq f(x_1) \cdot f(x_2)$, and statement III is NOT true. Since statements I and II are true and statement III is not true, choice (C) is correct.

Question 49

Choice (E) is the correct answer. It is helpful to draw a figure to solve the problem. Pyramid T with a triangular base has 4 faces. Therefore, the greatest possible number of sides for a figure created by a plane intersecting pyramid T is 4. The plane must intersect the pyramid in all 4 faces.

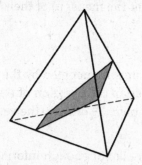

Choice (D) is incorrect. This would be the result of a plane intersecting with only 3 of the 4 faces of pyramid T.

Question 50

Choice (B) is the correct answer. It is helpful to use the given figure to solve the problem. Draw the altitude from vertex B to $\overline{AC}$. The altitude is perpendicular to $\overline{AC}$ and bisects $\overline{AC}$, since $AB = BC$.

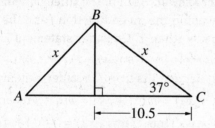

Thus, $\cos 37° = \dfrac{10.5}{x}$ and $x = \dfrac{10.5}{\cos 37°} \approx 13.1474$. Therefore, the perimeter of $\triangle ABC$ is $2x + 21 \approx 47.3$.

Choice (C) is incorrect. This is the result of incorrectly thinking that $\sin 37° = \dfrac{10.5}{x}$ and $x = \dfrac{10.5}{\sin 37°} \approx 17.4472$. Using this gives a perimeter of $2x + 21 \approx 55.9$.

Mathematics Level 1 – Practice Test 2

Practice Helps

The test that follows is an actual, previously administered SAT Subject Test in Mathematics Level 1. To get an idea of what it's like to take this test, practice under conditions that are much like those of an actual test administration.

- Set aside an hour when you can take the test uninterrupted.

- Sit at a desk or table with no other books or papers. Dictionaries, other books, or notes are not allowed in the test room.

- Remember to have a scientific or graphing calculator with you.

- Tear out an answer sheet from the back of this book and fill it in just as you would on the day of the test. One answer sheet can be used for up to three Subject Tests.

- Read the instructions that precede the practice test. During the actual administration you will be asked to read them before answering test questions.

- Use a clock or kitchen timer to time yourself.

- After you finish the practice test, read the sections "How to Score the SAT Subject Test in Mathematics Level 1" and "How Did You Do on the Subject Test in Mathematics Level 1?"

- The appearance of the answer sheet in this book may differ from the answer sheet you see on test day.

MATHEMATICS LEVEL 1 TEST

The top portion of the page of the answer sheet that you will use to take the Mathematics Level 1 Test must be filled in exactly as illustrated below. When your supervisor tells you to fill in the circle next to the name of the test you are about to take, mark your answer sheet as shown.

○ Literature	● Mathematics Level 1	○ German	○ Chinese Listening	○ Japanese Listening
○ Biology E	○ Mathematics Level 2	○ Italian	○ French Listening	○ Korean Listening
○ Biology M	○ U.S. History	○ Latin	○ German Listening	○ Spanish Listening
○ Chemistry	○ World History	○ Modern Hebrew		
○ Physics	○ French	○ Spanish	**Background Questions:** ① ② ③ ④ ⑤ ⑥ ⑦ ⑧ ⑨	

After filling in the circle next to the name of the test you are taking, locate the Background Questions section, which also appears at the top of your answer sheet (as shown above). This is where you will answer the following Background Questions on your answer sheet.

BACKGROUND QUESTIONS

Please answer Part I and Part II below by filling in the appropriate circle in the Background Questions box on your answer sheet. The information you provide is for statistical purposes only and will not affect your test score.

Part I. Which of the following describes a mathematics course you have taken or are currently taking? (FILL IN **ALL** CIRCLES THAT APPLY.)

- Algebra I or Elementary Algebra **OR** Course I of a college preparatory mathematics sequence   —Fill in circle 1.

- Geometry **OR** Course II of a college preparatory mathematics sequence   —Fill in circle 2.

- Algebra II or Intermediate Algebra **OR** Course III of a college preparatory mathematics sequence   —Fill in circle 3.

- Elementary Functions (Precalculus) and/or Trigonometry **OR** beyond Course III of a college preparatory mathematics sequence   —Fill in circle 4.

- Advanced Placement Mathematics (Calculus AB or Calculus BC)   —Fill in circle 5.

Part II. What type of calculator did you bring to use for this test? (FILL IN THE **ONE** CIRCLE THAT APPLIES. If you did not bring a scientific or graphing calculator, do not fill in any of circles 6-9.)

- Scientific   —Fill in circle 6.

- Graphing (Fill in the circle corresponding to the model you used.)

    Casio 9700, Casio 9750, Casio 9800, Casio 9850, Casio 9860, Casio FX 1.0, Casio CG-10, Sharp 9200, Sharp 9300, Sharp 9600, Sharp 9900, TI-82, TI-83, TI-83 Plus, TI-83 Plus Silver, TI-84 Plus, TI-84 Plus CE, TI-84 Plus Silver, TI-84 Plus C Silver, TI-85, TI-86, TI-Nspire, or TI-Nspire CX   —Fill in circle 7.

    Casio 9970, Casio Algebra FX 2.0, HP 38G, HP 39 series, HP 40 series, HP 48 series, HP 49 series, HP 50 series, HP Prime, TI-89, TI-89 Titanium, TI-Nspire CAS, or TI-Nspire CX CAS   —Fill in circle 8.

    Some other graphing calculator   —Fill in circle 9.

When the supervisor gives the signal, turn the page and begin the Mathematics Level 1 Test. There are 100 numbered circles on the answer sheet and 50 questions in the Mathematics Level 1 Test. Therefore, use only circles 1 to 50 for recording your answers.

MATHEMATICS LEVEL 1 TEST

REFERENCE INFORMATION

THE FOLLOWING INFORMATION IS FOR YOUR REFERENCE IN ANSWERING SOME OF THE QUESTIONS IN THIS TEST.

Volume of a right circular cone with radius r and height h: $V = \frac{1}{3}\pi r^2 h$

Volume of a sphere with radius r: $V = \frac{4}{3}\pi r^3$

Volume of a pyramid with base area B and height h: $V = \frac{1}{3}Bh$

Surface Area of a sphere with radius r: $S = 4\pi r^2$

DO NOT DETACH FROM BOOK.

GO ON TO THE NEXT PAGE

MATHEMATICS LEVEL 1 TEST

For each of the following problems, decide which is the BEST of the choices given. If the exact numerical value is not one of the choices, select the choice that best approximates this value. Then fill in the corresponding circle on the answer sheet.

Notes: (1) A scientific or graphing calculator will be necessary for answering some (but not all) of the questions in this test. For each question you will have to decide whether or not you should use a calculator.

(2) The only angle measure used on this test is degree measure. Make sure your calculator is in the degree mode.

(3) Figures that accompany problems in this test are intended to provide information useful in solving the problems. They are drawn as accurately as possible EXCEPT when it is stated in a specific problem that its figure is not drawn to scale. All figures lie in a plane unless otherwise indicated.

(4) Unless otherwise specified, the domain of any function f is assumed to be the set of all real numbers x for which $f(x)$ is a real number. The range of f is assumed to be the set of all real numbers $f(x)$, where x is in the domain of f.

(5) Reference information that may be useful in answering the questions in this test can be found on the page preceding Question 1.

USE THIS SPACE FOR SCRATCH WORK.

1. If $x^3 + y^2 = 23$ and $y^2 = 15$, what is the value of x ?

(A) –2   (B) 2   (C) 2.8   (D) 3.4   (E) 6.2

GO ON TO THE NEXT PAGE

MATHEMATICS LEVEL 1 TEST—*Continued*

2. A folder contains 23 sheets of paper—3 blue, 5 yellow, 6 red, and 9 white. If a sheet is selected from the folder at random, what is the probability that the sheet is blue or white?

(A) $\dfrac{3}{23}$ (B) $\dfrac{9}{23}$ (C) $\dfrac{11}{23}$ (D) $\dfrac{12}{23}$ (E) $\dfrac{27}{23^2}$

USE THIS SPACE FOR SCRATCH WORK.

3. If $a = \dfrac{x+3}{2}$ and $b = x - 6,$ for what value of x does $a = b$?

(A) −9   (B) −3   (C) 9   (D) 15   (E) 18

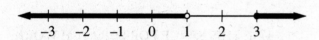

4. The graph in the figure above is the set of all x such that

(A) $x \le 3$
(B) $1 < x \le 3$
(C) $x \le 1$ or $x > 3$
(D) $x \le 1$ or $x \ge 3$
(E) $x < 1$ or $x \ge 3$

GO ON TO THE NEXT PAGE

MATHEMATICS LEVEL 1 TEST—*Continued*

5. A physics class launched a projectile from the roof of the school building and found that the projectile's height above the ground, in meters, was modeled by $h(t) = -4.9t^2 + 12t + 10,$ where t is the time, in seconds, after the launch. How many meters above the ground was the projectile 2 seconds after it was launched?

(A) 3.0
(B) 10.0
(C) 14.4
(D) 17.3
(E) 24.2

USE THIS SPACE FOR SCRATCH WORK.

6. What is the slope of the line in the xy-plane with equation $2x - 3y = 4$?

(A) $-\dfrac{3}{2}$

(B) $-\dfrac{2}{3}$

(C) $\dfrac{2}{3}$

(D) $\dfrac{3}{2}$

(E) 2

GO ON TO THE NEXT PAGE

MATHEMATICS LEVEL 1 TEST—*Continued*

USE THIS SPACE FOR SCRATCH WORK.

7. For what values of x is $\frac{1}{x} + \frac{1}{x-1}$ undefined?

(A) 0 only

(B) $\frac{1}{2}$ only

(C) 1 only

(D) 0 and 1 only

(E) 0, $\frac{1}{2}$, and 1

8. Susan has 4 times as many rocks as seashells. If the combined number of Susan's rocks and seashells is 120, how many seashells does she have?

(A) 20 (B) 24 (C) 30 (D) 96 (E) 100

9. What is the circumference of a circle with an area of 9π ?

(A) 6.0 (B) 9.4 (C) 13.3 (D) 18.8 (E) 63.6

10. For which of the following values of x is $(4 - x)(2x - 11)$ positive?

(A) 5 (B) 4 (C) 3 (D) 0 (E) -4

GO ON TO THE NEXT PAGE

USE THIS SPACE FOR SCRATCH WORK.

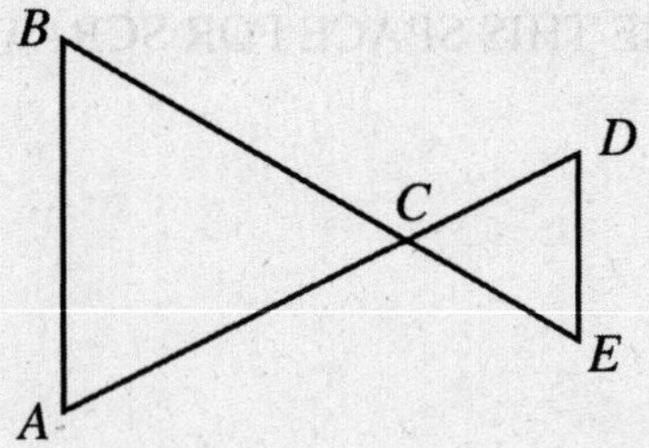

Note: Figure not drawn to scale.

11. In the figure above, $\overline{AB} \| \overline{DE}$. Which of the
following must be true about $\triangle ABC$ and
$\triangle DEC$?

(A) The triangles are similar.
(B) The triangles are congruent.
(C) The triangles are isosceles.
(D) The area of $\triangle ABC$ is twice the area
of $\triangle DEC$.
(E) The perimeter of $\triangle ABC$ is twice the
perimeter of $\triangle DEC$.

12. Five points, A, B, C, D, and E, lie on a line in
that order. If $AD = 15$, $BE = 13$, and $DE = 4$,
then $AB =$

(A) 2   (B) 4   (C) 6   (D) 8   (E) 10

GO ON TO THE NEXT PAGE

MATHEMATICS LEVEL 1 TEST—*Continued*

USE THIS SPACE FOR SCRATCH WORK.

13. If the ordered pairs $\left(x - 8, \frac{y}{3} + 1 \right)$ and $(2x + 5, 2)$

are equal, then $(x, y) =$

(A) $(-13, -1)$

(B) $(-13, 3)$

(C) $(-13, 9)$

(D) $(-3, -1)$

(E) $(-3, 3)$

14. If t is a negative number, which of the following must be a positive number?

(A) $10 - t$

(B) $t - 3$

(C) $t + 5$

(D) $2t$

(E) $\frac{-t}{-2}$

$$0, 1, 5, 14, 30, \ldots$$

15. The sequence above starts with 0 and the numbers increase by the squares of consecutive integers. What is the 6th number in the sequence?

(A) 46   (B) 47   (C) 55   (D) 61   (E) 66

GO ON TO THE NEXT PAGE

MATHEMATICS LEVEL 1 TEST—*Continued*

16. If $y = 4x$, $x = 2z$, and $z = 3a$, what is the value of $y - x$ in terms of a ?

(A) $-20a$
(B) $-18a$
(C) $6a$
(D) $18a$
(E) $20a$

USE THIS SPACE FOR SCRATCH WORK.

17. If x is a real number such that $x^2 < 5$, which of the following CANNOT be true?

(A) x is an integer.

(B) $|x| = \sqrt{5}$

(C) $x + 1 = 3$

(D) $\dfrac{1}{x} < 3$

(E) $3x + 2 > x$

18. If $f(x) = 2.4x^2 - 8x + 5.1$ and
$g(x) = 3.1x - 11$, what is the value
of $f(4) + (g(4))^2$?

(A) 12.9
(B) 13.46
(C) 14.3
(D) 133.65
(E) 166.41

GO ON TO THE NEXT PAGE

MATHEMATICS LEVEL 1 TEST—*Continued*

19. In the *xy*-plane, what is the *x*-coordinate of the vertex of the graph of $y = -6x^2 + 3x + 8$?

    (A) −0.5
    (B) −0.25
    (C)   0.25
    (D)   0.5
    (E)   2

USE THIS SPACE FOR SCRATCH WORK.

20. If *a* and *b* are positive, and $a > b$, which of the following must be true?

    I. $a > -b$
    II. $-a > b$
   III. $-a < -b$

    (A) I only
    (B) II only
    (C) III only
    (D) I and II
    (E) I and III

21. A farmer used 204 feet of fencing to enclose a garden in the shape of a rectangle. If the length of the garden is twice the width, what is the width of the garden?

    (A) 34 ft
    (B) 40.8 ft
    (C) 51 ft
    (D) 68 ft
    (E) 81.6 ft

GO ON TO THE NEXT PAGE

MATHEMATICS LEVEL 1 TEST—*Continued*

USE THIS SPACE FOR SCRATCH WORK.

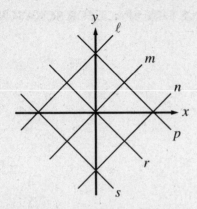

22. Which of the lines in the figure above is the result of reflecting line ℓ over the y-axis?

(A) m (B) n (C) p (D) r (E) s

TEST SCORES

7	3 5 6
8	2 2 4
9	0 3 5 7 9

Note: 7|3 represents 73.

23. The stem-and-leaf plot above shows the scores for eleven students on a driver education test. What is the median of the eleven scores?

(A) 82   (B) 83   (C) 84   (D) 86   (E) 87

GO ON TO THE NEXT PAGE

MATHEMATICS LEVEL 1 TEST—*Continued*

24. The number x is 15 less than the number y. The sum of three times x and twice y is 80. What is the value of $x + y$?

   (A) 15   (B) 23   (C) 29   (D) 35   (E) 45

USE THIS SPACE FOR SCRATCH WORK.

All integers that are factors of 18 are also factors of 24.

25. Which of the following integers can be used to show that the statement above is <u>false</u>?

   (A) 3   (B) 4   (C) 5   (D) 9   (E) 12

26. Last semester the mean of the amounts spent by 5 students on textbooks was $375. Four of the students each spent $300 or less. What is the least amount the fifth student could have spent on textbooks?

   (A) $375
   (B) $450
   (C) $675
   (D) $750
   (E) $875

27. For what value of k does the equation $x^2 + 6x - k = 0$ have equal roots?

   (A) 12   (B) 9   (C) 3   (D) –3   (E) –9

GO ON TO THE NEXT PAGE

MATHEMATICS LEVEL 1 TEST—*Continued*

28. A bottle of 500 cubic centimeters of fluid contains 125 units of medication. If a patient needs 8 units of medication per hour, how many cubic centimeters of the fluid must be administered per hour?

    (A) 0.5   (B) 2   (C) 4   (D) 16   (E) 32

USE THIS SPACE FOR SCRATCH WORK.

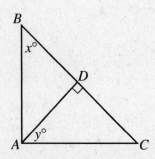

    Note: Figure not drawn to scale.

29. In $\triangle ABC$ above, $\angle BAC$ is a right angle. If $x = 40$, what is the value of y ?

    (A) 40   (B) 45   (C) 50   (D) 60   (E) 90

30. The rate at which crickets chirp depends on the temperature. If $c = t - 40$, where c is the number of chirps every 15 seconds and t is the temperature in degrees Fahrenheit, what is the temperature when the number of chirps is 40 per minute?

    (A)   0°F
    (B) 40°F
    (C) 50°F
    (D) 60°F
    (E) 80°F

GO ON TO THE NEXT PAGE

MATHEMATICS LEVEL 1 TEST—*Continued*

USE THIS SPACE FOR SCRATCH WORK.

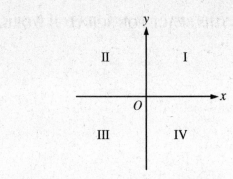

31. The figure above shows an *xy*-plane. The graph of
the line (not shown) with equation $y = mx + b$,
where $m < 0$ and $b > 0$, contains points in
which of the following quadrants?

(A) I and II only
(B) I and IV only
(C) II and III only
(D) I, II, and IV only
(E) I, III, and IV only

32. If a, b, and c are the lengths of the sides of a
triangle, which of the following must be true?

(A) $a^2 + b^2 > c^2$
(B) $a^2 + b^2 = c^2$
(C) $ab > c$
(D) $a - b > c$
(E) $a + b > c$

GO ON TO THE NEXT PAGE

MATHEMATICS LEVEL 1 TEST—*Continued*

33. Which of the following is a polynomial function?

USE THIS SPACE FOR SCRATCH WORK.

(A) $f(x) = x^{-1}$

(B) $f(x) = x + \dfrac{1}{x}$

(C) $f(x) = x^{\frac{2}{3}}$

(D) $f(x) = \dfrac{3}{x^2}$

(E) $f(x) = \dfrac{x^2}{3}$

34. What is the surface area, in square feet, of a cube with a volume of 0.125 cubic feet?

(A) 0.015   (B) 0.25   (C) 1   (D) 1.5   (E) 15

GO ON TO THE NEXT PAGE

MATHEMATICS LEVEL 1 TEST—*Continued*

USE THIS SPACE FOR SCRATCH WORK.

35. The function f is given by $f(x) = x^3$. In the xy-plane, the graph of f is shifted horizontally 2 units to the left to produce the graph of the function g. Which of the following represents $g(x)$?

(A) $g(x) = \dfrac{1}{2}x^3$

(B) $g(x) = x^3 - 2$

(C) $g(x) = x^3 + 2$

(D) $g(x) = (x - 2)^3$

(E) $g(x) = (x + 2)^3$

36. The distance to the furthest point on Earth's surface that a person can see in one direction out of the window of an airplane can be approximated by the formula $k = 35\sqrt{a}$, where a is the altitude of the plane in kilometers and k is the distance in kilometers. What is the distance in kilometers that a person can see from an altitude of 12,496 <u>meters</u>?

(A)   39
(B)   112
(C)   124
(D)   391
(E)   3,912

GO ON TO THE NEXT PAGE

37. If $f(2) > f(3)$, which of the following could be a graph of $y = f(x)$?

I.

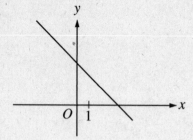

II.

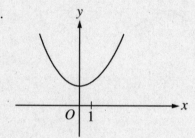

III.

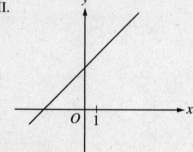

(A) I only
(B) II only
(C) III only
(D) I and II
(E) II and III

GO ON TO THE NEXT PAGE

MATHEMATICS LEVEL 1 TEST—*Continued*

38. If $f(x) = 2x + 3$ and $f(g(x)) = 8x - 1$, which
    of the following equals $g(x)$?

    (A) $4x - 2$
    (B) $4x - 1$
    (C) $8x - 4$
    (D) $8x - 1$
    (E) $16x + 23$

USE THIS SPACE FOR SCRATCH WORK.

39. A right circular cylindrical solid has height 10 and
    a base with diameter 6. A rectangular solid has
    height 10 and a square base with side of length 6.
    The volume of the rectangular solid is how many
    times the volume of the cylinder?

    (A) 4
    (B) 1.27
    (C) 0.76
    (D) 0.32
    (E) 0.13

GO ON TO THE NEXT PAGE

MATHEMATICS LEVEL 1 TEST—*Continued*

200 ft

A   *B*

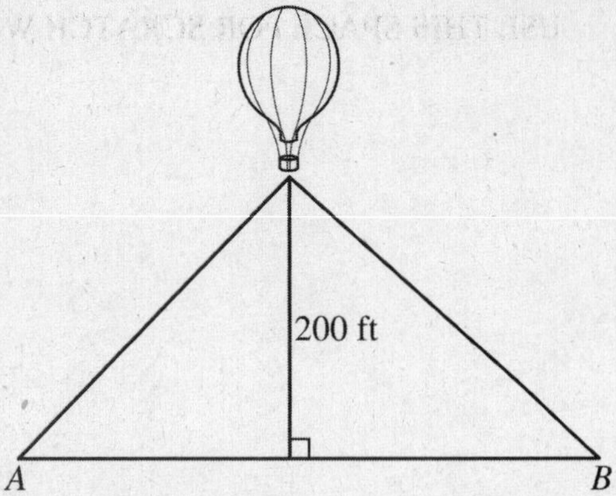

Note: Figure not drawn to scale.

40. In the figure above, two people on level ground
    at points *A* and *B* are observing a hot-air
    balloon from angles of elevation of 80° and 75°,
    respectively. If the height of the balloon is
    200 feet, how far apart are the two people?

    (A)   35 ft
    (B)   54 ft
    (C)   89 ft
    (D)   410 ft
    (E) 1,881 ft

41. In a circle with center *O*, the length of radius
    OB is 5. If the length of chord *CD* is 8, and if
    $\overline{CD} \perp \overline{OB}$, then $\sin \angle OCD =$

    (A) $\dfrac{3}{5}$ (B) $\dfrac{3}{4}$ (C) $\dfrac{4}{5}$ (D) $\dfrac{4}{3}$ (E) $\dfrac{5}{3}$

GO ON TO THE NEXT PAGE

MATHEMATICS LEVEL 1 TEST—*Continued*

USE THIS SPACE FOR SCRATCH WORK.

UNITED STATES POPULATION IN 2000

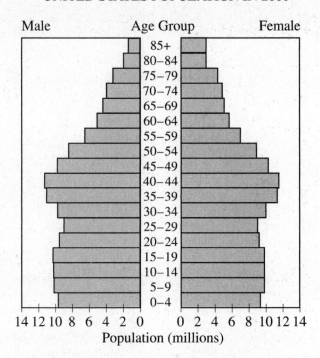

42. The graph above shows the age and gender distributions of the United States population in 2000. In which of the following time periods was the greatest number of individuals in this population born?

(A) 1946–1950
(B) 1951–1955
(C) 1956–1960
(D) 1961–1965
(E) 1981–1985

GO ON TO THE NEXT PAGE

MATHEMATICS LEVEL 1 TEST—*Continued*

USE THIS SPACE FOR SCRATCH WORK.

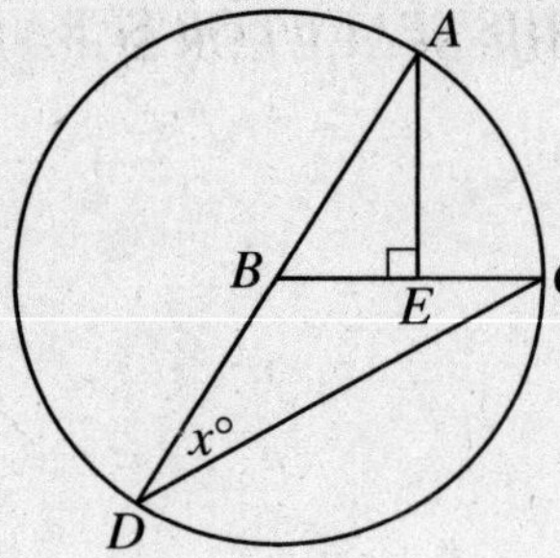

43. In the figure above, if $\overline{AD}$ is a diameter and $\overline{AE}$ bisects radius BC, what is the value of x ?

(A) 15
(B) 30
(C) 45
(D) 60
(E) It cannot be determined from the information given.

44. Which of the following is equal to $1 - \sin^2(4\theta)$ for all possible values of θ ?

(A) 4
(B) $4\sin\theta\cos\theta$
(C) $(1 - \sin(2\theta))(1 + \sin(2\theta))$
(D) $\tan^2(4\theta)$
(E) $\cos^2(4\theta)$

GO ON TO THE NEXT PAGE

MATHEMATICS LEVEL 1 TEST—*Continued*

45. A sphere has radius 6 inches. What is the radius, in inches, of the circle formed by the intersection of the sphere and a plane 3 inches from the sphere's center?

(A) 3

(B) $\sqrt{18}$

(C) $\sqrt{27}$

(D) $\dfrac{\sqrt{45}}{2}$

(E) $\sqrt{45}$

USE THIS SPACE FOR SCRATCH WORK.

46. What is the area, in square units, of a square whose diagonal is 1 unit longer than the length of a side?

(A) 3.83
(B) 4.41
(C) 4.83
(D) 5.83
(E) 9.66

47. If $5x - y = 8y + 12x$ and $xy \neq 0$, what is the ratio of x to y ?

(A) −1.29
(B) −0.78
(C)　0.78
(D)　1.29
(E)　1.89

GO ON TO THE NEXT PAGE

MATHEMATICS LEVEL 1 TEST—*Continued*

USE THIS SPACE FOR SCRATCH WORK.

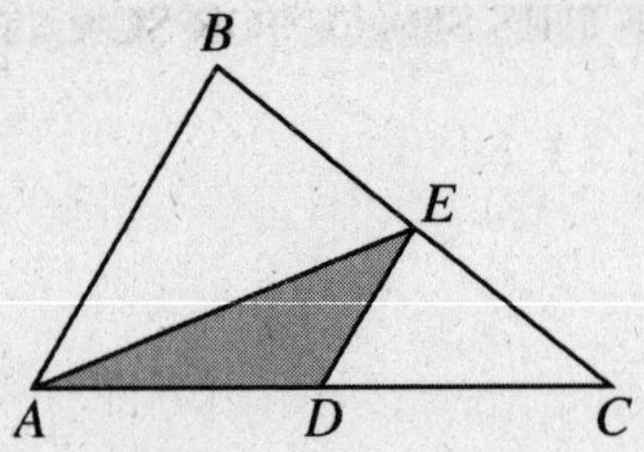

48. In the figure above, D is the midpoint of side AC, and E is the midpoint of side BC. If the area of $\triangle ABC$ is 24, what is the area of $\triangle ADE$?

(A) 4   (B) 6   (C) 8   (D) 10   (E) 12

49. Each year Luis and Patricia share the annual income from an investment so that Luis gets $\frac{3}{5}$ as much as Patricia. If d represents the annual income from the investment, which of the following is an expression for Luis's share?

(A) $\frac{3}{10}d$

(B) $\frac{3}{8}d$

(C) $\frac{2}{5}d$

(D) $\frac{3}{5}d$

(E) $\frac{5}{8}d$

GO ON TO THE NEXT PAGE

MATHEMATICS LEVEL 1 TEST—*Continued*

50. The function f is defined by

$f(x) = x^3 - 11x^2 + 30x + 5$ for

$0 \le x \le 7$. Of the following, which best describes the range of f?

(A) $1.81 < f(x) < 5.52$
(B) $3.62 < f(x) < 29.20$
(C) $5.00 \le f(x) \le 19.00$
(D) $5.00 < f(x) < 29.20$
(E) $5.52 < f(x) < 29.20$

USE THIS SPACE FOR SCRATCH WORK.

STOP

**IF YOU FINISH BEFORE TIME IS CALLED, YOU MAY CHECK YOUR WORK ON THIS TEST ONLY.
DO NOT TURN TO ANY OTHER TEST IN THIS BOOK.**

How to Score the SAT Subject Test in Mathematics Level 1

When you take an actual SAT Subject Test in Mathematics Level 1, your answer sheet will be "read" by a scanning machine that will record your response to each question. Then a computer will compare your answers with the correct answers and produce your raw score. You get one point for each correct answer. For each wrong answer, you lose one-fourth of a point. Questions you omit (and any for which you mark more than one answer) are not counted. This raw score is converted to a scaled score that is reported to you and to the colleges you specify.

Worksheet 1. Finding Your Raw Test Score

STEP 1: Table A on the following page lists the correct answers for all the questions on the Subject Test in Mathematics Level 1 that is reproduced in this book. It also serves as a worksheet for you to calculate your raw score.

- Compare your answers with those given in the table.

- Put a check in the column marked "Right" if your answer is correct.

- Put a check in the column marked "Wrong" if your answer is incorrect.

- Leave both columns blank if you omitted the question.

STEP 2: Count the number of right answers.

Enter the total here: _____

STEP 3: Count the number of wrong answers.

Enter the total here: _____

STEP 4: Multiply the number of wrong answers by .250.

Enter the product here: _____

STEP 5: Subtract the result obtained in Step 4 from the total you obtained in Step 2.

Enter the result here: _____

STEP 6: Round the number obtained in Step 5 to the nearest whole number.

Enter the result here: _____

The number you obtained in Step 6 is your raw score.

Answers to Practice Test 2 for Mathematics Level 1

Table A
Answers to the Subject Test in Mathematics Level 1 - Practice Test 2 and Percentage of Students Answering Each Question Correctly

Question Number	Correct Answer	Right	Wrong	Percent Answering Correctly*	Question Number	Correct Answer	Right	Wrong	Percent Answering Correctly*
1	B			91	26	C			80
2	D			93	27	E			62
3	D			90	28	E			75
4	E			83	29	A			81
5	C			91	30	C			69
6	C			84	31	D			75
7	D			85	32	E			58
8	B			82	33	E			29
9	D			76	34	D			57
10	A			87	35	E			61
11	A			76	36	C			63
12	C			85	37	A			62
13	B			83	38	A			69
14	A			84	39	B			51
15	C			79	40	C			60
16	D			85	41	A			26
17	B			73	42	C			72
18	B			85	43	B			24
19	C			66	44	E			59
20	E			79	45	C			15
21	A			75	46	D			31
22	C			67	47	A			31
23	C			79	48	B			31
24	D			72	49	B			35
25	D			75	50	B			16

* These percentages are based on an analysis of the answer sheets for a random sample of 11,483 students who took the original administration of this test and whose mean score was 618. They may be used as an indication of the relative difficulty of a particular question. Each percentage may also be used to predict the likelihood that a typical Subject Test in Mathematics Level 1 candidate will answer correctly that question on this edition of this test.

Finding Your Scaled Score

When you take SAT Subject Tests, the scores sent to the colleges you specify are reported on the College Board scale, which ranges from 200–800. You can convert your practice test score to a scaled score by using Table B. To find your scaled score, locate your raw score in the left-hand column of Table B; the corresponding score in the right-hand column is your scaled score. For example, a raw score of 30 on this particular edition of the Subject Test in Mathematics Level 1 corresponds to a scaled score of 610.

Raw scores are converted to scaled scores to ensure that a score earned on any one edition of a particular Subject Test is comparable to the same scaled score earned on any other edition of the same Subject Test. Because some editions of the tests may be slightly easier or more difficult than others, College Board scaled scores are adjusted so that they indicate the same level of performance regardless of the edition of the test taken and the ability of the group that takes it. Thus, for example, a score of 500 on one edition of a test taken at a particular administration indicates the same level of achievement as a score of 500 on a different edition of the test taken at a different administration.

When you take the SAT Subject Tests during a national administration, your scores are likely to differ somewhat from the scores you obtain on the tests in this book. People perform at different levels at different times for reasons unrelated to the tests themselves. The precision of any test is also limited because it represents only a sample of all the possible questions that could be asked.

Table B
Scaled Score Conversion Table
Subject Test in Mathematics Level 1 - Practice Test 2

Raw Score	Reported Score	Raw Score	Reported Score	Raw Score	Reported Score
50	800	29	600	8	420
49	800	28	590	7	420
48	790	27	580	6	410
47	780	26	570	5	400
46	770	25	560	4	390
45	760	24	550	3	380
44	750	23	540	2	370
43	740	22	530	1	360
42	730	21	520	0	350
41	720	20	520	−1	330
40	720	19	510	−2	320
39	710	18	500	−3	310
38	700	17	490	−4	290
37	680	16	480	−5	280
36	670	15	480	−6	270
35	660	14	470	−7	260
34	650	13	460	−8	250
33	640	12	450	−9	240
32	630	11	450	−10	240
31	620	10	440	−11	240
30	610	9	430	−12	240

How Did You Do on the Subject Test in Mathematics Level 1?

After you score your test and analyze your performance, think about the following questions:

Did you run out of time before reaching the end of the test?

If so, you may need to pace yourself better. For example, maybe you spent too much time on one or two hard questions. A better approach might be to skip the ones you can't answer right away and try answering all the questions that remain on the test. Then if there's time, go back to the questions you skipped.

Did you take a long time reading the directions?

You will save time when you take the test by learning the directions to the Subject Test in Mathematics Level 1 ahead of time. Each minute you spend reading directions during the test is a minute that you could use to answer questions.

How did you handle questions you were unsure of?

If you were able to eliminate one or more of the answer choices as wrong and guess from the remaining ones, your approach probably worked to your advantage. On the other hand, making haphazard guesses or omitting questions without trying to eliminate choices could cost you valuable points.

How difficult were the questions for you compared with other students who took the test?

Table A shows you how difficult the multiple-choice questions were for the group of students who took this test during its national administration. The right-hand column gives the percentage of students that answered each question correctly.

A question answered correctly by almost everyone in the group is obviously an easier question. For example, 76 percent of the students answered question 11 correctly. But only 26 percent answered question 41 correctly.

Keep in mind that these percentages are based on just one group of students. They would probably be different with another group of students taking the test.

If you missed several easier questions, go back and try to find out why: Did the questions cover material you haven't yet reviewed? Did you misunderstand the directions?

Answer Explanations

For Practice Test 2

The solutions presented here provide one method for solving each of the problems on this test. Other mathematically correct approaches are possible.

Question 1

Choice (B) is the correct answer. Since $y^2 = 15$, substituting 15 for y^2 in the second equation yields $x^3 + 15 = 23$; that is, $x^3 = 23 - 15 = 8$. Thus, $x = 2$.

Choice (C) is incorrect. Mistakenly removing y^2 from the equation $x^3 + y^2 = 23$ gives $x^3 = 23$ or $x \approx 2.8439$, which rounds to 2.8.

Question 2

Choice (D) is the correct answer. Of 23 sheets, 3 are blue and 9 are white. So, 12 out of 23 sheets are either blue or white. Therefore, the probability that the selected sheet is blue or white is $\frac{12}{23}$.

Choice (C) is incorrect. This is the probability that the selected sheet is neither blue nor white; that is, $\frac{23 - 12}{23} = \frac{11}{23}$.

Question 3

Choice (D) is the correct answer. To find the value of x such that $a = b$, one can substitute $\frac{x + 3}{2}$ for a and $x - 6$ for b, giving the equation $\frac{x + 3}{2} = x - 6$. Multiplying both sides of the equation by 2 yields $x + 3 = 2x - 12$, which results in $x = 15$.

Choice (C) is incorrect. If one multiplies both sides of the equation $\frac{x + 3}{2} = x - 6$ by 2 and does not correctly distribute the 2 on the right-hand side of the equation, one gets $x + 3 = 2x - 6$, which results in $x = 9$.

Question 4

Choice (E) is the correct answer. The graph on the number line consists of two separate rays. The ray on the left side extends left from number 1 without terminating. The open dot at 1 indicates that 1 is not included in the graph but that the ray represents all numbers to the left of 1 or all numbers less than 1. The other ray on the right side extends right from number 3 without terminating. The solid dot at 3 indicates that 3 is included in the graph and that the ray includes 3 and represents all numbers to the right of 3 or all numbers greater than or equal to 3. Thus, the graph is the set of numbers that are $x < 1$ or $x \geq 3$.

Choice (B) is incorrect. It results from incorrectly interchanging "less than" with "greater than" in $x < 1$ and incorrectly interchanging "greater than or equal to" with "less than or equal to" in $x \geq 3$.

Question 5

Choice (C) is the correct answer. Plugging $t = 2$ into the model yields $h(2) = -4.9(2^2) + 12(2) + 10 = 14.4$. So, the projectile is 14.4 meters above ground 2 seconds after it is launched.

Choice (E) is incorrect. If one mistakes the height given in the model as the height above the roof, one would add the height of the roof, which is 10 meters (when $t = 0$), to 14.4 meters and get 24.4 meters, which is closest to 24.2 meters.

Question 6

Choice (C) is the correct answer. It is helpful to rewrite the equation in the slope-intercept form. Adding $3y$ to both sides of the equation and subtracting 4 from both sides of the equation yields $3y = 2x - 4$. Dividing both sides of this equation by 3 yields $y = \frac{2}{3}x - \frac{4}{3}$. So, the slope is $\frac{2}{3}$.

Choice (B) is incorrect. This results from not changing the sign when expressing y in terms of x.

Question 7

Choice (D) is the correct answer. Since rational expressions are undefined when the denominator is zero, the expression $\frac{1}{x}$ is undefined when $x = 0$ and the expression $\frac{1}{x-1}$ is undefined when $x = 1$.

Therefore, the expression $\frac{1}{x} + \frac{1}{x-1}$ is undefined when $x = 0$ and $x = 1$.

Choice (A) is incorrect. This comes from incorrectly thinking that only the first fraction, $\frac{1}{x}$, needs to be undefined, which incorrectly indicates that the expression is undefined for only one value, $x = 0$.

Question 8

Choice (B) is the correct answer. Let r be the number of rocks Susan has and s be the number of seashells she has. One can then set up a system of equations in the two variables $r = 4s$ and $r + s = 120$. Substituting $4s$ for r into $r + s = 120$ yields $5s = 120$ or $s = 24$.

Choice (D) is incorrect. If one misinterprets the statement "4 times as many rocks as seashells" to mean the number of seashells is 4 time the number of rocks, then the system of equations determined would be $s = 4r$ and $r + s = 120$, which yields s is 96; this is incorrect.

Question 9

Choice (D) is the correct answer. Given that the area of the circle is 9π, if the radius of the circle is r, then $\pi r^2 = 9\pi$. From this it follows that the radius r equals 3. Therefore, the circumference of the circle is $2\pi r$ or 6π, which rounds to 18.8.

Choice (A) is incorrect. This is the diameter of the circle, not the circumference of the circle.

Question 10

Choice (A) is the correct answer. If $(4 - x)(2x - 11)$ is positive, there are two cases to consider: both factors are positive or both factors are negative.

Case I. $4 - x > 0$ and $2x - 11 > 0$. Solving the two inequalities gives $x < 4$ and $x > \frac{11}{2}$. Since $4 < \frac{11}{2}$, there is no such value of x that is less than 4 and greater than $\frac{11}{2}$. So, no values of x make $(4 - x)(2x - 11)$ positive in this case.

Case II. $4 - x < 0$ and $2x - 11 < 0$. Solving these two inequalities gives $x > 4$ and $x < \frac{11}{2}$. Since $4 < \frac{11}{2}$, all the values that are greater than 4 and less than $\frac{11}{2}$ make $(4 - x)(2x - 11)$ positive. And the number 5 is the only value among the choices that is such a value.

Choice (B) is incorrect. If $x = 4$, the expression $(4 - x)(2x - 11)$ is equal to 0. Thus, the expression $(4 - 4)(2 \cdot 4 - 11)$ is not positive.

Question 11

Choice (A) is the correct answer. Since $\overline{AB} \parallel \overline{DE}$, alternate interior angles are congruent. So, you have $\angle B \cong \angle E$ and $\angle A \cong \angle D$. Also, $\angle BCA$ and $\angle DCE$ are vertical angles; so, $\angle BCA \cong \angle DCE$. Therefore, $\triangle ABC$ and $\triangle DEC$ are similar because all three pairs of corresponding angles are congruent.

Choice (E) is incorrect. The figure drawn seems to suggest that the length of each side of $\triangle ABC$ is twice the length of the corresponding side of $\triangle DEC$. However, the note given under the figure indicates that one should not draw a conclusion based on the size of the figure.

Question 12.

Choice (C) is the correct answer. It is helpful to draw a figure with the points on the number line as described in the question.

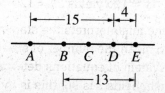

One can see from the figure shown above that $AB = AE - BE$. Since $AE = AD + DE = 15 + 4 = 19$ and $BE = 13$, you get $AB = 19 - 13 = 6$.

Choice (A) is incorrect. This results from mistaking $AD = 15$ for the total length AE and then subtracting 13 from 15 to get 2.

Question 13

Choice (B) is the correct answer. If the two ordered pairs are equal, then the corresponding coordinates are equal. Thus, $x - 8 = 2x + 5$ and $\frac{y}{3} + 1 = 2$. Solving these two equations yields $x = -13$ and $y = 3$.

Choice (E) is incorrect. In solving the first equation $x - 8 = 2x + 5$ for x, forgetting to change the sign of 5 incorrectly yields $-8 + 5 = x$ or $x = -3$.

Question 14

Choice (A) is the correct answer. Each of the five choices needs to be examined. One may start with choice (A). If t is negative, then $-t$ is always positive. And so $10 - t = 10 + (-t)$ is a positive number.

Choice (B) is incorrect because $t - 3$ remains negative when t is negative.

Choice (C) is incorrect because $t + 5$ can be a negative number. For example, when $t = -6$, one gets $t + 5 = -1$.

Choice (D) is incorrect because $2t$ remains negative when t is negative.

Choice (E) is incorrect because $\frac{-t}{-2} = \frac{t}{2}$ remains negative when t is negative.

Question 15

Choice (C) is the correct answer. The sequence starts with 0, and each subsequent term is obtained by adding the square of the corresponding consecutive integers 1, 2, 3, ... to its preceding term. For example, the <u>second</u> term is obtained by adding the square of the <u>first</u> consecutive integer, 1, to the preceding term 0 to get $0 + 1^2 = 1$; the <u>third</u> term is obtained by adding the square of the <u>second</u> consecutive integer, 2, to the preceding term, 1, to get $1 + 2^2 = 5$. Similarly, the <u>sixth</u> term is obtained by adding the square of the <u>fifth</u> consecutive integer, 5, to the preceding term, 30, to get $30 + 5^2 = 55$.

Choice (E) is incorrect. This results from incorrectly adding the square of the sixth (instead of the fifth) consecutive integer to the preceding term to get the sixth term, which gives 66.

Question 16

Choice (D) is the correct answer. Substituting $x = 2z$ and $z = 3a$ into $y = 4x$ yields $y = 4x = 4(2(3a)) = 24a$. Since $x = 2z$ and $z = 3a$, this yields $x = 6a$. Thus, $y - x = 24a - 6a = 18a$.

Choice (C) is incorrect. This is the value of x in terms of a and not the value of $y - x$ in terms of a.

Question 17

Choice (B) is the correct answer. Each of the five choices needs to be examined. Solving $x^2 < 5$ yields $|x| < \sqrt{5}$ or $-\sqrt{5} < x < \sqrt{5}$. Choice (B) cannot be true, since $|x| < \sqrt{5}$; therefore, $|x| \neq \sqrt{5}$.

Choice (A) is true when $x = 1$, since 1 is an integer and $1 < \sqrt{5}$.

Choices (C) is true when $x = 2$, since $2 < \sqrt{5}$.

Choices (D) and (E) are true when $x = 1$, since $1 < \sqrt{5}$.

Question 18

Choice (B) is the correct answer. Plugging $x = 4$ into $f(x) = 2.4x^2 - 8x + 5.1$ gives $f(4) = 2.4(4^2) - 8(4) + 5.1 = 11.5$. Similarly, plugging $x = 4$ into $g(x) = 3.1x - 11$ gives $g(4) = 3.1(4) - 11 = 1.4$. Thus, $f(4) + (g(4))^2 = 11.5 + 1.4^2 = 13.46$.

Choice (A) is incorrect. This results from calculating $f(4) + g(4)$, which is 12.9, instead of calculating $f(4) + (g(4))^2$.

Question 19

Choice (C) is the correct answer. If one can use a graphing calculator to graph $y = -6x^2 + 3x + 8$, one will find that $x = 0.25$ is the x-coordinate of the vertex of the graph. An alternate approach is that since the graph of $y = -6x^2 + 3x + 8$ is a parabola that opens downward, the vertex of the graph is the maximum point. To find the maximum value of y, it is useful to rewrite it as follows.

$$y = -6x^2 + 3x + 8$$
$$= -6\left(x^2 - \frac{1}{2}x\right) + 8$$
$$= -6\left[\left(x - \frac{1}{4}\right)^2 - \left(\frac{1}{4}\right)^2\right] + 8$$
$$= -6\left(x - \frac{1}{4}\right)^2 + 8.375$$

With the equation written in this form, one can see that when $x = \frac{1}{4}$ or 0.25, the graph reaches its maximum value at 8.375. Thus, the vertex of the parabola is $(0.25, 8.375)$ and its x-coordinate is 0.25.

Choice (D) is incorrect. Using the alternate approach above and making an error in completing the square with $x^2 - \frac{1}{2}x$ into $\left(x - \frac{1}{2}\right)^2 - \left(\frac{1}{2}\right)^2$ would lead to $x = \frac{1}{2}$ or 0.5 as the answer.

Question 20

Choice (E) is the correct answer. Each of the three statements must be analyzed separately. The problem gives $a > 0$ and $b > 0$; thus, $-a < 0$ and $-b < 0$. Consider statement I. Since $a > 0$ and $-b < 0$, it follows that $a > 0 > -b$ and the statement must be true. Consider statement II. Since $b > 0$ and $-a < 0$, it follows that $b > 0 > -a$ and the statement $-a > b$ is false. Consider statement III. Since the problem gives $a > b$, multiplying this inequality by -1 changes the direction of inequality and yields $-a < -b$. Thus, the statement must be true. Since statements I and III must be true, choice (E) is correct.

Question 21

Choice (A) is the correct answer. Let x and y be the width and length, in feet, of the garden, respectively. Then, $y = 2x$ and $2x + 2y = 204$. Substituting $y = 2x$ into $2x + 2y = 204$ yields $2x + 4x = 204$. Solving the equation yields $6x = 204$ or $x = 34$.

Choice (D) is incorrect. This results from incorrectly providing the length instead of the width of the garden.

Question 22

Choice (C) is the correct answer. When line ℓ is reflected over the y-axis, the point where line ℓ intersects the y-axis will remain the same, and the point where line ℓ intersects the x-axis will be the point on the x-axis that is an equal distance from the origin on the other side of the y-axis. Since line p passes through these two points, line p is the reflection of line ℓ with respect to the y-axis.

Choice (B) is incorrect. This results from incorrectly reflecting line ℓ with respect to the origin, which yields line n.

Question 23

Choice (C) is the correct answer. The median of the 11 scores in the stem-and-leaf plot is the 6th score when all the scores are listed in increasing order; that is, 84.

Choice (A) is incorrect. This could result from providing the mode of the scores instead of the median of the scores.

Question 24

Choice (D) is the correct answer. The statements translate to the equations $x = y - 15$ and $3x + 2y = 80$. Solving this system of equations for x and y is one way to then obtain the sum $x + y$.

Using the first equation to substitute $y - 15$ for x into the second equation yields $3(y - 15) + 2y = 80$, which gives $5y = 125$ or $y = 25$. So, $x = y - 15 = 25 - 15 = 10$. Thus, $x + y = 35$.

Choice (C) is incorrect. In the system of the equations above, if the first equation is replaced by $x - 15 = y$, which is an incorrect translation of "the number x is 15 less than the number y," one would get $x = 22$ and $y = 7$. Thus, $x + y = 29$.

Question 25

Choice (D) is the correct answer. Each of the five choices needs to be examined. One can see that 9 is a factor of 18 but is not a factor of 24. So, the statement is false for integer 9. Since the integers 4, 5, and 12 are not factors of 18, the statement does not apply. The statement is <u>true</u> for integer 3.

Question 26

Choice (C) is the correct answer. The total amount spent by the 5 students is $\$375 \times 5 = \$1,875$. Since 4 of the students together spent $\$300 \times 4 = \$1,200$ or less, the fifth student will spend the least amount when the 4 students spend the maximum amount they can spend. Thus, the least amount the fifth student could have spent is $\$1,875 - \$1,200 = \$675$.

Choice (B) is incorrect. Only adding $\$75$, instead of $\$75 \times 4 = \$300$, to the mean when calculating the least amount that the fifth student could have spent results in $\$375 + \$75 = \$450$.

Question 27

Choice (E) is the correct answer. The solutions of a quadratic

equation of the form $ax^2 + bx + c = 0$ are $x = \dfrac{-b + \sqrt{b^2 - 4ac}}{2a}$ and

$x = \dfrac{-b - \sqrt{b^2 - 4ac}}{2a}$. If $b^2 - 4ac = 0$, then the two solutions are equal roots of the equation. Therefore, the quadratic equation $x^2 + 6x - k = 0$ has equal roots when $6^2 - 4(-k) = 0$. Solving this equation yields $k = -9$.

Choice (B) is incorrect. This could result from evaluating $b^2 - 4ac$ and getting $6^2 - 4k$, which is 0 when k is 9.

Question 28

Choice (E) is the correct answer. Since 1 unit contains $\dfrac{500}{125}$ or 4 cubic centimeters of fluid, 8 units contain $4 \times 8 = 32$ cubic centimeters of fluid.

Choice (B) is incorrect. Mistaking $\frac{125}{500}$ or $\frac{1}{4}$ for the number of cubic centimeters of fluid that 1 unit contains will give $\frac{1}{4} \times 8 = 2$ cubic centimeters of fluid that 8 units contain.

Question 29

Choice (A) is the correct answer. It is given that $\angle BAC$ is a right angle, so $\triangle BAC$ is a right triangle. Note that $\triangle ADC$ is also a right triangle. In these two right triangles, $\angle C$ is a common angle to both triangles; therefore, the corresponding complementary angles, $\angle DAC$ and $\angle ABC$, must be congruent. Thus, $y = x$. And it is given that $x = 40$. So, $y = 40$.

Choice (C) is incorrect. From the figure, incorrectly assuming $\angle DAC$ to be congruent to $\angle C$ would lead $\angle DAC$ to be equal to $50°$ because $\angle C$ is the complementary angle of $\angle B$, whose degree measure is $40°$.

Question 30

Choice (C) is the correct answer. The rate of 40 chirps per minute is equivalent to $\frac{40}{60}$ or $\frac{2}{3}$ chirps per second; that is, $\frac{2}{3} \times 15 = 10$ chirps every 15 seconds. Substituting 10 for c in the equation and solving the equation $10 = t - 40$ yields $t = 50$.

Choice (E) is incorrect. Mistaking 40 chirps per minute for the number of chirps every 15 seconds leads to solving the equation $40 = t - 40$, which gives $t = 80$.

Question 31

Choice (D) is the correct answer. Based on the information $m < 0$ and $b > 0$, the line $y = mx + b$ slants downward and to the right and has a positive y-intercept (i.e., lies above the origin when $x = 0$). It can pass through any point in the xy-plane except Quadrant III. You can also conclude this from the equation $y = mx + b$. If $x < 0$, then $mx > 0$. And since $b > 0$, you get $y = mx + b > 0$. That is, the line does not contain points with negative x and negative y coordinates.

Choice (A) is incorrect. Only focusing on the part of the line that is above the x-axis confines the line to Quadrants I and II only.

Question 32

Choice (E) is the correct answer. In a triangle with sides of lengths a, b, and c, since each of the angles is less than $180°$, the combined length, $a + b$, of any two sides is longer than the length, c, of the third side; that is, $a + b > c$ is always true. This is the triangle inequality theorem.

Choice (B) is incorrect. This results from incorrectly assuming the triangle is a right triangle.

Question 33

Choice (E) is the correct answer. Recall that a polynomial function has the form $f(x) = a_n x^n + a_{n-1} x^{n-1} + \ldots + a_1 x + a_0$, where n is a nonnegative integer and a_n, a_{n-1}, ..., a_0 are real numbers. Among the answer choices, only $\dfrac{x^2}{3}$ has this form.

Choice (B) is incorrect. The function f given by $f(x) = x + \dfrac{1}{x} = x + x^{-1}$ does not have the form of a polynomial given that it includes a term with a power of x that is a negative integer.

Question 34

Choice (D) is the correct answer. If x feet is the length of the edge of the cube, then because the volume of the cube is 0.125 cubic feet $x^3 = 0.125$ and $x = 0.5$. The area of each face of the cube is x^2 square feet, and the surface of the cube has 6 faces; so, the surface area of the cube, in square feet, is $6x^2$, which is 6×0.5^2 or 1.5.

Choice (B) is incorrect. This is only the area of one face of the cube.

Question 35

Choice (E) is the correct answer. In the xy-plane, shifting the graph of f horizontally 2 units to the left to be the graph of g means that for every point $(a, g(a))$ on the graph of g, the value $g(a)$ equals the value of $f(x)$ at $x = a + 2$; that is, $g(a) = f(a + 2)$. Since a is an arbitrary number, it concludes that $g(x) = f(x + 2)$ for values of x.

Choice (C) is incorrect. This results from incorrectly shifting the graph of $y = x^3$ vertically by 2 units up to get the graph of $y = x^3 + 2$.

Question 36

Choice (C) is the correct answer. An altitude of 12,496 meters equals 12.496 kilometers. Substituting $a = 12.496$ into the formula $k = 35\sqrt{a}$ yields $k = 35\sqrt{12.496} \approx 123.7239$, which is rounded to 124 kilometers.

Choice (E) is incorrect. Mistaking 12,496 meters for 12,496 kilometers in the formula leads to 3,912 for the value of k.

Question 37

Choice (A) is the correct answer. Each of the 3 figures must be analyzed separately. Consider the figure in I. The figure shows a line that slants downward and to the right, and the point $(2, a)$ is higher than the point $(3, b)$; thus, $a > b$. So, the line could be the graph of a function satisfying $f(2) > f(3)$. Figure II shows a curve that goes upward and to the right for $x > 1$, and the point $(2, a)$ is lower than the point $(3, b)$; thus, $a < b$. So, the curve could not be the graph of a function satisfying $f(2) > f(3)$. Figure III shows a line that slants upward and to the right, and the point $(2, a)$ is lower than the point $(3, b)$; thus, $a < b$. So, the line could not be the graph of a function satisfying $f(2) > f(3)$. Since only figure I could be the graph of $y = f(x)$, choice (A) is correct.

Question 38

Choice (A) is the correct answer. If $f(x) = 2x + 3$, then $f(g(x)) = 2g(x) + 3$. Since it is given that $f(g(x)) = 8x - 1$, it follows that $2g(x) + 3 = 8x - 1$. Subtracting 3 from both sides of this equation gives $2g(x) = 8x - 4$, and dividing both sides of that result by 2 results in $g(x) = \dfrac{8x - 4}{2} = 4x - 2$.

Choice (B) is incorrect. Making an error in simplifying $2g(x) + 3 = 8x - 1$ to $2g(x) = 8x - 2$ leads to $g(x) = 4x - 1$.

Question 39

Choice (B) is the correct answer. The volume of the cylinder is $\pi\left(\dfrac{6}{2}\right)^2 (10) = 90\pi$. The volume of the rectangular solid is $\left(6^2\right)(10)$ or 360. Therefore, the volume of the rectangular solid is $\dfrac{360}{90\pi} = \dfrac{4}{\pi}$ times the volume of the cylinder. Using a calculator, you get $\dfrac{4}{\pi} \approx 1.2732$, which rounds to 1.27.

Choice (A) is incorrect. Overlooking π in the volume of the cylinder gives 90, which incorrectly makes the volume of the rectangular solid $\dfrac{360}{90} = 4$ times the volume of the cylinder.

Question 40

Choice (C) is the correct answer. It is useful to label the figure in the problem as indicated below.

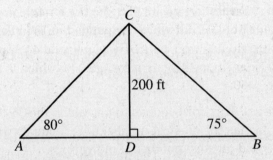

To find AB, you need to find AD and DB. In right triangle ACD, $\tan 80° = \dfrac{200}{AD}$, so $AD = \dfrac{200}{\tan 80°} \approx 35.2654$. Similarly, in right triangle CBD, you get $DB = \dfrac{200}{\tan 75°} \approx 53.5898$. Then,

$AB = AD + DB \approx 35.2654 + 53.5898 = 88.8552$, which rounds to 89.

Choice (D) is incorrect. It results from mistakenly using the sine function in place of the tangent function to get

$$AD = \frac{200}{\sin 80°} \approx 203.0853 \text{ and } DB = \frac{200}{\sin 75°} \approx 207.0552, \text{ thus getting}$$

$AB = AD + DB \approx 203.0853 + 207.0552 = 410.1405$, which rounds to 410.

Question 41

Choice (A) is the correct answer. Drawing a figure as indicated below helps to see how the angle OCD is formed.

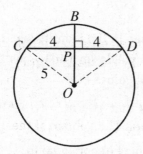

In the figure, $\overline{OC}$ and $\overline{OD}$ are radii of the circle, and $\triangle CPO$ and $\triangle DPO$ are right triangles. In the two right triangles, since $\overline{OC}$ and $\overline{OD}$ have equal length and $\overline{OP}$ is a side common to both triangles, $\triangle CPO$ and $\triangle DPO$ are congruent by the Hypotenuse Leg Theorem. Thus, $CD = 8$ implies $CP = PD = 4$. In right triangle CPO, by the Pythagorean Theorem, $OP = 3$. Therefore, $\sin \angle OCD = \dfrac{OP}{OC} = \dfrac{3}{5}$.

Choice (C) is incorrect. This may result from mistakenly finding the cosine instead of the sine and getting $\cos \angle OCD = \dfrac{CP}{OC} = \dfrac{4}{5}$.

Question 42

Choice (C) is the correct answer. From the bar graph, the longest bar for male and the longest bar for female are both for the 40–44 age group, so the greatest number of individuals in the population is in the 40–44 age group. Those individuals who were between 40 and 44 years old in 2000 were born between 40 to 44 years prior to 2000, which is between the years 1956 and 1960.

Choice (D) is incorrect. This corresponds to mistaking the 35–39 age group as the one that has the greatest number of individuals when it actually has the second-greatest number of individuals.

Question 43

Choice (B) is the correct answer. Since $\overline{AD}$ is a diameter and $\overline{BC}$ is a radius, point B is the center of the circle and $\overline{AB}$ is a radius. It is given that segment AE bisects segment BC, so $BE = \dfrac{1}{2} BC$ and $BE = \dfrac{1}{2} AB$.

Note that in $\triangle AEB$, $\angle AEB$ is a right angle and $\cos \angle ABE = \dfrac{BE}{AB} = \dfrac{1}{2}$, so you have m$\angle ABE = 60°$. It is observed that inscribed angle $\angle ADC$ and central angle $\angle ABC$ intercept the same arc AC, so the measure of $\angle ADC$ is $\dfrac{1}{2}$ the measure of $\angle ABC$. However, $\angle ABC$ is congruent to $\angle ABE$, so $x = \dfrac{1}{2}(60) = 30$.

Choice (A) is incorrect. In the above argument, this may result from mistaking $\cos \angle ABE = \dfrac{1}{2}$ for $\sin \angle ABE = \dfrac{1}{2}$, which would lead to m$\angle ABE = 30°$. And so $x = \dfrac{1}{2}(30) = 15$, which is incorrect.

Question 44

Choice (E) is the correct answer. In the identity $\sin^2 x + \cos^2 x = 1$ for all values of x, replacing x by 4θ yields $\sin^2(4\theta) + \cos^2(4\theta) = 1$; that is, $1 - \sin^2(4\theta) = \cos^2(4\theta)$ for all values of θ.

Choice (C) is incorrect. Recall that $a^2 - b^2 = (a + b)(a - b)$ for all values of a and b. You can write $1 - \sin^2(4\theta) = 1^2 - (\sin(4\theta))^2 = (1 + \sin(4\theta))(1 - \sin(4\theta))$, which is not equal to $(1 - \sin(2\theta))(1 + \sin(2\theta))$.

Question 45

Choice (C) is the correct answer. It is helpful to sketch a sphere intersected by a plane as shown below.

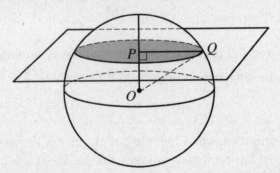

In the figure above, point O is the center of the sphere. Point P is the center of the circle that is the intersection of the sphere and a plane 3 inches above the sphere's center, and $\overline{PQ}$ is the radius of the circle. Since $\overline{PQ}$ lies on the plane, $\overline{PQ}$ is perpendicular to $\overline{OP}$. Thus, $\triangle OPQ$ is a right triangle. In the right triangle, $OP = 3$ and $OQ = 6$; therefore, $PQ = \sqrt{OQ^2 - OP^2} = \sqrt{6^2 - 3^2} = \sqrt{27}$.

Choice (A) is incorrect. It results from mistakenly treating the radius of the circle as the distance from the center of the circle to the center of the sphere.

Question 46

Choice (D) is the correct answer. If the length of a side of the square is x units, then by the Pythagorean Theorem $x^2 + x^2 = (x + 1)^2$. Solving for x yields $x = 1 \pm \sqrt{2}$. But $x > 0$, so $x = 1 + \sqrt{2} \approx 2.4142$ and $x^2 \approx 5.8284$, which rounds to 5.83; that is, the area of the square is 5.83 square units.

Choice (C) is incorrect. It results from multiplying the x value by 2 instead of squaring it to get the area.

Question 47

Choice (A) is the correct answer. The equation can be rewritten as $5x - 12x = 8y + y$ or $-7x = 9y$. Since $xy \neq 0$, dividing both sides of the equation by $-7y$ yields $\dfrac{x}{y} = -\dfrac{9}{7}$. So, the ratio of x to y is $-\dfrac{9}{7}$ or approximately -1.29.

Choice (B) is incorrect. This results from using the ratio of y to x instead of the ratio of x to y.

Question 48

Choice (B) is the correct answer.

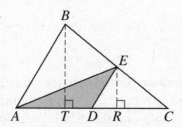

It would be useful to add $\overline{BT}$ and $\overline{ER}$ to the given figure to help represent the areas, where $\overline{BT}$ is the height of $\triangle ABC$ with base $\overline{AC}$ and $\overline{ER}$ is the height of $\triangle AEC$ with base $\overline{AC}$.

In the figure above, $\triangle ADE$ has base $\overline{AD}$ and the corresponding height $\overline{ER}$. So, the area of $\triangle ADE$ is $\dfrac{1}{2}(AD)(ER)$. Note that $\overline{ER}$ is also the height of $\triangle DEC$ with base $\overline{DC}$, and $AD = DC$, so the area of $\triangle DEC$ equals the area of $\triangle ADE$. Therefore, the area of $\triangle ADE$ is $\dfrac{1}{2}$ the area of $\triangle AEC$.

On the other hand, $\triangle AEC$ has base $\overline{AC}$ and height $\overline{ER}$, so the area of $\triangle AEC$ is equal to $\dfrac{1}{2}(AC)(ER)$. Note that $\triangle ABC$ has base $\overline{AC}$ and height $\overline{BT}$, so the area of $\triangle ABC$ is $\dfrac{1}{2}(AC)(BT)$. Comparing these two area expressions, if you can show that $ER = \dfrac{1}{2}BT$, you will get that the area of $\triangle AEC$ equals $\dfrac{1}{2}$ the area of $\triangle ABC$, and therefore the area of $\triangle ADE$ is $\dfrac{1}{4}$ the area of $\triangle ABC$, that is, $\dfrac{1}{4}(24) = 6$.

To show $ER = \frac{1}{2}BT$, you look at $\triangle ERC$ and $\triangle BTC$. Since these two triangles are right triangles and angle C is common to both triangles, the two triangles are similar. Recall that $EC = \frac{1}{2}BC$ or $\frac{EC}{BC} = \frac{1}{2}BC$, so you get $\frac{ER}{BT} = \frac{EC}{BC} = \frac{1}{2}$; that is, $ER = \frac{1}{2}BT$.

Choice (C) is incorrect. From the figure, it may incorrectly appear that the area of $\triangle AED$ is $\frac{1}{3}$ the area of $\triangle ABC$. Since the area of $\triangle ABC$ is 24, the area of $\triangle AED$ would incorrectly then result in $\frac{1}{3}(24)$ or 8.

Question 49

Choice (B) is the correct answer. Let L and P represent Luis's and Patricia's share from the investment, respectively. Then you will get $d = L + P$ and $L = \frac{3}{5}P$. Replacing P in the second equation by $P = d - L$ yields $L = \frac{3}{5}(d - L)$. Solving this equation for L gives $L = \frac{3}{8}d$.

Choice (D) is incorrect. This may result from misinterpreting Luis's share that is $\frac{3}{5}$ Patricia's share as $\frac{3}{5}$ of the total annual income from the investment; that is, $\frac{3}{5}d$.

Question 50

Choice (B) is the correct answer. Since the question is asking for the local behavior of the function f that is a cubic polynomial, a graphing calculator is best to use to help find the details of the graph of f for $0 \leq x \leq 7$. A suitable viewing window is $[0, 7]$ for x-values and $[0, 30]$ for y-values. By graphing $y = f(x)$ in this window, you are able to view the local maximum value of $f(x)$, which is approximately 29.1926, and the local minimum value of $f(x)$, which is approximately 3.6222. Using the graph, you can determine that the range of the function f is between 3.62217 and 29.1926; that is, $3.6222 < f(x) < 29.1926$. But $3.62 < 3.6222$ and $29.1926 < 29.20$, so it follows that $3.62 < f(x) < 29.20$.

Choice (C) is incorrect. Mistakenly assuming the function f is increasing in the interval $0 \leq x \geq 7$ would incorrectly lead you to find its minimum at $x = 0$ and its maximum at $x = 7$; that is, $f(0) = 5$ is incorrectly determined to be the minimum and $f(7) = 19$ is incorrectly determined to be the maximum. So, the range would incorrectly be identified as $5 \leq f(x) \leq 19$.

Mathematics Level 1 – Practice Test 3

Practice Helps

The test that follows is an actual, previously administered SAT Subject Test in Mathematics Level 1. To get an idea of what it's like to take this test, practice under conditions that are much like those of an actual test administration.

- Set aside an hour when you can take the test uninterrupted.

- Sit at a desk or table with no other books or papers. Dictionaries, other books, or notes are not allowed in the test room.

- Remember to have a scientific or graphing calculator with you.

- Tear out an answer sheet from the back of this book and fill it in just as you would on the day of the test. One answer sheet can be used for up to three Subject Tests.

- Read the instructions that precede the practice test. During the actual administration you will be asked to read them before answering test questions.

- Use a clock or kitchen timer to time yourself.

- After you finish the practice test, read the sections "How to Score the SAT Subject Test in Mathematics Level 1" and "How Did You Do on the Subject Test in Mathematics Level 1?"

- The appearance of the answer sheet in this book may differ from the answer sheet you see on test day.

MATHEMATICS LEVEL 1 TEST

The top portion of the page of the answer sheet that you will use to take the Mathematics Level 1 Test must be filled in exactly as illustrated below. When your supervisor tells you to fill in the circle next to the name of the test you are about to take, mark your answer sheet as shown.

○ Literature	● Mathematics Level 1	○ German	○ Chinese Listening	○ Japanese Listening
○ Biology E	○ Mathematics Level 2	○ Italian	○ French Listening	○ Korean Listening
○ Biology M	○ U.S. History	○ Latin	○ German Listening	○ Spanish Listening
○ Chemistry	○ World History	○ Modern Hebrew		
○ Physics	○ French	○ Spanish	**Background Questions:** ① ② ③ ④ ⑤ ⑥ ⑦ ⑧ ⑨	

After filling in the circle next to the name of the test you are taking, locate the Background Questions section, which also appears at the top of your answer sheet (as shown above). This is where you will answer the following Background Questions on your answer sheet.

BACKGROUND QUESTIONS

Please answer Part I and Part II below by filling in the appropriate circle in the Background Questions box on your answer sheet. The information you provide is for statistical purposes only and will not affect your test score.

<u>Part I.</u>   Which of the following describes a mathematics course you have taken or are currently taking? (FILL IN **ALL** CIRCLES THAT APPLY.)

- Algebra I or Elementary Algebra **OR** Course I of a college preparatory mathematics sequence   —Fill in circle 1.

- Geometry **OR** Course II of a college preparatory mathematics sequence   —Fill in circle 2.

- Algebra II or Intermediate Algebra **OR** Course III of a college preparatory mathematics sequence   —Fill in circle 3.

- Elementary Functions (Precalculus) and/or Trigonometry **OR** beyond Course III of a college preparatory mathematics sequence   —Fill in circle 4.

- Advanced Placement Mathematics (Calculus AB or Calculus BC)   —Fill in circle 5.

<u>Part II.</u>   What type of calculator did you bring to use for this test? (FILL IN THE **ONE** CIRCLE THAT APPLIES. If you did not bring a scientific or graphing calculator, do not fill in any of circles 6-9.)

- Scientific   —Fill in circle 6.

- Graphing (Fill in the circle corresponding to the model you used.)

    Casio 9700, Casio 9750, Casio 9800, Casio 9850, Casio 9860, Casio FX 1.0, Casio CG-10, Sharp 9200, Sharp 9300, Sharp 9600, Sharp 9900, TI-82, TI-83, TI-83 Plus, TI-83 Plus Silver, TI-84 Plus, TI-84 Plus CE, TI-84 Plus Silver, TI-84 Plus C Silver, TI-85, TI-86, TI-Nspire, or TI-Nspire CX   —Fill in circle 7.

    Casio 9970, Casio Algebra FX 2.0, HP 38G, HP 39 series, HP 40 series, HP 48 series, HP 49 series, HP 50 series, HP Prime, TI-89, TI-89 Titanium, TI-Nspire CAS, or TI-Nspire CX CAS   —Fill in circle 8.

    Some other graphing calculator   —Fill in circle 9.

When the supervisor gives the signal, turn the page and begin the Mathematics Level 1 Test. There are 100 numbered circles on the answer sheet and 50 questions in the Mathematics Level 1 Test. Therefore, use only circles 1 to 50 for recording your answers.

MATHEMATICS LEVEL 1 TEST

REFERENCE INFORMATION

THE FOLLOWING INFORMATION IS FOR YOUR REFERENCE IN ANSWERING SOME OF THE QUESTIONS IN THIS TEST.

Volume of a right circular cone with radius r and height h: $V = \frac{1}{3}\pi r^2 h$

Volume of a sphere with radius r: $V = \frac{4}{3}\pi r^3$

Volume of a pyramid with base area B and height h: $V = \frac{1}{3}Bh$

Surface Area of a sphere with radius r: $S = 4\pi r^2$

DO NOT DETACH FROM BOOK.

GO ON TO THE NEXT PAGE

MATHEMATICS LEVEL 1 TEST

For each of the following problems, decide which is the BEST of the choices given. If the exact numerical value is not one of the choices, select the choice that best approximates this value. Then fill in the corresponding circle on the answer sheet.

Notes: (1) A scientific or graphing calculator will be necessary for answering some (but not all) of the questions in this test. For each question you will have to decide whether or not you should use a calculator.

(2) The only angle measure used on this test is degree measure. Make sure your calculator is in the degree mode.

(3) Figures that accompany problems in this test are intended to provide information useful in solving the problems. They are drawn as accurately as possible EXCEPT when it is stated in a specific problem that its figure is not drawn to scale. All figures lie in a plane unless otherwise indicated.

(4) Unless otherwise specified, the domain of any function f is assumed to be the set of all real numbers x for which $f(x)$ is a real number. The range of f is assumed to be the set of all real numbers $f(x)$, where x is in the domain of f.

(5) Reference information that may be useful in answering the questions in this test can be found on the page preceding Question 1.

USE THIS SPACE FOR SCRATCHWORK.

1. If $xy + 7y = 84$ and $x + 7 = 3$, what is the value of y ?

   (A) −4
   (B) 4.9
   (C) 8.4
   (D) 12
   (E) 28

GO ON TO THE NEXT PAGE

MATHEMATICS LEVEL 1 TEST—*Continued*

USE THIS SPACE FOR SCRATCHWORK.

2. When four given numbers are multiplied together, the product is negative. Which of the following could be true about the four numbers?

   (A) One is negative, two are positive, and one is zero.
   (B) Two are negative, one is positive, and one is zero.
   (C) Two are negative and two are positive.
   (D) Three are negative and one is positive.
   (E) Four are negative.

3. If $x + y = 5$ and $x - y = 3$, then $x^2 - y^2 =$

   (A) 9   (B) 15   (C) 16   (D) 25   (E) 34

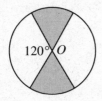

4. In the figure above, what fraction of the circular region with center O is shaded?

   (A) $\dfrac{1}{6}$ (B) $\dfrac{1}{5}$ (C) $\dfrac{1}{4}$ (D) $\dfrac{1}{3}$ (E) $\dfrac{3}{5}$

GO ON TO THE NEXT PAGE

MATHEMATICS LEVEL 1 TEST—*Continued*

5. Which of the following is the graph of a linear function with both a negative slope and a negative y-intercept?

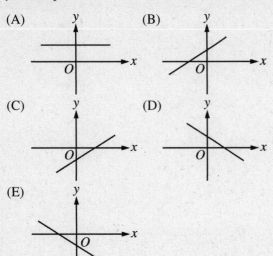

(A)   (B)

(C)   (D)

(E)

6. If $k^2 - 4 = 4 - k^2$, what are all possible values of k ?

(A)   0 only
(B)   2 only
(C)   4 only
(D)   −2 and 2 only
(E)   −2, 0, and 2

7. If $b^{2x+1} = b^{3x-1}$ for all values of b, what is the value of x ?

(A) 2   (B) $\frac{3}{2}$ (C) $\frac{2}{3}$ (D) −2   (E) −3

GO ON TO THE NEXT PAGE

MATHEMATICS LEVEL 1 TEST—*Continued*

USE THIS SPACE FOR SCRATCHWORK.

8. At North High School, the number of students taking French is decreasing by 20 students per year and the number of students taking Spanish is increasing by 10 students per year. This year 250 students are taking French, and 100 students are taking Spanish. Which of the following equations could be used to find the number of years n until the number of students is the same in both courses?

(A) $250 - 20n = 100 + 10n$
(B) $250 + 10n = 100 - 20n$
(C) $250 + 20n = 100 - 10n$
(D) $20n - 250 = 100 + 10n$
(E) $n(250 - 20) = n(100 + 10)$

9. If $y = x^3 - 1.5$, for what value of x is $y = 2$?

(A) 0.79
(B) 1.14
(C) 1.52
(D) 1.87
(E) 6.50

10. The length of a rectangle is four times its width. If the perimeter of the rectangle is 40 centimeters, what is its area?

(A)   4 cm^2
(B) 16 cm^2
(C) 20 cm^2
(D) 40 cm^2
(E) 64 cm^2

GO ON TO THE NEXT PAGE

MATHEMATICS LEVEL 1 TEST—Continued

11. The function g, where $g(t) = 0.066t + 0.96$, can be used to represent the relation between grade point average $g(t)$ and the number of hours t spent studying each week. Based on this function, a student with a grade point average of 3.5 studied how many hours per week?

    (A) 0.96
    (B) 1.2
    (C) 14.5
    (D) 38.5
    (E) 67.8

12. $x^2 - 2x + 3 = x^3 + 2x + x^2$ is equivalent to

    (A) 0
    (B) $2x^2 - 4x = 0$
    (C) $-x^3 + 4x - 3 = 0$
    (D) $x^3 - 2x^2 - 3 = 0$
    (E) $x^3 + 4x - 3 = 0$

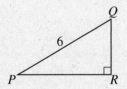

13. In right triangle PQR in the figure above, $\sin P = 0.5$. What is the length of side QR ?

    (A) 2
    (B) 3
    (C) 5
    (D) 6
    (E) 12

GO ON TO THE NEXT PAGE

MATHEMATICS LEVEL 1 TEST—*Continued*

USE THIS SPACE FOR SCRATCHWORK.

14. Which of the following numbers is a
    COUNTEREXAMPLE to the statement
    "All odd numbers greater than 2 are prime
    numbers" ?

    (A) 2   (B) 3   (C) 5   (D) 7   (E) 9

15. If $f(x) = \dfrac{2x - 1}{x^2}$, what is the value of $f(-0.1)$?

    (A) −120
    (B) −100
    (C)   100
    (D)   120
    (E)   220

16. On a blueprint, 0.4 inch represents 6 feet. If the
    actual distance between two buildings is 76 feet,
    what would be the distance between the corre-
    sponding buildings on the blueprint?

    (A)   3.2 in
    (B)   5.1 in
    (C) 12.7 in
    (D) 30.4 in
    (E) 31.7 in

GO ON TO THE NEXT PAGE

MATHEMATICS LEVEL 1 TEST—*Continued*

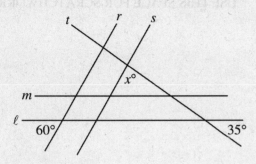

17. In the figure above, if $\ell \parallel m$ and $r \parallel s$, what is the value of x ?

    (A) 65
    (B) 80
    (C) 85
    (D) 95
    (E) 115

18. For what value of x is $\dfrac{2x}{3x-1}$ undefined?

    (A) $-\dfrac{1}{3}$ (B) 0   (C) $\dfrac{1}{3}$ (D) $\dfrac{1}{2}$ (E) 1

19. A sales team sold an average (arithmetic mean) of 10.375 mobile phones per week during the first 8 weeks of the last quarter of the year. The members of the sales team will receive a bonus if they sell a total of 185 phones for the quarter. What must their average sales, in phones per week, be for the remaining 5 weeks of the quarter if they are to receive the bonus?

    (A)   4.2
    (B)   20.4
    (C)   83
    (D) 102
    (E) 174.6

GO ON TO THE NEXT PAGE

MATHEMATICS LEVEL 1 TEST—*Continued*

20. What is the y-coordinate of the point at which the
line whose equation is $3x - 2y - 7 = 0$ crosses
the y-axis?

(A) $-\dfrac{7}{2}$

(B) $-\dfrac{7}{3}$

(C) $\dfrac{7}{3}$

(D) $\dfrac{7}{2}$

(E) 7

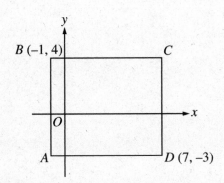

21. In the figure above, the sides of rectangle $ABCD$
are parallel to the axes. What is the distance
between point A and point C ?

(A) 6.07
(B) 7
(C) 10.1
(D) 10.6
(E) 15

GO ON TO THE NEXT PAGE

MATHEMATICS LEVEL 1 TEST—*Continued*

USE THIS SPACE FOR SCRATCHWORK.

22. Four signal flags — one red, one blue, one yellow, and one green — can be arranged from top to bottom on a signal pole. Every arrangement of the four flags is a different signal. How many different signals using all four flags have the red flag at the top?

    (A) 3   (B) 4   (C) 6   (D) 16   (E) 24

23. Triangle *FGH* is similar to triangle *JKL*. The length of side *GH* is 2.1 meters, the length of corresponding side *KL* is 1.4 meters, and the perimeter of $\triangle JKL$ is 3.6 meters. What is the perimeter of $\triangle FGH$?

    (A) 2.4 m
    (B) 3.3 m
    (C) 4.3 m
    (D) 5.1 m
    (E) 5.4 m

24. Which of the following is an equation of a line that is parallel to the line with equation $2x - y = 7$?

    (A) $y = -2x - 7$

    (B) $y = -2x + 7$

    (C) $y = -\frac{1}{2}x - 7$

    (D) $y = \frac{1}{2}x - 7$

    (E) $y = 2x + 7$

GO ON TO THE NEXT PAGE

MATHEMATICS LEVEL 1 TEST—*Continued*

USE THIS SPACE FOR SCRATCHWORK.

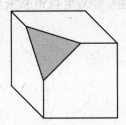

25. A tetrahedron was cut from the corner of the
cube shown above, with three of its vertices
at the midpoints of three edges of the cube. If
tetrahedrons of the same size are cut from the
remaining seven corners of the cube, how many
faces will the resulting solid have?

    (A) 6   (B) 8   (C) 12   (D) 14   (E) 16

26. The consecutive vertices of a certain parallelogram
are A, B, C, and D. Which of the following are
NOT necessarily congruent?

    (A) $\angle A$ and $\angle C$
    (B) $\angle B$ and $\angle D$
    (C) $\overline{AC}$ and $\overline{BD}$
    (D) $\overline{AB}$ and $\overline{CD}$
    (E) $\overline{AD}$ and $\overline{BC}$

GO ON TO THE NEXT PAGE

MATHEMATICS LEVEL 1 TEST—*Continued*

USE THIS SPACE FOR SCRATCHWORK.

27. A car traveled 200 miles at an average speed of 45 miles per hour. Of the following, which is the closest approximation to the amount of time that could be saved on this 200-mile trip if the average speed had increased 20 percent?

    (A) 1 hour

    (B) $\frac{3}{4}$ hour

    (C) $\frac{1}{2}$ hour

    (D) $\frac{1}{4}$ hour

    (E) $\frac{1}{5}$ hour

28. If c is a negative integer, for which of the following values of d is $|c - d|$ greatest?

    (A) −10   (B) −4   (C) 0   (D) 4   (E) 10

29. In $\triangle PQR$, $\angle Q$ is a right angle. Which of the following is equal to $\cos P$?

    (A) $\frac{PQ}{PR}$

    (B) $\frac{PR}{PQ}$

    (C) $\frac{PR}{QR}$

    (D) $\frac{QR}{PQ}$

    (E) $\frac{QR}{PR}$

GO ON TO THE NEXT PAGE

MATHEMATICS LEVEL 1 TEST—*Continued*

USE THIS SPACE FOR SCRATCHWORK.

30. The junior class is sponsoring a drama production to raise funds and plans to charge the same price for all admission tickets. The class has \$700 in expenses for this production. If 300 tickets are sold, the class will make a profit of \$1,100. What will be the profit for the class if 500 tickets are sold?

(A) \$1,133
(B) \$1,833
(C) \$2,300
(D) \$3,000
(E) \$3,700

31. In the *xy*-plane, the point (6, 3) is the midpoint of the line segment with endpoints $(x, 5)$ and $(9, y)$. What is the value of $x + y$?

(A) 4 (B) 9 (C) 14 (D) 18 (E) 32

32. If $\frac{1}{2}$ is $\frac{3}{4}$ of $\frac{4}{5}$ of a certain number, what is that number?

(A) $\frac{3}{10}$

(B) $\frac{5}{6}$

(C) $\frac{11}{10}$

(D) $\frac{6}{5}$

(E) $\frac{10}{3}$

GO ON TO THE NEXT PAGE

MATHEMATICS LEVEL 1 TEST—Continued

USE THIS SPACE FOR SCRATCHWORK.

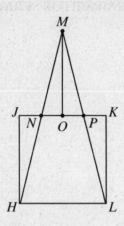

33. In the figure above, *HJKL* is a square and
$JN = NO = OP = PK$. What is the ratio of the
area of $\triangle MNP$ to the area of square *HJKL* ?

(A) $\frac{1}{8}$ (B) $\frac{1}{4}$ (C) $\frac{1}{3}$ (D) $\frac{3}{8}$ (E) $\frac{1}{2}$

34. Which of the following numbers is NOT
contained in the domain of the function f
if $f(x) = \dfrac{x+2}{x+3} - \dfrac{1}{x}$?

(A) -3 (B) -2 (C) 1   (D) $\sqrt{3}$ (E) 3

35. Which of the following is the graph of all values
of x for which $1 \le x^2 \le 4$?

(A) ←——+——+——+——●——————→
　　　 −2　−1　　0　　1　　2

(B) ←——●——●——+——●——+——→
　　　 −2　−1　　0　　1　　2

(C) ←——●————————————●——→
　　　 −2　−1　　0　　1　　2

(D) ←——+——+——+——+——●——→
　　　 −2　−1　　0　　1　　2

(E) ←——●——●——+——+——●——→
　　　 −2　−1　　0　　1　　2

GO ON TO THE NEXT PAGE ⇒

USE THIS SPACE FOR SCRATCHWORK.

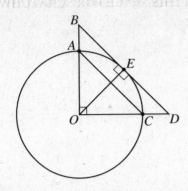

36. The circle in the figure above has center O and radius r. If $OB = OD$, how many of the line segments shown (with labeled endpoints) have length r?

    (A) Two
    (B) Three
    (C) Four
    (D) Five
    (E) Six

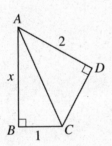

37. In the figure above, if $\triangle ABC$ and $\triangle ADC$ are right triangles, then $CD =$

    (A) $\sqrt{x^2 - 3}$

    (B) $\sqrt{x^2 + 1}$

    (C) $\sqrt{x^2 + 1} + 2$

    (D) $\sqrt{x^2 + 3}$

    (E) $x^2 + 5$

GO ON TO THE NEXT PAGE

USE THIS SPACE FOR SCRATCHWORK.

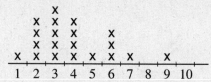

Number of red candies in sample

38. Each of 20 students in a class took a sample
of 10 candies from a large bag and counted the
number of red candies in the sample. The distribution of red candies in their samples is shown
above. If one of the students were chosen at
random, what is the probability that the student's
sample would have at least 5 red candies?

(A) $\dfrac{3}{5}$

(B) $\dfrac{3}{10}$

(C) $\dfrac{1}{4}$

(D) $\dfrac{3}{20}$

(E) $\dfrac{1}{20}$

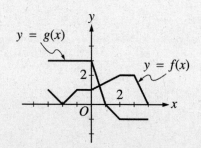

39. The figure above shows the graphs of functions f
and g. What is the value of $f(g(3))$?

(A) −2   (B) −1   (C) 0   (D) 1   (E) 2

GO ON TO THE NEXT PAGE

MATHEMATICS LEVEL 1 TEST—*Continued*

USE THIS SPACE FOR SCRATCHWORK.

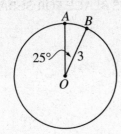

40. If O is the center of the circle in the figure above, what is the length of minor arc AB ?

(A) 0.65
(B) 1.27
(C) 1.31
(D) 1.40
(E) 1.96

41. In the xy-plane, which of the following are the points of intersection of the circles whose equations are $x^2 + y^2 = 4$ and $(x - 2)^2 + y^2 = 4$?

(A) $(-1, \sqrt{3}), (-1, -\sqrt{3})$

(B) $(1, \sqrt{3}), (1, -\sqrt{3})$

(C) $(1, \sqrt{3}), (-1, \sqrt{3})$

(D) $(1, 1), (-1, 1)$

(E) $(1, 1), (1, -2)$

GO ON TO THE NEXT PAGE

42. The area of one face of a cube is x square meters. Which of the following gives an expression for the volume of this cube, in cubic meters?

(A) $x\sqrt{x}$

(B) $3\sqrt{x}$

(C) $x^2\sqrt{x}$

(D) x^3

(E) $3x^3$

43. For which of the following equations is it true that the sum of the roots equals the product of the roots?

(A) $x^2 - 4 = 0$
(B) $x^2 - 2x + 1 = 0$
(C) $x^2 - 4x + 4 = 0$
(D) $x^2 - 5x + 6 = 0$
(E) $x^2 + 4x + 4 = 0$

44. If the positive integers, starting with 1, are written consecutively, what will be the 90th digit written?

(A) 0   (B) 1   (C) 5   (D) 8   (E) 9

GO ON TO THE NEXT PAGE

MATHEMATICS LEVEL 1 TEST—*Continued*

USE THIS SPACE FOR SCRATCHWORK.

45. The function f is defined by
$f(x) = x^4 - 4x^2 + x + 1$ for $-5 \le x \le 5$.
In which of the following intervals does the
minimum value of f occur?

(A) $-5 < x < -3$
(B) $-3 < x < -1$
(C) $-1 < x < 1$
(D) $1 < x < 3$
(E) $3 < x < 5$

46. In convex polygon P, the sum of the measures
of the interior angles is $1,800°$. How many sides
does P have?

(A) 8   (B) 10   (C) 12   (D) 14   (E) 18

47. What is the least integer value of k such that
$x^2(3k + 1) - 6x + 2 = 0$ has no real roots?

(A) 5   (B) 2   (C) 1   (D) −1   (E) −2

48. If $\angle A$ is an acute angle and $\dfrac{\sin^2 A}{\cos^2 A} = 2.468$,

what is the value of $\tan A$?

(A) 1.234
(B) 1.571
(C) 2.468
(D) 4.936
(E) 6.091

GO ON TO THE NEXT PAGE

MATHEMATICS LEVEL 1 TEST—*Continued*

USE THIS SPACE FOR SCRATCHWORK.

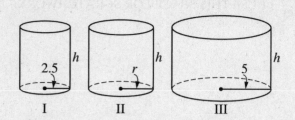

I   II   III

49. In the figure above, all of the right circular cylinders have height h. Cylinders I and III have a base
radius of 2.5 and 5, respectively. If the volume of
cylinder II is the mean of the volumes of cylinders
I and III, what is the radius r of cylinder II?

(A) 1.98
(B) 3.75
(C) 3.95
(D) 4.00
(E) 15.63

50. If f and g are functions, where
$f(x) = x^3 - 10x^2 + 27x - 18$ and
$g(x) = x^3 - x^2 - 6x$, which of the following
gives a relationship between f and g ?

(A) $g(x) = 3f(x)$
(B) $g(x) = f(x) - 3$
(C) $g(x) = f(x) + 3$
(D) $g(x) = f(x - 3)$
(E) $g(x) = f(x + 3)$

S T O P

**IF YOU FINISH BEFORE TIME IS CALLED, YOU MAY CHECK YOUR WORK ON THIS TEST ONLY.
DO NOT TURN TO ANY OTHER TEST IN THIS BOOK.**

How to Score the SAT Subject Test in Mathematics Level 1

When you take an actual SAT Subject Test in Mathematics Level 1, your answer sheet will be "read" by a scanning machine that will record your responses to each question. Then a computer will compare your answers with the correct answers and produce your raw score. You get one point for each correct answer. For each wrong answer, you lose one-quarter of a point. Questions you omit (and any for which you mark more than one answer) are not counted. This raw score is converted to a scaled score that is reported to you and to the colleges you specify.

Worksheet 1. Finding Your Raw Test Score

STEP 1: Table A on the following page lists the correct answers for all the questions on the Subject Test in Mathematics Level 1 that is reproduced in this book. It also serves as a worksheet for you to calculate your raw score.

- Compare your answers with those given in the table.
- Put a check in the column marked "Right" if your answer is correct.
- Put a check in the column marked "Wrong" if your answer is incorrect.
- Leave both columns blank if you omitted the question.

STEP 2: Count the number of right answers.

Enter the total here: _____

STEP 3: Count the number of wrong answers.

Enter the total here: _____

STEP 4: Multiply the number of wrong answers by .250.

Enter the product here: _____

STEP 5: Subtract the result obtained in Step 4 from the total you obtained in Step 2.

Enter the result here: _____

STEP 6: Round the number obtained in Step 5 to the nearest whole number.

Enter the result here: _____

The number you obtained in Step 6 is your raw score.

Answers to Practice Test 3 for Mathematics Level 1

Table A
Answers to the Subject Test in Mathematics Level 1 – Practice Test 3 and Percentage of Students Answering
Each Question Correctly

Question Number	Correct Answer	Right	Wrong	Percentage of Students Answering the Question Correctly*	Question Number	Correct Answer	Right	Wrong	Percentage of Students Answering the Question Correctly*
1	E			92	26	C			64
2	D			95	27	B			68
3	B			83	28	E			59
4	D			91	29	A			71
5	E			91	30	C			53
6	D			83	31	A			59
7	A			90	32	B			56
8	A			83	33	B			53
9	C			88	34	A			66
10	E			85	35	B			45
11	D			84	36	D			49
12	E			84	37	A			41
13	B			81	38	B			49
14	E			89	39	D			41
15	A			70	40	C			42
16	B			87	41	B			36
17	C			89	42	A			33
18	C			81	43	C			29
19	B			78	44	C			29
20	A			75	45	B			30
21	D			77	46	C			28
22	C			63	47	B			18
23	E			75	48	B			46
24	E			78	49	C			37
25	D			70	50	E			41

* These percentages are based on an analysis of the answer sheets of a representative sample of 21,848 students who took the original administration of this test and whose mean score was 605. They may be used as an indication of the relative difficulty of a particular question.

Finding Your Scaled Score

When you take SAT Subject Tests, the scores sent to the colleges you specify are reported on the College Board scale, which ranges from 200 to 800. You can convert your practice test raw score to a scaled score by using Table B. To find your scaled score, locate your raw score in the left-hand column of Table B; the corresponding score in the right-hand column is your scaled score. For example, a raw score of 28 on this particular edition of the Subject Test in Mathematics Level 1 corresponds to a scaled score of 600.

Raw scores are converted to scaled scores to ensure that a score earned on any one edition of a particular Subject Test is comparable to the same scaled score earned on any other edition of the same Subject Test. Because some editions of the tests may be slightly easier or more difficult than others, College Board scaled scores are adjusted so that they indicate the same level of performance regardless of the edition of the test taken and the ability of the group that takes it. Thus, for example, a score of 400 on one edition of a test taken at a particular administration indicates the same level of achievement as a score of 400 on a different edition of the test taken at a different administration.

When you take the SAT Subject Tests during a national administration, your scores are likely to differ somewhat from the scores you obtain on the tests in this book. People perform at different levels at different times for reasons unrelated to the tests themselves. The precision of any test is also limited because it represents only a sample of all the possible questions that could be asked.

Table B
Scaled Score Conversion Table
Subject Test in Mathematics Level 1 – Practice Test 3

Raw Score	Scaled Score	Raw Score	Scaled Score	Raw Score	Scaled Score
50	800	28	600	6	390
49	800	27	580	5	390
48	790	26	570	4	380
47	780	25	560	3	370
46	770	24	550	2	360
45	760	23	540	1	360
44	750	22	530	0	350
43	740	21	520	−1	340
42	730	20	510	−2	330
41	720	19	500	−3	330
40	720	18	490	−4	320
39	710	17	490	−5	310
38	700	16	480	−6	300
37	690	15	470	−7	290
36	680	14	460	−8	280
35	670	13	450	−9	270
34	660	12	440	−10	260
33	650	11	440	−11	260
32	640	10	430	−12	250
31	630	9	420		
30	620	8	410		
29	610	7	400		

How Did You Do on the Subject Test in Mathematics Level 1?

After you score your test and analyze your performance, think about the following questions:

Did you run out of time before reaching the end of the test?

If so, you may need to pace yourself better. For example, maybe you spent too much time on one or two hard questions. A better approach might be to skip the ones you can't answer right away and try answering all the remaining questions on the test. Then if there's time, go back to the questions you skipped.

Did you take a long time reading the directions?

You will save time when you take the test by learning the directions to the Subject Test in Mathematics Level 1 ahead of time. Each minute you spend reading directions during the test is a minute that you could use to answer questions.

How did you handle questions you were unsure of?

If you were able to eliminate one or more of the answer choices as wrong and guess from the remaining ones, your approach probably worked to your advantage. On the other hand, making haphazard guesses or omitting questions without trying to eliminate choices could cost you valuable points.

How difficult were the questions for you compared with other students who took the test?

Table A shows you how difficult the multiple-choice questions were for the group of students who took this test during its national administration. The right-hand column gives the percentage of students that answered each question correctly.

A question answered correctly by almost everyone in the group is obviously an easier question. For example, 89 percent of the students answered question 14 correctly. However, only 29 percent answered question 43 correctly.

Keep in mind that these percentages are based on just one group of students. They would probably be different with another group of students taking the test.

If you missed several easier questions, go back and try to find out why: Did the questions cover material you haven't yet reviewed? Did you misunderstand the directions?

Answer Explanations

For Practice Test 3

The solutions presented here provide one method for solving each of the problems on this test. Other mathematically correct approaches are possible.

Question 1

Choice (E) is the correct answer. Since $x + 7 = 3$, $x = -4$. Thus,

$$-4y + 7y = 84$$
$$3y = 84$$
$$y = 28$$

Question 2

Choice (D) is the correct answer. For the product of the numbers to be negative, an odd number of them must be negative, and none of the numbers can be zero. This is true for choice (D) only.

Question 3

Choice (B) is the correct answer. Since $x^2 - y^2 = (x + y)(x - y)$, $x^2 - y^2 = (5)(3) = 15$.

Question 4

Choice (D) is the correct answer. Two diameters of the circle are drawn. The central angle of each of the shaded sectors is 60°. Each shaded sector is $\frac{60}{360}$ or $\frac{1}{6}$ of the circular region. Therefore, $\frac{1}{3}$ of the circular region is shaded.

Question 5

Choice (E) is the correct answer. A line with a negative slope slants downward from left to right, and a line with a negative y-intercept crosses the negative y-axis. Only choice (E) satisfies both of these conditions. Choice (A) is incorrect. The line is horizontal so its slope is 0, and the y-intercept is positive. Choice (B) is incorrect. The slope of the line is positive, and the y-intercept is positive. Choice (C) is incorrect. Although the y-intercept is negative, the slope of the line is positive. Choice (D) is incorrect. Although the slope of the line is negative, the y-intercept is positive.

Question 6

Choice (D) is the correct answer. The left and right sides of the equation are opposites of each other. The only number equal to its opposite is 0, so you should find the values of k for which $k^2 - 4 = 0$. These are 2 and –2, which is choice (D). You could also solve the equation by combining like terms. If $k^2 - 4 = 4 - k^2$, then $2k^2 - 8 = 0$ or $k^2 = 4$.

Question 7

Choice (A) is the correct answer. Since $b^{2x+1} = b^{3x-1}$, $2x + 1 = 3x - 1$ and $x = 2$.

Question 8

Choice (A) is the correct answer. The number of students taking French is decreasing by 20 students per year. After n years, there will be $20n$ fewer students taking French. Currently, there are 250 students taking French. Thus, after n years, there will be $250 - 20n$ students taking French. The number of students taking Spanish is increasing by 10 students per year. After n years, there will be $10n$ more students taking Spanish. Currently, there are 100 students taking Spanish. Thus, after n years, there will be $100 + 10n$ students taking Spanish. To find when the number of students is the same in both courses, set the two expressions equal to each other; $250 - 20n = 100 + 10n$.

Question 9

Choice (C) is the correct answer. To find the value of x when $y = 2$, you need to solve the equation $2 = x^3 - 1.5$, which is equivalent to $3.5 = x^3$. Taking the cube root of both sides of the equation yields $x \approx 1.52$.

Question 10

Choice (E) is the correct answer. If the width of the rectangle is w, then the length of the rectangle is $4w$, and the perimeter is $w + 4w + w + 4w = 10w = 40$. Thus, the width of the rectangle is 4 centimeters, and the length is 16 centimeters. Therefore, the area is equal to $4 \cdot 16 = 64$ cm^2. Choice (A) is incorrect. This is the width of the rectangle. Choice (B) is incorrect. This is the length of the rectangle. Choice (D) is incorrect. This is the perimeter of the rectangle.

Question 11

Choice (D) is the correct answer. According to the function, if a student has a grade point average of 3.5, then $3.5 = 0.066t + 0.96$ and $2.54 = 0.066t$. Thus, $t \approx 38.48$, meaning that a student with a grade point average of 3.5 studied approximately 38.5 hours per week.

Question 12

Choice (E) is the correct answer. Since x^2 is on both sides of the equation, the equation can be written as

$$-2x + 3 = x^3 + 2x$$
$$3 = x^3 + 4x$$
$$0 = x^3 + 4x - 3$$

Question 13

Choice (B) is the correct answer. In a right triangle, the sine of an angle is equal to the ratio of the length of the opposite side to the length of the hypotenuse. If $\sin P = 0.5$, then $\frac{QR}{PQ} = \frac{1}{2}$. So, $\frac{QR}{6} = \frac{1}{2}$ and $QR = 3$.

Question 14

Choice (E) is the correct answer. A counterexample to the statement "All odd numbers greater than 2 are prime numbers" would be an odd number greater than 2 that is <u>not</u> a prime number. Choice (A) is not odd, so it cannot be a counterexample. Choices (B), (C), and (D) are odd numbers greater than 2, but they are prime numbers, so they are not counterexamples. Choice (E) is odd and it is greater than 2. However, since 9 is equal to 3 × 3, it is not a prime number. Therefore 9 is a counterexample to the statement.

Question 15

Choice (A) is the correct answer. $f(-0.1) = \dfrac{2(-0.1) - 1}{(-0.1)^2} = \dfrac{-0.2 - 1}{0.01} = -120.$

Question 16

Choice (B) is the correct answer. To solve the problem, set up a proportion, where x represents the distance between the buildings on the blueprint.

$$\frac{0.4 \text{ in}}{6 \text{ ft}} = \frac{x \text{ in}}{76 \text{ ft}}$$
$$\frac{76(0.4)}{6} = x$$
$$x = 5.0\overline{6} \approx 5.1$$

Question 17

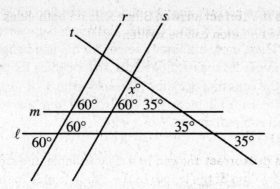

Choice (C) is the correct answer. Using the fact that vertical angles are congruent and corresponding angles are congruent, you can determine the measures of five additional angles as shown in the figure above. Since the sum of the degree measures of the interior angles in a triangle is 180, $x = 180 - (60 + 35) = 85$.

Question 18

Choice (C) is the correct answer. The expression $\frac{2x}{3x-1}$ is undefined when $3x - 1$ is equal to 0. If $3x - 1 = 0$, then $x = \frac{1}{3}$.

Question 19

Choice (B) is the correct answer. The total number of phones sold in the first 8 weeks of the last quarter is equal to $8 \cdot 10.375 = 83$. In order to sell 185 phones for the quarter, the team must sell 102 phones during the last five weeks, resulting in an average of 20.4[$102 \div 5$] phones to be sold per week for the last five weeks. Choice (C) is incorrect. This is the total number of phones sold in the first 8 weeks. Choice (D) is incorrect. This is the total number of phones the team needs to sell for the remaining 5 weeks.

Question 20

Choice (A) is the correct answer. At the point where a line crosses the *y*-axis, the value of the *x*-coordinate will be 0. When 0 is substituted into the equation, the result is $-2y - 7 = 0$. Solving for *y* produces a value of $-\frac{7}{2}$ for the *y*-coordinate.

Question 21

Choice (D) is the correct answer. Because *ABCD* is a rectangle, it has congruent diagonals. The distance from *A* to *C* is the same as the distance from *B* to *D*. You can use the distance formula to get $BD = \sqrt{(-1 - 7)^2 + (4 - (-3))^2} = \sqrt{64 + 49} = \sqrt{113} \approx 10.6$.

Question 22

Choice (C) is the correct answer. Since the red flag must be at the top, only the order of the blue, yellow, and green flags needs to be considered. Thus, there are three choices for the flag beneath the red one, 2 choices for the next position, and 1 choice for the lowest spot. Using the counting principle, the answer is $3 \cdot 2 \cdot 1 = 6$, which is choice (C). Choice (E) is incorrect. This results from allowing any flag at the top and computing $4 \cdot 3 \cdot 2 \cdot 1 = 24$.

Question 23

Choice (E) is the correct answer. Since the triangles are similar, the lengths of the sides and the perimeters are in proportion. If $\dfrac{GH}{KL} = \dfrac{2.1}{1.4} = 1.5$, then $\dfrac{\text{perimeter of } \triangle FGH}{\text{perimeter of } \triangle JKL} = 1.5$. Thus, $\dfrac{\text{perimeter of } \triangle FGH}{3.6} = 1.5$, so the perimeter of $\triangle FGH$ is $(3.6)(1.5) = 5.4$ meters, which is choice (E). Choice (A) is incorrect. This results from recognizing that KL is $\dfrac{2}{3}$ of GH and multiplying 3.6 by $\dfrac{2}{3}$ instead of $\dfrac{3}{2}$. Choice (C) is incorrect. This results from reasoning that since $GH - KL = 0.7$, the perimeter of $\triangle FGH$ is $3.6 + 0.7 = 4.3$.

Question 24

Choice (E) is the correct answer. The line with equation $2x - y = 7$ can be written in $y = mx + b$ form as $y = 2x - 7$. The slope of the line is 2, and any line parallel to the line will also have a slope of 2.

Question 25

Choice (D) is the correct answer. Since the original cube has 6 faces and 8 corners, placing a new face on each corner will add 8 faces to the resulting solid for a total of 14 faces.

Question 26

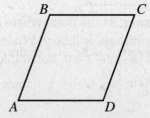

Choice (C) is the correct answer. It is helpful to draw and label a parallelogram to answer this question. In a parallelogram, opposite angles are congruent, so $\angle A$ and $\angle C$ are congruent, and $\angle B$ and $\angle D$ are congruent. Opposite sides are also congruent, so $\overline{AB} \cong \overline{CD}$ and $\overline{BC} \cong \overline{AD}$. However, $\overline{AC}$ and $\overline{BD}$ are not necessarily congruent, as shown in the figure.

Question 27

Choice (B) is the correct answer. At a rate of 45 miles per hour, the time it takes to go 200 miles is $\frac{200}{45} \approx 4.44$ hours. If the speed increases by 20 percent, the new speed will be $45 \cdot 1.2 = 54$ miles per hour. At 54 miles per hour, it would take $\frac{200}{54} \approx 3.70$ hours to travel 200 miles. The time saved by going at the faster speed would be approximately $4.44 - 3.70 = 0.74$ hour, or approximately $\frac{3}{4}$ of an hour, which is choice (B). Choice (E) is incorrect. It results from assuming that an increase in speed of 20 percent yields a reduction in time of 20 percent of an hour.

Question 28

Choice (E) is the correct answer. To solve the problem, it is helpful to think of the absolute value of the difference of two quantities as the distance between their corresponding points on the number line. Thus, you have to determine which of the five choices is furthest from c. Since c is negative, c is to the left of 0, 4, and 10 on the number line. Therefore, c is further from 10 than from either 0 or 4. To see that c is also further from 10 than -10 and -4, consider two cases. Case (1): c is between -10 and 0. Then, c is less than 10 units from -10 and -4. Since c is more than 10 units from 10, c is further from 10 than from either -10 or -4. Case (2): c is less than -10. Then, it is obvious that c is further from 10 than from either -10 or -4. Thus, in all cases, c is furthest from 10 than it is from -10, -4, 0, and 4.

Question 29

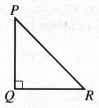

Choice (A) is the correct answer. It is helpful to draw and label ΔPQR

$\cos P = \dfrac{\text{length of adjacent side}}{\text{length of hypotenuse}} = \dfrac{PQ}{PR}$, which is choice (A).

Choice (B) is incorrect.

$\dfrac{PR}{PQ} = \dfrac{\text{length of hypotenuse}}{\text{length of adjacent side}}$ and $\cos P = \dfrac{\text{length of adjacent side}}{\text{length of hypotenuse}}$.

This is the reciprocal of the correct answer, or sec P.

Choice (C) is incorrect.

$$\frac{PR}{QR} = \frac{\text{length of hypotenuse}}{\text{length of opposite side}} \text{ and } \cos P = \frac{\text{length of adjacent side}}{\text{length of hypotenuse}}.$$

$$\frac{PR}{QR} = \csc P.$$

Choice (D) is incorrect.

$$\frac{QR}{PQ} = \frac{\text{length of opposite side}}{\text{length of adjacent side}} \text{ and } \cos P = \frac{\text{length of adjacent side}}{\text{length of hypotenuse}}.$$

$$\frac{QR}{PQ} = \tan P.$$

Choice (E) is incorrect.

$$\frac{QR}{PR} = \frac{\text{length of opposite side}}{\text{length of hypotenuse}} \text{ and } \cos P = \frac{\text{length of adjacent side}}{\text{length of hypotenuse}}.$$

$$\frac{QR}{PR} = \sin P.$$

Question 30

Choice (C) is the correct answer. To answer this question, you must use the fact that profit is equal to revenue minus expenses. The class has $700 in expenses. The problem gives the profit when 300 tickets are sold. If x represents the price per ticket, in dollars, the revenue for this sale is $300x$. Therefore, $\$1,100 = 300x - 700$, which implies that the price per ticket is $6. If 500 tickets are sold at the same price, the revenue is $500 \cdot \$6 = \$3,000$. The profit on the sale of the 500 tickets would be $\$3,000 - \$700 = \$2,300$.

Question 31

Choice (A) is the correct answer. The midpoint of the line segment that has endpoints $(x, 5)$ and $(9, y)$ is given by $\left(\frac{x+9}{2}, \frac{5+y}{2}\right)$. Thus, $\frac{x+9}{2} = 6$ yielding $x = 3$, and $\frac{5+y}{2} = 3$ yielding $y = 1$. The sum of x and y is 4.

Question 32

Choice (B) is the correct answer. If $\frac{1}{2}$ is $\frac{3}{4}$ of $\frac{4}{5}$ of a number n, then $\frac{1}{2} = \frac{3}{4} \cdot \frac{4}{5} n$.

$$\frac{1}{2} = \frac{3}{5} n$$

$$\frac{5}{2} = 3n$$

$$\frac{5}{6} = n$$

Question 33

Choice (B) is the correct answer. In $\triangle MHL$, $\overline{NP}$ is a midsegment because $\overline{NP} \parallel \overline{HL}$ and $NP = \frac{1}{2}HL$. Because $\overline{NP}$ is a midsegment of $\triangle MHL$, $HN = NM$. Since vertical angles are congruent, $\angle JNH \cong \angle ONM$. Together with the given information that $JN = NO$, you can conclude that $\triangle HJN \cong \triangle MON$ by side-angle-side congruence. Corresponding parts of congruent triangles are congruent, so $JH = MO$.

$$\text{Area of } \triangle MNP = \frac{1}{2}(NP)(MO)$$

$$= \frac{1}{2}\left(\frac{1}{2}HL\right)(JH)$$

$$= \left(\frac{1}{4}\right)(HL)(JH)$$

$$= \frac{1}{4} \text{ (area of square } HJKL)$$

This shows that the area of $\triangle MNP$ is $\frac{1}{4}$ the area of square $HJKL$.

Question 34

Choice (A) is the correct answer. The function f given by $f(x) = \frac{x+2}{x+3} - \frac{1}{x}$ is not defined for values of x that result in a denominator of 0. The value $x = -3$ results in a denominator of 0 in $\frac{x+2}{x+3}$, and the value $x = 0$ results in a denominator of 0 in $\frac{1}{x}$. The only choice given that is not contained in the domain of f is -3.

Question 35

Choice (B) is the correct answer. If x^2 must be between 1 and 4, then the absolute value of x must be between 1 and 2. If x is positive, then $1 \leq x \leq 2$. If x is negative, then $-2 \leq x \leq -1$. Choice (B) shows the graph of all numbers x such that $-2 \leq x \leq -1$ or $1 \leq x \leq 2$.

Question 36

Choice (D) is the correct answer. $\overline{OA}$, $\overline{OE}$, and $\overline{OC}$ are radii of the circle, so they all have length r. Since $OB = OD$, angles B and D are each 45°. Thus, $OE = ED$ and $OE = BE$. So, there are five labeled segments with length r: $\overline{OA}$, $\overline{OE}$, $\overline{OC}$, $\overline{BE}$, and $\overline{ED}$.

Question 37

Choice (A) is the correct answer. To solve the problem, you will need to use the Pythagorean theorem twice. In right triangle ABC,

$$(AC)^2 = (AB)^2 + (BC)^2$$
$$(AC)^2 = x^2 + 1^2 = x^2 + 1$$
$$AC = \sqrt{x^2 + 1}$$

In right triangle ADC,

$$(AC)^2 = (AD)^2 + (CD)^2$$
$$\left(\sqrt{x^2 + 1}\right)^2 = 2^2 + (CD)^2$$
$$x^2 + 1 = 4 + (CD)^2$$
$$x^2 - 3 = (CD)^2$$
$$CD = \sqrt{x^2 - 3}$$

Choice (B) is incorrect. $\sqrt{x^2 + 1} = AC$, not CD. Choice (D) is incorrect. It results from using 3 instead of -3 in the solution. Choice (E) is incorrect. If you added 4 instead of subtracting 4 from both sides of the equation, and you also forgot to take the square root of both sides, you would have chosen choice (E).

Question 38

Choice (B) is the correct answer. To answer this question, you need to determine the number of students that have at least 5 red candies. From the distribution, there are 6 students who each had at least 5 red candies. Therefore, the probability that the student's sample would have at least 5 red candies is equal to $\frac{6}{20}$ or $\frac{3}{10}$.

Question 39

Choice (D) is the correct answer. From the graph, you can determine $g(3) = -1$. Thus, $f(g(3)) = f(-1)$. From the graph, you can determine that $f(-1)$ is 1.

Question 40

Choice (C) is the correct answer. The measure of $\angle AOB$ is 25°, which is $\frac{25}{360}$ of the circle, so the length of $\overset{\frown}{AB}$ is $\frac{25}{360}$ of the circumference of the circle. Since the radius of the circle is 3, the circumference of the circle is $2\pi r = 6\pi$. Thus, the length of $\overset{\frown}{AB}$ is $\frac{25}{360}(6\pi) \approx 1.31$.

Question 41

Choice (B) is the correct answer. To find the points of intersection, you need to solve the system $\begin{cases} x^2 + y^2 = 4 \\ (x-2)^2 + y^2 = 4 \end{cases}$ for x and y. One way to solve the system is to subtract the second equation from the first and solve for x and y.

$$x^2 + y^2 = 4$$
$$-\left[(x-2)^2 + y^2 = 4\right]$$
$$x^2 - (x-2)^2 = 0$$
$$x^2 - (x^2 - 4x + 4) = 0$$
$$4x - 4 = 0$$
$$x = 1$$

If $x = 1$, then $1^2 + y^2 = 4$. Thus, $y^2 = 3$ and $y = \pm\sqrt{3}$. The points of intersection are $(1, \sqrt{3})$ and $(1, -\sqrt{3})$.

Question 42

Choice (A) is the correct answer. If the area of one face of the cube is x, then the length of each edge of the cube is $\sqrt{x}$. Therefore, the volume of the cube is equal to $(\sqrt{x})^3 = x\sqrt{x}$.

Question 43

Choice (C) is the correct answer. The quadratic equation $ax^2 + bx + c = 0$ with $a \neq 0$ has solutions $x = \dfrac{-b+\sqrt{b^2-4ac}}{2a}$ and $\dfrac{-b-\sqrt{b^2-4ac}}{2a}$, so the sum of the two roots is $-\dfrac{b}{a}$, and their product is $\dfrac{c}{a}$. Therefore, you need an equation in which $-\dfrac{b}{a} = \dfrac{c}{a}$, or $-b = c$. The only choice satisfying this condition is choice (C).

You could also solve this problem by finding the actual roots of each of the five given equations, either by factoring, using the quadratic formula, or using a graphing calculator. After you find the two roots of an equation, find their sum and product and compare them. Choice (A) is incorrect. The roots of the equation are –2 and 2. The sum of the roots is 0, and the product is –4. Choice (B) is incorrect. $x^2 - 2x + 1 = (x - 1)^2$, so there is a double root at $x = 1$. The sum of the roots is 2, and the product is 1. Choice (D) is incorrect. $x^2 - 5x + 6 = (x - 3)(x - 2)$, so the roots are 3 and 2. The sum of the roots is 5, and the product is 6. Choice (E) is incorrect. $x^2 + 4x + 4 = (x + 2)^2$, so there is a double root at $x = -2$. The sum of the roots is –4, and the product is 4.

Question 44

Choice (C) is the correct answer. Of the 90 digits you need to write, the first 9 digits correspond to the integers 1–9, and the next 81 digits come from two-digit positive integers (10, 11, ...). Because each of these are two-digit positive integers, there will be 40 complete two-digit positive integers written, and the 90th digit will be the tens digit of the 41st two-digit positive integer. Since 10 is the first two-digit positive integer, 50 is the 41st two-digit positive integer. Thus, the 90th digit will be 5.

Question 45

Choice (B) is the correct answer. In this question, it is helpful to use a graphing calculator to graph $y = x^4 - 4x^2 + x + 1$. Since the domain of the function is $-5 \le x \le 5$, set the viewing window to go from $x = -5$ to $x = 5$, and graph the function. The minimum value of the function occurs when $x \approx -1.473$, which is in the interval $-3 < x < -1$. Choice (A) is incorrect. The minimum value of the function is $y \approx -4.444$, which is $f(-1.473)$. The question asks for the interval in which the minimum value of f occurs. Choice (A) results from confusing x with y, since the minimum value of the function is $y \approx -4.444$.

Question 46

Choice (C) is the correct answer. The sum of the measures of the interior angles of a convex polygon with n sides is equal to $(n-2)180°$. Thus, $(n-2)180° = 1{,}800°$ and $n-2 = 10$, so $n = 12$.

Question 47

Choice (B) is the correct answer. The quadratic equation $ax^2 + bx + c = 0$ has no real roots if $b^2 - 4ac < 0$. Thus, the equation $x^2(3k+1) - 6x + 2 = 0$ has no real roots if $(-6)^2 - 4(3k+1)(2) < 0$. This simplifies to $28 - 24k < 0$. The least integer value of k that satisfies this inequality is 2.

Question 48

Choice (B) is the correct answer. Since $\dfrac{\sin^2 A}{\cos^2 A} = \tan^2 A = 2.468$,

$\tan A = \sqrt{2.468} \approx 1.571$.

Question 49

Choice (C) is the correct answer. The volume of a cylinder with radius r and height h is equal to $\pi r^2 h$. Thus, the volume of cylinder I is $\pi(2.5)^2 h = 6.25\pi h$, and the volume of cylinder III is $25\pi h$. The volume of cylinder II is the mean of the volumes of cylinders I and III. Thus, $\pi r^2 h = \dfrac{6.25\pi h + 25\pi h}{2} = 15.625\pi h$ and $r^2 = 15.625$. The value of r is $\sqrt{15.625}$, which is approximately 3.95. Choice (B) is incorrect. This is the mean of the radii of cylinders I and III. Using this value for r will not give a volume for cylinder II that is the mean of the volumes of cylinders I and III. Choice (E) is incorrect. This is the value of r^2. You need to take the square root of this value to find the radius of cylinder II.

Question 50

Choice (E) is the correct answer. A graphing calculator is helpful for this problem. If you graph functions f and g in a standard viewing window of $[-10, 10]$ by $[-10, 10]$, you can see that the graph of g is identical to the graph of f, but it is shifted 3 units to the left. Thus, $g(x) = f(x+3)$.

Mathematics Level 1 – Practice Test 4

Practice Helps

The test that follows is an actual, previously administered SAT Subject Test in Mathematics Level 1. To get an idea of what it's like to take this test, practice under conditions that are much like those of an actual test administration.

- Set aside an hour when you can take the test uninterrupted.

- Sit at a desk or table with no other books or papers. Dictionaries, other books, or notes are not allowed in the test room.

- Remember to have a scientific or graphing calculator with you.

- Tear out an answer sheet from the back of this book and fill it in just as you would on the day of the test. One answer sheet can be used for up to three Subject Tests.

- Read the instructions that precede the practice test. During the actual administration you will be asked to read them before answering test questions.

- Use a clock or kitchen timer to time yourself.

- After you finish the practice test, read the sections "How to Score the SAT Subject Test in Mathematics Level 1" and "How Did You Do on the Subject Test in Mathematics Level 1?"

- The appearance of the answer sheet in this book may differ from the answer sheet you see on test day.

MATHEMATICS LEVEL 1 TEST

The top portion of the page of the answer sheet that you will use to take the Mathematics Level 1 Test must be filled in exactly as illustrated below. When your supervisor tells you to fill in the circle next to the name of the test you are about to take, mark your answer sheet as shown.

◯ Literature	● Mathematics Level 1	◯ German	◯ Chinese Listening	◯ Japanese Listening
◯ Biology E	◯ Mathematics Level 2	◯ Italian	◯ French Listening	◯ Korean Listening
◯ Biology M	◯ U.S. History	◯ Latin	◯ German Listening	◯ Spanish Listening
◯ Chemistry	◯ World History	◯ Modern Hebrew		
◯ Physics	◯ French	◯ Spanish	**Background Questions:** ① ② ③ ④ ⑤ ⑥ ⑦ ⑧ ⑨	

After filling in the circle next to the name of the test you are taking, locate the Background Questions section, which also appears at the top of your answer sheet (as shown above). This is where you will answer the following Background Questions on your answer sheet.

BACKGROUND QUESTIONS

Please answer Part I and Part II below by filling in the appropriate circle in the Background Questions box on your answer sheet. The information you provide is for statistical purposes only and will not affect your test score.

Part I. Which of the following describes a mathematics course you have taken or are currently taking? (FILL IN **ALL** CIRCLES THAT APPLY.)

- Algebra I or Elementary Algebra **OR** Course I of a college preparatory mathematics sequence — Fill in circle 1.

- Geometry **OR** Course II of a college preparatory mathematics sequence — Fill in circle 2.

- Algebra II or Intermediate Algebra **OR** Course III of a college preparatory mathematics sequence — Fill in circle 3.

- Elementary Functions (Precalculus) and/or Trigonometry **OR** beyond Course III of a college preparatory mathematics sequence — Fill in circle 4.

- Advanced Placement Mathematics (Calculus AB or Calculus BC) — Fill in circle 5.

Part II. What type of calculator did you bring to use for this test? (FILL IN THE **ONE** CIRCLE THAT APPLIES. If you did not bring a scientific or graphing calculator, do not fill in any of circles 6-9.)

- Scientific — Fill in circle 6.

- Graphing (Fill in the circle corresponding to the model you used.)

    Casio 9700, Casio 9750, Casio 9800, Casio 9850, Casio 9860, Casio FX 1.0, Casio CG-10, Sharp 9200, Sharp 9300, Sharp 9600, Sharp 9900, TI-82, TI-83, TI-83 Plus, TI-83 Plus Silver, TI-84 Plus, TI-84 Plus CE, TI-84 Plus Silver, TI-84 Plus C Silver, TI-85, TI-86, TI-Nspire, or TI-Nspire CX — Fill in circle 7.

    Casio 9970, Casio Algebra FX 2.0, HP 38G, HP 39 series, HP 40 series, HP 48 series, HP 49 series, HP 50 series, HP Prime, TI-89, TI-89 Titanium, TI-Nspire CAS, or TI-Nspire CX CAS — Fill in circle 8.

    Some other graphing calculator — Fill in circle 9.

When the supervisor gives the signal, turn the page and begin the Mathematics Level 1 Test. There are 100 numbered circles on the answer sheet and 50 questions in the Mathematics Level 1 Test. Therefore, use only circles 1 to 50 for recording your answers.

MATHEMATICS LEVEL 1 TEST

REFERENCE INFORMATION

THE FOLLOWING INFORMATION IS FOR YOUR REFERENCE IN ANSWERING SOME OF THE QUESTIONS IN THIS TEST.

Volume of a right circular cone with radius r and height h: $V = \dfrac{1}{3}\pi r^2 h$

Volume of a sphere with radius r: $V = \dfrac{4}{3}\pi r^3$

Volume of a pyramid with base area B and height h: $V = \dfrac{1}{3}Bh$

Surface Area of a sphere with radius r: $S = 4\pi r^2$

DO NOT DETACH FROM BOOK.

GO ON TO THE NEXT PAGE

MATHEMATICS LEVEL 1 TEST

For each of the following problems, decide which is the BEST of the choices given. If the exact numerical value is not one of the choices, select the choice that best approximates this value. Then fill in the corresponding circle on the answer sheet.

Notes: (1) A scientific or graphing calculator will be necessary for answering some (but not all) of the questions in this test. For each question you will have to decide whether or not you should use a calculator.

(2) The only angle measure used on this test is degree measure. Make sure your calculator is in the degree mode.

(3) Figures that accompany problems in this test are intended to provide information useful in solving the problems. They are drawn as accurately as possible EXCEPT when it is stated in a specific problem that its figure is not drawn to scale. All figures lie in a plane unless otherwise indicated.

(4) Unless otherwise specified, the domain of any function f is assumed to be the set of all real numbers x for which $f(x)$ is a real number. The range of f is assumed to be the set of all real numbers $f(x)$, where x is in the domain of f.

(5) Reference information that may be useful in answering the questions in this test can be found on the page preceding Question 1.

1. If $2t + 3t = 4t + 6t - 10$, then $t =$

   (A) -1 (B) 0 (C) $\frac{1}{2}$ (D) 1 (E) 2

2. For all $x \neq 0, \dfrac{1}{\left(\dfrac{2}{x^2}\right)} =$

   (A) $\dfrac{x^2}{2}$ (B) $\dfrac{x^2}{4}$ (C) $\dfrac{2}{x^2}$ (D) $\dfrac{1}{2x^2}$ (E) $2x^2$

3. If $x = 1$, then $(x - 5)(x + 2) =$

   (A) -12 (B) -3 (C) -1 (D) 3 (E) 12

GO ON TO THE NEXT PAGE

MATHEMATICS LEVEL 1 TEST—*Continued*

USE THIS SPACE FOR SCRATCH WORK.

4. In rectangle $ABCD$ in Figure 1, what are the coordinates of vertex C ?

(A) $(1, 4)$
(B) $(1, 5)$
(C) $(5, 7)$
(D) $(7, 4)$
(E) $(7, 5)$

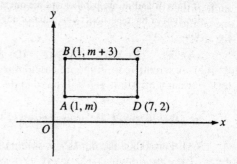

Figure 1

5. $(a + b + 2)(a + b + 2) =$

(A) $(a + b)^2 + 4$
(B) $(a + b)^2 + 4(a + b)$
(C) $(a + b)^2 + 4(a + b) + 4$
(D) $a^2 + b^2 + 4$
(E) $a^2 + b^2 + 4ab$

6. At what point does the graph of $2x + 3y = 12$ intersect the y-axis?

(A) $(0, -6)$
(B) $(0, -2)$
(C) $(0, 3)$
(D) $(0, 4)$
(E) $(0, 12)$

7. If $12x^2 = 7$, then $7\left(12x^2\right)^2 =$

(A)   49
(B)   84
(C)   98
(D)   144
(E)   343

GO ON TO THE NEXT PAGE

MATHEMATICS LEVEL 1 TEST—*Continued*

USE THIS SPACE FOR SCRATCH WORK.

8. If lines ℓ and m are parallel and are intersected by line t, what is the sum of the measures of the interior angles on the same side of line t ?

(A) 90°   (B) 180°   (C) 270°   (D) 360°   (E) 540°

9. If $x + y = 5$ and $x - y = 3$, then $x =$

(A) 4   (B) 2   (C) 1   (D) 0   (E) –1

10. If the cube root of the square root of a number is 2, what is the number?

(A)   16
(B)   32
(C)   36
(D)   64
(E)   256

11. Each face of the cube in Figure 2 consists of nine small squares. The shading on three of the faces is shown, and the shading on the other three faces is such that on opposite faces the reverse squares are shaded. For example, if one face has only the center square shaded, its opposite face will have eight of the nine squares shaded (the center square will not be shaded). What is the total number of shaded squares on all six faces of the cube?

(A) 12   (B) 16   (C) 18   (D) 27   (E) 54

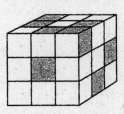

Figure 2

12. For three bins, A, B, and C, the volume of A is one-half that of B and the volume of B is two-thirds that of C. If A has a volume of 210 cubic meters, what is the volume of C, in cubic meters?

(A) 630   (B) 315   (C) 280   (D) 140   (E) 70

GO ON TO THE NEXT PAGE

MATHEMATICS LEVEL 1 TEST—*Continued*

13. In Figure 3, when ray *OA* is rotated clockwise 7 degrees about point *O*, ray *OA* will be perpendicular to ray *OB*. What is the measure of ∠*AOB* before this rotation?

    (A) 97°   (B) 90°   (C) 87°   (D) 83°   (E) 80°

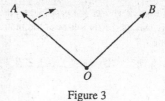

Figure 3

14. If $x + x + x = y$, then $x - y =$

    (A) $-3x$ (B) $-2x$ (C) $-\dfrac{x}{2}$ (D) $\dfrac{2}{3}x$ (E) $2x$

15. If $f(x) = \dfrac{1}{x}$ for $x > 0$, then $f(1.5) =$

    (A) $\dfrac{3}{4}$ (B) $\dfrac{2}{3}$ (C) $\dfrac{1}{2}$ (D) $\dfrac{1}{3}$ (E) $\dfrac{1}{4}$

16. If $15^m = 3^4 \cdot 5^4$, what is the value of m ?

    (A) 4   (B) 8   (C) 16   (D) 32   (E) 128

17. What are all values of x for which $|x - 2| < 3$?

    (A) $x < -1$ or $x > 5$
    (B) $x < -1$
    (C) $x > 5$
    (D) $-5 < x < 1$
    (E) $-1 < x < 5$

GO ON TO THE NEXT PAGE

MATHEMATICS LEVEL 1 TEST—*Continued*

USE THIS SPACE FOR SCRATCH WORK.

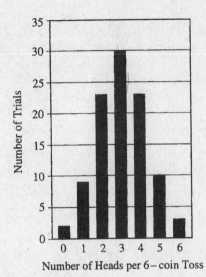

18. An algebra class conducted a coin-tossing experiment. Each trial of the experiment consisted of tossing 6 coins and counting the number of heads that resulted. The results for 100 trials are pictured in the graph above. In approximately what percent of the trials were there 3 or more heads?

(A) 32%   (B) 36%   (C) 50%   (D) 60%   (E) 66%

19. The circle in Figure 4 has center *J* and radius 6. What is the length of chord *GH* ?

(A) 6   (B) 8.49   (C) 10.39   (D) 12   (E) 16.97

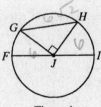

Figure 4

GO ON TO THE NEXT PAGE

MATHEMATICS LEVEL 1 TEST—*Continued*

USE THIS SPACE FOR SCRATCH WORK.

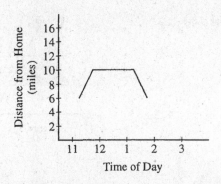

20. The graph above shows the distance of Janet's car from her home over a period of time on a given day. Which of the following situations best fits the information?

    (A) Janet leaves her workplace, drives to a restaurant for lunch, and then returns to her workplace.
    (B) Janet leaves her workplace, drives home, and stays at home.
    (C) Janet leaves home, drives to a friend's house, and stays at the friend's house.
    (D) Janet drives from home to the grocery store and then returns home.
    (E) Janet is at the grocery store, takes the groceries home, and then drives back to the grocery store.

$X = \{2, 3, 4, 5, 6, 7, 8, 9\}$
$Y = \{0, 1\}$
$Z = \{0, 1, 2, 3, 4, 5, 6, 7, 8, 9\}$

21. Before 1990, telephone area codes in the United States were three-digit numbers of the form xyz. Shown above are sets X, Y, and Z from which the digits x, y, and z, respectively, were chosen. How many possible area codes were there?

    (A) 919   (B) 160   (C) 144   (D) 126   (E) 20

GO ON TO THE NEXT PAGE

USE THIS SPACE FOR SCRATCH WORK.

22. In Figure 5, $\triangle ABC$ is equilateral and $EF \parallel DG \parallel AC$. What is the perimeter of the shaded region?

    (A) 4   (B) 6   (C) 8   (D) 9   (E) 10

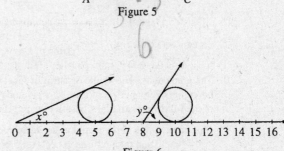

Figure 5

23. In Figure 6, two congruent circles are tangent to the number line at points 5 and 10, respectively, and tangent to rays from points 0 and 8, respectively. The circle at 10 is to be moved to the right along the number line, and the ray from point 8 is to be rotated so that it is tangent to the circle at its new position and $\tan x° = \tan y°$. How many units to the right must the circle be moved?

    (A) 1   (B) 2   (C) 3   (D) 4   (E) 5

GO ON TO THE NEXT PAGE

MATHEMATICS LEVEL 1 TEST—*Continued*

USE THIS SPACE FOR SCRATCH WORK.

24. A beacon that rotates in a complete circle at a constant rate throws a single beam of light that is seen every 9 seconds at a point four miles away. How many degrees does the beacon turn in 1 second?

(A) 6° (B) 20° (C) 40° (D) 54° (E) 60°

25. If $i^2 = -1$ and if $\left(\left(i^2 \right)^3 \right)^k = 1$, then the least positive integer value of k is

(A) 1 (B) 2 (C) 4 (D) 6 (E) 8

26. In Figure 7, if $\theta = 44°$, what is the value of c ?

(A) 6.94 (B) 7.19 (C) 9.66 (D) 10.36 (E) 13.90

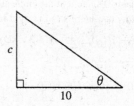

Note: Figure not drawn to scale.

Figure 7

GO ON TO THE NEXT PAGE

MATHEMATICS LEVEL 1 TEST—*Continued*

USE THIS SPACE FOR SCRATCH WORK.

27. The thickness of concrete that lines a swimming pool is a function of the depth of the pool. If d represents the depth, in feet, of the pool and $t(d)$ represents the thickness, in inches, of the concrete, then $t(d) = \frac{1}{12}\left(d^2 - 2d + 6\right)$.

    Of the following, which is the closest approximation to the thickness, in inches, of the concrete at a depth of 10 feet?

    (A) 0.5   (B) 1.5   (C) 6.2   (D) 7.2   (E) 10.5

28. Of the following, which has the greatest value?

    (A) 10^{100}

    (B) 100^{10}

    (C) $\left(10 \cdot 10^{10}\right)^{10}$

    (D) $(100 \cdot 10)^{10}$

    (E) $10,000,000,000$

29. In the xy-plane, the points $O(0, 0)$, $P(-6, 0)$, $R(-7, 5)$, and $S(-1, 1)$ can be connected to form line segments. Which two segments have the same length?

    (A) OP and OR
    (B) OP and OS
    (C) OR and RS
    (D) OS and PR
    (E) PR and PS

30. A total of 9 students took a test and their average (arithmetic mean) score was 86. If the average score for 4 of the students was 81, what was the average score for the remaining 5 students?

    (A) 87   (B) 88   (C) 89   (D) 90   (E) 91

GO ON TO THE NEXT PAGE

MATHEMATICS LEVEL 1 TEST—*Continued*

31. Line ℓ has a positive slope and a negative y-intercept.
    Line m is parallel to ℓ and has a positive y-intercept.
    The x-intercept of m must be

    (A) negative and greater than the x-intercept of ℓ
    (B) negative and less than the x-intercept of ℓ
    (C) zero
    (D) positive and greater than the x-intercept of ℓ
    (E) positive and less than the x-intercept of ℓ

32. Figure 8 is a right rectangular prism. Which of the given points is
    located in the plane determined by the vertices G, H, and B ?

    (A) A (B) C (C) D (D) E (E) F

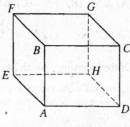

Figure 8

33. The sum of the two roots of a quadratic equation is 5 and their
    product is -6. Which of the following could be the equation?

    (A) $x^2 - 6x + 5 = 0$
    (B) $x^2 - 5x - 6 = 0$
    (C) $x^2 - 5x + 6 = 0$
    (D) $x^2 + 5x - 6 = 0$
    (E) $x^2 + 6x + 5 = 0$

34. In Figure 9, triangles ABC and DEC are similar and $w = 5$.
    What is the value of $\dfrac{x}{y}$?

    (A) $\dfrac{2}{5}$ (B) $\dfrac{3}{5}$ (C) $\dfrac{2}{3}$ (D) $\dfrac{3}{2}$ (E) $\dfrac{5}{2}$

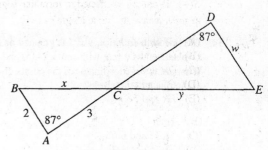

Note: Figure not drawn to scale.

Figure 9

35. $\left(\sin^2\theta + \cos^2\theta - 3\right)^4 =$

    (A) 256   (B) 81   (C) 64   (D) 32   (E) 16

GO ON TO THE NEXT PAGE

USE THIS SPACE FOR SCRATCH WORK.

36. In Figure 10, if $\triangle ABC$ is reflected across line ℓ, what will be the coordinates of the reflection of point A ?

    (A) $(5, 1)$ (B) $(8, 1)$ (C) $(9, 1)$ (D) $(11, 1)$ (E) $(13, 1)$

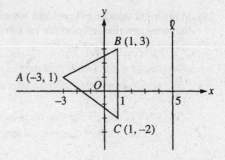

Figure 10

37. In Figure 11, the cube has edge of length 2. What is the distance from vertex A to the midpoint C of edge BD ?

    (A) $\sqrt{7}$
    (B) $2\sqrt{2}$
    (C) 3
    (D) 5
    (E) $\sqrt{29}$

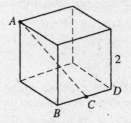

Figure 11

38. The line with equation $y = 7$ is graphed on the same xy-plane as the circle with center $(4, 5)$ and radius 3. What are the x-coordinates of the points of intersection of the line and the circle?

    (A) -5 and 5
    (B) -1 and 1
    (C) 1.35 and 6.65
    (D) 1.76 and 6.24
    (E) 2 and 6

GO ON TO THE NEXT PAGE

MATHEMATICS LEVEL 1 TEST—*Continued*

USE THIS SPACE FOR SCRATCH WORK.

39. In Figure 12, if $60 < q + s < 160$, which of the following describes all possible values of $t + r$?

    (A) $0 < t + r < 60$
    (B) $60 < t + r < 120$
    (C) $120 < t + r < 200$
    (D) $200 < t + r < 300$
    (E) $420 < t + r < 520$

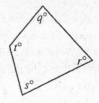

Figure 12

40. At the end of 1990, the population of a certain town was 6,250. If the population increases at the rate of 3.5 percent each year, what will the population of the town be at the end of 2005 ?

    (A)   9,530
    (B)   9,740
    (C)   9,950
    (D)   10,260
    (E)   10,470

41. If points R, S, and T lie on a circle and if the center of the circle lies on segment RT, then $\triangle RST$ must be

    (A) acute
    (B) obtuse
    (C) right
    (D) isosceles
    (E) equilateral

42. The function f, where $f(x) = (1 + x)^2$, is defined for $-2 \leq x \leq 2$. What is the range of f ?

    (A) $0 \leq f(x) \leq 4$
    (B) $0 \leq f(x) \leq 9$
    (C) $1 \leq f(x) \leq 4$
    (D) $1 \leq f(x) \leq 5$
    (E) $1 \leq f(x) \leq 9$

GO ON TO THE NEXT PAGE

USE THIS SPACE FOR SCRATCH WORK.

43. In the right circular cylinder shown in Figure 13, P and O are the centers of the bases and segment AB is a diameter of one of the bases. What is the perimeter of $\triangle ABO$ if the height of the cylinder is 5 and the radius of the base is 3 ?

    (A) 11.83
    (B) 14.66
    (C) 16
    (D) 16.66
    (E) 17.66

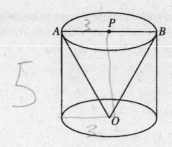

Figure 13

44. Sequential arrangements of squares are formed according to a pattern. Each arrangement after the first one is generated by adding a row of squares to the bottom of the previous arrangement, as shown in Figure 14. If this pattern continues, which of the following gives the number of squares in the nth arrangement?

    (A) $2n^2$

    (B) $2(2n-1)$

    (C) $n(n-1)$

    (D) $\frac{1}{2}n(n+1)$

    (E) $n(n+1)$

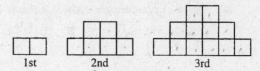

1st   2nd   3rd

Figure 14

45. If $f(x) = x^3 + 1$ and if f^{-1} is the inverse function of f, what is $f^{-1}(4)$?

    (A) 0.02   (B) 1.44   (C) 1.71   (D) 27   (E) 65

GO ON TO THE NEXT PAGE

MATHEMATICS LEVEL 1 TEST—*Continued*

46. Two positive integers j and k satisfy the relation $j\mathbf{R}k$ if and only if $j = k^2 + 1$. If m, n, and p satisfy the relations $m\mathbf{R}n$ and $n\mathbf{R}p$, what is the value of m in terms of p ?

    (A) $p^2 + 1$

    (B) $p^2 + 2$

    (C) $\left(p^2 + 1\right)^2$

    (D) $\left(p^2 + 1\right)^2 + 1$

    (E) $\left(p^2 + 2\right)^2$

47. The area of parallelogram $ABCD$ in Figure 15 is

    (A) 12   (B) $6\sqrt{3}$ (C) 20   (D) $12\sqrt{3}$ (E) 24

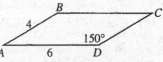

Figure 15

48. In Figure 16, the area of the shaded region bounded by the graph of the parabola $y = f(x)$ and the x-axis is 3. What is the area of the region bounded by the graph of $y = f(x - 2)$ and the x-axis?

    (A) 1   (B) $\dfrac{3}{2}$ (C) 2   (D) 3   (E) 6

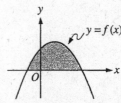

Figure 16

GO ON TO THE NEXT PAGE

MATHEMATICS LEVEL 1 TEST—*Continued*

USE THIS SPACE FOR SCRATCH WORK.

49. Marigolds are to be planted inside a circular flower garden so that there are 4 marigolds per square foot. The circumference of the garden is 20 feet. If marigolds are available only in packs of 6, how many packs of 6 flowers are needed?

(A) 6 (B) 13 (C) 14 (D) 20 (E) 22

50. A solution is made by mixing concentrate with water. How many liters of concentrate should be mixed with 2 liters of water so that 32 percent of the solution is concentrate?

(A) 0.63
(B) 0.64
(C) 0.68
(D) 0.94
(E) 1.06

STOP

IF YOU FINISH BEFORE TIME IS CALLED, YOU MAY CHECK YOUR WORK ON THIS TEST ONLY.
DO NOT TURN TO ANY OTHER TEST IN THIS BOOK.

How to Score the SAT Subject Test in Mathematics Level 1

When you take an actual SAT Subject Test in Mathematics Level 1, your answer sheet will be "read" by a scanning machine that will record your responses to each question. Then a computer will compare your answers with the correct answers and produce your raw score. You get one point for each correct answer. For each wrong answer, you lose one-quarter of a point. Questions you omit (and any for which you mark more than one answer) are not counted. This raw score is converted to a scaled score that is reported to you and to the colleges you specify.

Worksheet 1. Finding Your Raw Test Score

Step 1: Table A on the following page lists the correct answers for all the questions on the SAT Subject Test in Mathematics Level 1 that is reproduced in this book. It also serves as a worksheet for you to calculate your raw score.

- Compare your answers with those given in the table.

- Put a check in the column marked "Right" if your answer is correct.

- Put a check in the column marked "Wrong" if your answer is incorrect.

- Leave both columns blank if you omitted the question.

Step 2: Count the number of right answers.

Enter the total here: _____

Step 3: Count the number of wrong answers.

Enter the total here: _____

Step 4: Multiply the number of wrong answers by .250.

Enter the product here: _____

Step 5: Subtract the result obtained in Step 4 from the total you obtained in Step 2.

Enter the result here: _____

Step 6: Round the number obtained in Step 5 to the nearest whole number.

Enter the result here: _____

The number you obtained in Step 6 is your raw score.

Answers to Practice Test 4 for Mathematics Level 1

Table A
Answers to the Subject Test in Mathematics Level 1 – Practice Test 4 and Percentage of Students Answering
Each Question Correctly

Question Number	Correct Answer	Right	Wrong	Percentage of Students Answering the Question Correctly*	Question Number	Correct Answer	Right	Wrong	Percentage of Students Answering the Question Correctly*
1	E			92	26	C			68
2	A			76	27	D			72
3	A			93	28	C			52
4	E			91	29	E			57
5	C			65	30	D			53
6	D			77	31	B			58
7	E			86	32	A			51
8	B			77	33	B			24
9	A			88	34	A			51
10	D			80	35	E			49
11	D			78	36	E			38
12	A			75	37	C			34
13	A			80	38	D			25
14	B			75	39	D			37
15	B			86	40	E			25
16	A			71	41	C			25
17	E			71	42	B			14
18	E			65	43	E			51
19	B			80	44	E			42
20	A			72	45	B			28
21	B			68	46	D			32
22	E			66	47	A			19
23	C			60	48	D			19
24	C			72	49	E			22
25	B			63	50	D			27

* These percentages are based on an analysis of the answer sheets of a representative sample of 9,999 students who took the original administration of this test and whose mean score was 564. They may be used as an indication of the relative difficulty of a particular question.

Finding Your Scaled Score

When you take SAT Subject Tests, the scores sent to the colleges you specify are reported on the College Board scale, which ranges from 200 to 800. You can convert your practice test raw score to a scaled score by using Table B. To find your scaled score, locate your raw score in the left-hand column of Table B; the corresponding score in the right-hand column is your scaled score. For example, a raw score of 30 on this particular edition of the SAT Subject Test in Mathematics Level 1 corresponds to a scaled score of 620.

Raw scores are converted to scaled scores to ensure that a score earned on any one edition of a particular Subject Test is comparable to the same scaled score earned on any other edition of the same Subject Test. Because some editions of tests may be slightly easier or more difficult than others, scaled scores are adjusted so that they indicate the same level of performance regardless of the edition of the test taken and the ability of the group that takes it. Thus, for example, a score of 400 on one edition of a test taken at a particular administration indicates the same level of achievement as a score of 400 on a different edition of the test taken at a different administration.

When you take the SAT Subject Tests during a national administration, your scores are likely to differ somewhat from the scores you obtain on the tests in this book. People perform at different levels at different times for reasons unrelated to the tests themselves. The precision of any test is also limited because it represents only a sample of all the possible questions that could be asked.

Table B
Scaled Score Conversion Table
Subject Test in Mathematics Level 1 – Practice Test 4

Raw Score	Scaled Score	Raw Score	Scaled Score	Raw Score	Scaled Score
50	800	28	590	6	390
49	790	27	580	5	380
48	780	26	570	4	380
47	780	25	560	3	370
46	770	24	550	2	360
45	750	23	540	1	350
44	740	22	530	0	340
43	740	21	520	−1	340
42	730	20	510	−2	330
41	720	19	500	−3	320
40	710	18	490	−4	310
39	710	17	480	−5	300
38	700	16	470	−6	300
37	690	15	460	−7	280
36	680	14	460	−8	270
35	670	13	450	−9	260
34	660	12	440	−10	260
33	650	11	430	−11	250
32	640	10	420	−12	240
31	630	9	420		
30	620	8	410		
29	600	7	400		

How Did You Do on the Subject Test in Mathematics Level 1?

After you score your test and analyze your performance, think about the following questions:

Did you run out of time before reaching the end of the test?

If so, you may need to pace yourself better. For example, maybe you spent too much time on one or two hard questions. A better approach might be to skip the ones you can't answer right away and try answering all the remaining questions on the test. Then if there's time, go back to the questions you skipped.

Did you take a long time reading the directions?

You will save time when you take the test by learning the directions to the Subject Test in Mathematics Level 1 ahead of time. Each minute you spend reading directions during the test is a minute that you could use to answer questions.

How did you handle questions you were unsure of?

If you were able to eliminate one or more of the answer choices as wrong and guess from the remaining ones, your approach probably worked to your advantage. On the other hand, making haphazard guesses or omitting questions without trying to eliminate choices could cost you valuable points.

How difficult were the questions for you compared with other students who took the test?

Table A shows you how difficult the multiple-choice questions were for the group of students who took this test during its national administration. The right-hand column gives the percentage of students that answered each question correctly.

A question answered correctly by almost everyone in the group is obviously an easier question. For example, 91 percent of the students answered question 4 correctly. However, only 19 percent answered question 47 correctly.

Keep in mind that these percentages are based on just one group of students. They would probably be different with another group of students taking the test.

If you missed several easier questions, go back and try to find out why: Did the questions cover material you haven't reviewed yet? Did you misunderstand the directions?

Answer Explanations

For Practice Test 4

The solutions presented here provide one method for solving each of the problems on this test. Other mathematically correct approaches are possible.

Question 1

Choice (E) is the correct answer. When like terms are combined, the equation simplifies to $5t = 10t - 10$. Solving for t gives $-5t = -10$ and $t = 2$.

Question 2

Choice (A) is the correct answer. If $x \neq 0$, then $\dfrac{1}{\left(\dfrac{2}{x^2}\right)} = \dfrac{x^2}{2}$.

Question 3

Choice (A) is the correct answer. Substituting $x = 1$ yields $(1 - 5)(1 + 2) = -4 \cdot 3 = -12$.

Question 4

Choice (E) is the correct answer. From the figure you can see that points A and D have the same y-coordinate. Thus, $m = 2$ and $m + 3 = 5$. The y-coordinate of vertex C is 5. The x-coordinates of C and D are equal. Thus, the coordinates of C are $(7, 5)$.

Question 5

Choice (C) is the correct answer. $(a + b + 2)(a + b + 2) = [(a + b) + 2]^2 = (a + b)^2 + 2 \cdot (a + b) \cdot 2 + 2^2 = (a + b)^2 + 4(a + b) + 4$.

Question 6

Choice (D) is the correct answer. The point of intersection of the graph of $2x + 3y = 12$ and the y-axis is simply the point at which $x = 0$, since $x = 0$ for all points on the y-axis. If $x = 0$, then $2x + 3y = 12$ simplifies to $3y = 12$ or $y = 4$. The graph of $2x + 3y = 12$ intersects the y-axis at $(0, 4)$.

Question 7

Choice (E) is the correct answer. Since $12x^2 = 7$, then $7(12x^2)^2 = 7(7)^2 = 7^3 = 343$.

Question 8

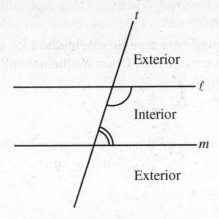

Choice (B) is the correct answer. It is helpful to draw a figure to solve the problem. Since $\ell \parallel m$, the sum of the interior angles on the same side of line t is 180°.

Question 9

Choice (A) is the correct answer. One way to solve for x is to set up the system of equations $\begin{cases} x+y=5 \\ x-y=3 \end{cases}$. Adding the two equations gives $2x = 8$ or $x = 4$. Choice (C) is incorrect. If you add the left hand sides of the equations but subtract the right hand sides, you get $2x = 2$ or $x = 1$.

Question 10

Choice (D) is the correct answer. The statement translates to the equation $\sqrt[3]{\sqrt{x}} = 2$. If you cube each side of the equation, you get $\sqrt{x} = 2^3 = 8$. Now if you square each side, you get $x = 8^2 = 64$. Choice (B) is incorrect. It results from thinking that $\sqrt[3]{\sqrt{x}} = 2$ is equal to $\sqrt[5]{x} = 2$, thereby getting $x = 32$.

Question 11

Choice (D) is the correct answer. One face of the cube has the center square shaded, which implies its opposite face has 8 shaded squares, for a total of 9 shaded squares. Another face has 3 squares shaded, which implies its opposite face has 6 shaded squares, for a total of 9 shaded squares. The last face has 5 squares shaded, which implies its opposite face has 4 shaded squares, for a total of 9 shaded squares. Thus, the number of shaded squares on the six faces of the cube is $3(9) = 27$. Choice (C) is incorrect. It results from counting the number of shaded squares shown and doubling that number.

Question 12

Choice (A) is the correct answer. If the volume of A is 210 cubic meters, then the volume of B is 420 cubic meters. Since the volume of B is $\frac{2}{3}$ the volume of C, $420 = \frac{2}{3}$ C and C = 630.

Question 13

Choice (A) is the correct answer. When ray OA is perpendicular to ray OB, the measure of $\angle AOB$ is 90°. Therefore, before ray OA is rotated 7 degrees clockwise, the measure of $\angle AOB$ is 97°.

Question 14

Choice (B) is the correct answer. Since $3x = y$, $x - y = x - 3x = -2x$.

Question 15

Choice (B) is the correct answer. f (1.5) is equal to $\frac{1}{1.5} = 0.667$ or $\frac{2}{3}$. Alternatively, f (1.5) can be expressed as $\frac{1}{\frac{3}{2}} = \frac{2}{3}$.

Question 16

Choice (A) is the correct answer. Since $3^4 \cdot 5^4 = 15^4$, $m = 4$. Choice (C) is incorrect. If you think $3^4 \cdot 5^4 = (3 \cdot 5)^{(4 \cdot 4)}$, you will get $15^m = 15^{16}$.

Question 17

Choice (E) is the correct answer. If $|x - 2| < 3$, then $-3 < x - 2 < 3$. This is equivalent to $-1 < x < 5$.

Question 18

Choice (E) is the correct answer. You need to add the number of trials in which there were 3 heads, 4 heads, 5 heads, and 6 heads. This is equal to $30 + 23 + 10 + 3 = 66$. Since there were 100 trials, $\frac{66}{100} = 66\%$.

Choice (B) is incorrect. This is the percent of trials for which there were more than 3 heads. Choice (C) is incorrect. This results from assuming that since the bar in the middle represents 3 heads, half of the trials had 3 or more heads.

Question 19

Choice (B) is the correct answer. In the figure, $JG = JH = 6$, since chords $\overline{JG}$ and $\overline{JH}$ are radii of the circle. Thus, $\triangle GHJ$ is an isosceles right triangle, and it follows from the Pythagorean theorem that $GH = 6\sqrt{2} \approx 8.49$. Choice (C) is incorrect. $10.39 \approx 6\sqrt{3}$ instead of $6\sqrt{2}$.

Question 20

Choice (A) is the correct answer. The graph represents a situation in which Janet starts out 6 miles from home. She departs there at about 11:00 a.m. and goes some place farther from home. She stays there for a while and then returns to a location 6 miles from home. Choices (B), (C), (D), and (E) are incorrect. In each of these situations, Janet is at home during some part of the time period. For Janet to be at home, Janet's distance from home would have to be 0.

Question 21

Choice (B) is the correct answer. There are 8 possible digits for the first digit, x, of the area code, 2 possible digits for y, and 10 possible digits for z. Therefore, the number of possible area codes would be $8 \cdot 2 \cdot 10 = 160$. Choice (E) is incorrect. It results from adding $8 + 2 + 10$.

Question 22

Choice (E) is the correct answer. Since $\overline{EF} \parallel \overline{DG} \parallel \overline{AC}$, triangles EBF and DBG are equilateral. Thus, $EF = DE = 2$ and $DG = 4$. The perimeter of the shaded region is $2 + 2 + 2 + 4 = 10$.

Question 23

Choice (C) is the correct answer. Since the circles are congruent, in order for $\tan x°$ to equal $\tan y°$, the distances from the vertex of each angle to the point where the circle touches the number line must be equal. Thus, the circle at 10 must be moved 3 units to the right.

Question 24

Choice (C) is the correct answer. Since the beam of light can be seen every 9 seconds, it takes 9 seconds for the beacon to completely rotate once. In 1 second, the beacon makes $\frac{1}{9}$ of a rotation. Since a full rotation is 360°, then $\frac{1}{9}$ of a rotation is 40°.

Question 25

Choice (B) is the correct answer. Since $i^2 = -1$, $(i^2)^3 = -1$. In order for $(-1)^k$ to equal 1, k must be even. Thus, the least positive integer value of k is 2.

Question 26

Choice (C) is the correct answer. In the figure, $\tan \theta = \frac{c}{10}$. Thus, $\tan 44° = \frac{c}{10}$ and $c = 10 \tan 44° \approx 9.66$. Choice (A) is incorrect. If you use $\sin 44° = \frac{c}{10}$ instead of $\tan 44° = \frac{c}{10}$, you will get $c \approx 6.94$. Choice (B) is incorrect. If you use $\cos 44° = \frac{c}{10}$ instead of $\tan 44° = \frac{c}{10}$, you will get $c \approx 7.19$. Choice (D) is incorrect. This is equal to $\frac{10}{\tan 44°}$ instead of $10 \tan 44°$. Choice (E) is incorrect. This is equal to $\frac{10}{\cos 44°}$ instead of $10 \tan 44°$.

Question 27

Choice (D) is the correct answer. The thickness, in inches, of the concrete at a depth of 10 feet is equal to $t(10) = \frac{1}{12}(10^2 - 2 \cdot 10 + 6) = \frac{86}{12} \approx 7.167$. This is closest to 7.2.

Question 28

Choice (C) is the correct answer. By applying the rules for exponents, each choice can be written as a power of 10. Choice (A) is incorrect, 10^{100}, is already written as a power of 10. Choice (B) is incorrect, 100^{10}, is equal to $(10^2)^{10} = 10^{20}$. Choice (C) is equal to $(10^{11})^{10} = 10^{110}$. Choice (D) is equal to $(10^2 \cdot 10)^{10} = (10^3)^{10} = 10^{30}$. Choice (E), 10,000,000,000 is equal to 10^{10}. Thus, the greatest value is $(10 \cdot 10^{10})^{10} = 10^{110}$.

Question 29

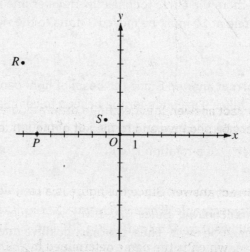

Choice (E) is the correct answer. It is helpful to draw a figure. From the figure, it is clear that $\overline{OS}$ is shorter than the other segments, so the answer cannot be choice (B) or choice (D).

$$OP = 6$$
$$OR = \sqrt{(-7)^2 + 5^2} = \sqrt{74}$$
$$RS = \sqrt{(-6)^2 + 4^2} = \sqrt{52}$$
$$PS = \sqrt{(-5)^2 + 1^2} = \sqrt{26}$$
$$PR = \sqrt{(-1)^2 + 5^2} = \sqrt{26}$$

$\overline{PS}$ and $\overline{PR}$ are the same length.

Question 30

Choice (D) is the correct answer. Since the mean score for the 9 students was 86, the total of the scores of the 9 students was $9 \cdot 86 = 774$. The total of the scores for 4 of the students was $4 \cdot 81 = 324$. The total of the scores for the remaining 5 students was $774 - 324 = 450$. Thus, the average score for the remaining 5 students was $\frac{450}{5} = 90$.

Question 31

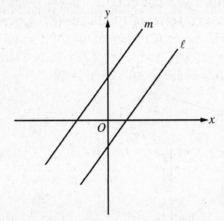

Choice (B) is the correct answer. It is helpful to draw a figure. The x-intercept of m must be negative and to the left of the x-intercept of ℓ.

Question 32

Choice (A) is the correct answer. Since the figure is a rectangular solid, each of the faces is a rectangle. Thus, $\overline{AB}$ is parallel to $\overline{EF}$, and $\overline{EF}$ is parallel to $\overline{GH}$. It follows that $\overline{AB}$ is parallel to $\overline{GH}$, and so $\overline{AB}$ and $\overline{GH}$ lie in the same plane, which is the plane determined by points G, H, and B. Therefore, A is in the same plane as G, H, and B.

Question 33

Choice (B) is the correct answer. One way to do this problem is to think about the properties of roots. Suppose the two roots of a quadratic equation are a and b. Then the quadratic equation can be written in factored form as $(x - a)(x - b) = 0$. The sum of the roots is $a + b$, and the product is ab. Note that $(x - a)(x - b) = x^2 - (a + b)x + ab$. In this question the sum of the roots is 5 and the product is –6. Therefore, $(a + b) = 5$ and $ab = -6$. The equation could be $x^2 - 5x - 6 = 0$. Note that the roots of this equation are 6 and –1. Their sum is 5 and their product is –6.

Question 34

Choice (A) is the correct answer. Since $\triangle ABC$ is similar to $\triangle DEC$, $\frac{AB}{DE} = \frac{BC}{EC}$. Thus, $\frac{2}{w} = \frac{x}{y}$. Since $w = 5$, $\frac{x}{y} = \frac{2}{5}$.

Question 35

Choice (E) is the correct answer. By the Pythagorean identity, $\sin^2 \theta + \cos^2 \theta = 1$. Therefore, $(\sin^2 \theta + \cos^2 \theta - 3)^4 = (1 - 3)^4 = (-2)^4 = 16$.

Question 36

Choice (E) is the correct answer. Point A is located 8 units to the left of line ℓ. Thus, when $\triangle ABC$ is reflected across line ℓ, the image of A will have a horizontal position 8 units to the right of line ℓ. Its vertical position will be the same as A. Thus, the coordinates of the image of A will be (13, 1).

Question 37

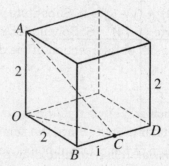

Choice (C) is the correct answer. In the figure, since the cube has edge of length 2, $AO = OB = 2$. Since C is the midpoint of edge BD, $BC = 1$. Using the Pythagorean theorem,

$$(OB)^2 + (BC)^2 = (OC)^2$$
$$4 + 1 = (OC)^2 \text{ and } OC = \sqrt{5}.$$

Using the Pythagorean theorem again,

$$(AO)^2 + (OC)^2 = (AC)^2$$
$$4 + 5 = (AC)^2 \text{ and } AC = \sqrt{9} = 3.$$

The distance from A to C is 3.

Question 38

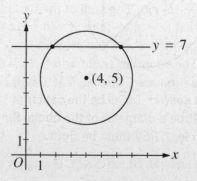

Choice (D) is the correct answer. It is helpful to draw a figure. The line $y = 7$ intersects the circle in 2 points. These 2 points and the center of the circle form a triangle with two sides of length 3, since the radius of the circle is 3. The triangle has height 2, since the distance between the point (4, 5) and the line $y = 7$ is the distance between (4, 5) and (4, 7).

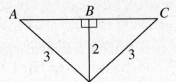

Using the Pythagorean theorem, you can find that $AB = \sqrt{5}$. The x-coordinate of point B is 4. Therefore, the x-coordinates of the points of intersection are $4 - \sqrt{5}$ and $4 + \sqrt{5}$ or 1.76 and 6.24. You could also solve the problem algebraically. The equation for a circle with center (4, 5) and radius 3 is $(x - 4)^2 + (y - 5)^2 = 9$. Substitute $y = 7$ into the equation, and it simplifies to $(x - 4)^2 = 5$. Solving for x produces the two x-coordinates of the points of intersection of the circle and the line.

Question 39

Choice (D) is the correct answer. The sum of the degree measures of the angles of a quadrilateral is 360°. Since the sum of q and s is between 60 and 160, the sum of t and r must be between $(360 - 60)$ and $(360 - 160)$. Thus, $200 < t + r < 300$.

Question 40

Choice (E) is the correct answer. Let P_0 represent the population of the town at the end of 1990. $P_0 = 6{,}250$. The population grows exponentially at the rate of 3.5% each year. The population of the town at the end of 15 years is given by $P_0(1.035)^{15} = 6{,}250(1.035)^{15} = 10{,}470.9 \approx 10{,}470$.

Question 41

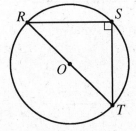

Choice (C) is the correct answer. Let O be the center of the circle. If O lies on $\overline{RT}$, then $\overline{RT}$ must be a diameter of the circle. Since $\angle RST$ is inscribed in the semicircle, $\triangle RST$ must be right.

Question 42

Choice (B) is the correct answer. Since $(1 + x)^2$ is a perfect square, the minimum value of the function is 0, which occurs when $x = -1$. The maximum value of f occurs when $x = 2$ and $f(2) = 9$. Thus, the range is $0 \le f(x) \le 9$. You can also graph the function and see what values the function takes on for the given domain. The graph is a parabola that opens upward and has a vertex at $(-1, 0)$. Choices (A), (C), (D), and (E) are incorrect and arise from several errors. Making the assumption that the left endpoint of the domain, $x = -2$, gives the minimum value for the range, yields $f(x) = 1$. Squaring an endpoint of the domain, $x = -2$ or $x = 2$, to give a maximum value for the range yields $f(x) = 4$. Lastly, incorrectly expanding $(1 + x)^2$ and getting $1 + x^2$, and then substituting $x = -2$ or $x = 2$ yields a maximum value of 5 for the range of f.

Question 43

Choice (E) is the correct answer. Since the radius of the base is 3, $AP = PB = 3$ and $AB = 6$. Since the height of the cylinder is 5, $OP = 5$. Using the Pythagorean theorem, $(OP)^2 + (PB)^2 = (OB)^2$. $25 + 9 = (OB)^2$ and $OB = \sqrt{34} \approx 5.831$. Since $OA = OB$, the perimeter of the triangle is $OA + OB + AB = 2\sqrt{34} + 6 \approx 17.66$.

Question 44

Choice (E) is the correct answer. The first arrangement has 2 squares. The second arrangement has 6 squares. The third arrangement has 12 squares. The fourth arrangement would add a row of 8 squares, giving a total of $12 + 8 = 20$ squares. Notice the pattern.

n	Number of Squares
1	$1 \cdot 2 = 2$
2	$2 \cdot 3 = 6$
3	$3 \cdot 4 = 12$
4	$4 \cdot 5 = 20$

The nth arrangement has $n(n+1)$ squares.

Question 45

Choice (B) is the correct answer. If $f(x) = x^3 + 1$, then $x = (f^{-1}(x))^3 + 1$ and $f^{-1}(x) = \sqrt[3]{x - 1}$. Thus, $f^{-1}(4) = \sqrt[3]{4 - 1} = \sqrt[3]{3} \approx 1.44$. Choice (A) is incorrect. $f^{-1}(x)$ is not equal to $\dfrac{1}{f(w)}$. Choice (C) is incorrect. It results from incorrectly taking the sum of 4 and 1 first and then evaluating the cube root of this sum: $\sqrt[3]{4 + 1} \approx 1.71$. Choice (D) is incorrect. It results from taking the cube of the difference of 4 and 1 instead of the cube root: $(4 - 1)^3 = 27$. Choice (E) is incorrect. It results from $f(4) = 4^3 + 1 = 65$.

Question 46

Choice (D) is the correct answer. Since mRn, then $m = n^2 + 1$. Since nRp, then $n = p^2 + 1$. Thus, $m = n^2 + 1 = (p^2 + 1)^2 + 1$.

Question 47

Choice (A) is the correct answer. Since the measure of $\angle D$ is 150° and $ABCD$ is a parallelogram, the measure of $\angle A$ is 30°. The area of the parallelogram can be found by $ab \sin A$, where A is the angle included between sides of length a and b. Thus, the area is equal to $(4)(6) \sin$ $30° = 24 \cdot \frac{1}{2} = 12$. Choice (D) is incorrect. It is equal to $ab \cos A$ instead of $ab \sin A$: $4 \cdot 6 \cdot \cos 30° = 24 \cdot \frac{\sqrt{3}}{2} = 12\sqrt{3}$. Choice (E) is incorrect. It results from simply multiplying 4 by 6 to get 24, but 4 is not the height of the parallelogram.

Question 48

Choice (D) is the correct answer. Since the graph of $y = f(x - 2)$ can be obtained from the graph of $y = f(x)$ by shifting the graph of $y = f(x)$ 2 units to the right, the shaded region will only be moved 2 units to the right. Therefore, there is no change in the shape or size of the shaded region. Thus, the area remains equal to 3.

Question 49

Choice (E) is the correct answer. The first step is to determine the area of the garden. Since the circumference is 20 feet, the radius is $\frac{20}{2\pi} = \frac{10}{\pi}$ and the area is $\pi r2$ or $\pi \left(\frac{10}{\pi} \right)^2 = \frac{100}{\pi}$ square feet. If there are 4 marigolds per square foot, $4 \cdot \frac{100}{\pi}$ marigolds are needed. To find out how many packs of 6 flowers are needed, divide $\frac{400}{\pi}$ by 6. The result is 21.22; thus, 22 packs would be needed. Choice (C) is incorrect. It results from using the circumference, 20, instead of the area, to determine the number of marigolds needed and getting $4 \cdot 20 = 80$. Since $80 \div 6 \approx 13.33$, 14 packs would be needed.

Question 50

Choice (D) is the correct answer. Let x be the number of liters of concentrate added to the water. You can set up the proportion $\frac{x}{2 + x} = \frac{32}{100}$.

$$100x = 64 + 32x$$
$$68x = 64$$
$$x = \frac{64}{68}$$
$$\approx 0.941$$

1 Your Name:
(Print)

Last   First   M.I.

I agree to the conditions on the front and back of the SAT Subject Tests™ book. I also agree with the SAT Test Security and Fairness policies and understand that any violation of these policies will result in score cancellation and may result in reporting of certain violations to law enforcement.

Signature: _____

Today's Date: ___/___/___
MM DD YY

Home Address: _____
(Print)
Number and Street   City   State/Country   Zip Code

Phone: (___)_____ Test Center: _____
(Print)   City   State/Country

2 YOUR NAME

Last Name (First 6 Letters) First Name (First 4 Letters) Mid. Init.

3 DATE OF BIRTH

MONTH | DAY | YEAR

○ Jan
○ Feb
○ Mar
○ Apr
○ May
○ Jun
○ Jul
○ Aug
○ Sep
○ Oct
○ Nov
○ Dec

4 REGISTRATION NUMBER
(Copy from Admission Ticket.)

Important: Fill in items 8 and 9 exactly as shown on the back of test book.

7 TEST BOOK SERIAL NUMBER
(Copy from front of test book.)

8 BOOK CODE
(Copy and grid as on back of test book.)

9 BOOK ID
(Copy from back of test book.)

PLEASE MAKE SURE to fill in these fields completely and correctly. If they are not correct, we won't be able to score your test(s)!

5 ZIP CODE

6 TEST CENTER
(Supplied by Test Center Supervisor.)

FOR OFFICIAL USE ONLY

PLEASE DO NOT WRITE IN THIS AREA

SERIAL #

You must use a No. 2 pencil and marks must be complete. Do not use a mechanical pencil. It is very important that you fill in the entire circle darkly and completely. If you change your response, erase as completely as possible. Incomplete marks or erasures may affect your score.

○ Literature
○ Biology E
○ Biology M
○ Chemistry
○ Physics

○ Mathematics Level 1
○ Mathematics Level 2
○ U.S. History
○ World History
○ French

○ German
○ Italian
○ Latin
○ Modern Hebrew
○ Spanish

○ Chinese Listening
○ French Listening
○ German Listening

○ Japanese Listening
○ Korean Listening
○ Spanish Listening

Background Questions: ① ② ③ ④ ⑤ ⑥ ⑦ ⑧ ⑨

1 Ⓐ Ⓑ Ⓒ Ⓓ Ⓔ 26 Ⓐ Ⓑ Ⓒ Ⓓ Ⓔ 51 Ⓐ Ⓑ Ⓒ Ⓓ Ⓔ 76 Ⓐ Ⓑ Ⓒ Ⓓ Ⓔ
2 Ⓐ Ⓑ Ⓒ Ⓓ Ⓔ 27 Ⓐ Ⓑ Ⓒ Ⓓ Ⓔ 52 Ⓐ Ⓑ Ⓒ Ⓓ Ⓔ 77 Ⓐ Ⓑ Ⓒ Ⓓ Ⓔ
3 Ⓐ Ⓑ Ⓒ Ⓓ Ⓔ 28 Ⓐ Ⓑ Ⓒ Ⓓ Ⓔ 53 Ⓐ Ⓑ Ⓒ Ⓓ Ⓔ 78 Ⓐ Ⓑ Ⓒ Ⓓ Ⓔ
4 Ⓐ Ⓑ Ⓒ Ⓓ Ⓔ 29 Ⓐ Ⓑ Ⓒ Ⓓ Ⓔ 54 Ⓐ Ⓑ Ⓒ Ⓓ Ⓔ 79 Ⓐ Ⓑ Ⓒ Ⓓ Ⓔ
5 Ⓐ Ⓑ Ⓒ Ⓓ Ⓔ 30 Ⓐ Ⓑ Ⓒ Ⓓ Ⓔ 55 Ⓐ Ⓑ Ⓒ Ⓓ Ⓔ 80 Ⓐ Ⓑ Ⓒ Ⓓ Ⓔ
6 Ⓐ Ⓑ Ⓒ Ⓓ Ⓔ 31 Ⓐ Ⓑ Ⓒ Ⓓ Ⓔ 56 Ⓐ Ⓑ Ⓒ Ⓓ Ⓔ 81 Ⓐ Ⓑ Ⓒ Ⓓ Ⓔ
7 Ⓐ Ⓑ Ⓒ Ⓓ Ⓔ 32 Ⓐ Ⓑ Ⓒ Ⓓ Ⓔ 57 Ⓐ Ⓑ Ⓒ Ⓓ Ⓔ 82 Ⓐ Ⓑ Ⓒ Ⓓ Ⓔ
8 Ⓐ Ⓑ Ⓒ Ⓓ Ⓔ 33 Ⓐ Ⓑ Ⓒ Ⓓ Ⓔ 58 Ⓐ Ⓑ Ⓒ Ⓓ Ⓔ 83 Ⓐ Ⓑ Ⓒ Ⓓ Ⓔ
9 Ⓐ Ⓑ Ⓒ Ⓓ Ⓔ 34 Ⓐ Ⓑ Ⓒ Ⓓ Ⓔ 59 Ⓐ Ⓑ Ⓒ Ⓓ Ⓔ 84 Ⓐ Ⓑ Ⓒ Ⓓ Ⓔ
10 Ⓐ Ⓑ Ⓒ Ⓓ Ⓔ 35 Ⓐ Ⓑ Ⓒ Ⓓ Ⓔ 60 Ⓐ Ⓑ Ⓒ Ⓓ Ⓔ 85 Ⓐ Ⓑ Ⓒ Ⓓ Ⓔ
11 Ⓐ Ⓑ Ⓒ Ⓓ Ⓔ 36 Ⓐ Ⓑ Ⓒ Ⓓ Ⓔ 61 Ⓐ Ⓑ Ⓒ Ⓓ Ⓔ 86 Ⓐ Ⓑ Ⓒ Ⓓ Ⓔ
12 Ⓐ Ⓑ Ⓒ Ⓓ Ⓔ 37 Ⓐ Ⓑ Ⓒ Ⓓ Ⓔ 62 Ⓐ Ⓑ Ⓒ Ⓓ Ⓔ 87 Ⓐ Ⓑ Ⓒ Ⓓ Ⓔ
13 Ⓐ Ⓑ Ⓒ Ⓓ Ⓔ 38 Ⓐ Ⓑ Ⓒ Ⓓ Ⓔ 63 Ⓐ Ⓑ Ⓒ Ⓓ Ⓔ 88 Ⓐ Ⓑ Ⓒ Ⓓ Ⓔ
14 Ⓐ Ⓑ Ⓒ Ⓓ Ⓔ 39 Ⓐ Ⓑ Ⓒ Ⓓ Ⓔ 64 Ⓐ Ⓑ Ⓒ Ⓓ Ⓔ 89 Ⓐ Ⓑ Ⓒ Ⓓ Ⓔ
15 Ⓐ Ⓑ Ⓒ Ⓓ Ⓔ 40 Ⓐ Ⓑ Ⓒ Ⓓ Ⓔ 65 Ⓐ Ⓑ Ⓒ Ⓓ Ⓔ 90 Ⓐ Ⓑ Ⓒ Ⓓ Ⓔ
16 Ⓐ Ⓑ Ⓒ Ⓓ Ⓔ 41 Ⓐ Ⓑ Ⓒ Ⓓ Ⓔ 66 Ⓐ Ⓑ Ⓒ Ⓓ Ⓔ 91 Ⓐ Ⓑ Ⓒ Ⓓ Ⓔ
17 Ⓐ Ⓑ Ⓒ Ⓓ Ⓔ 42 Ⓐ Ⓑ Ⓒ Ⓓ Ⓔ 67 Ⓐ Ⓑ Ⓒ Ⓓ Ⓔ 92 Ⓐ Ⓑ Ⓒ Ⓓ Ⓔ
18 Ⓐ Ⓑ Ⓒ Ⓓ Ⓔ 43 Ⓐ Ⓑ Ⓒ Ⓓ Ⓔ 68 Ⓐ Ⓑ Ⓒ Ⓓ Ⓔ 93 Ⓐ Ⓑ Ⓒ Ⓓ Ⓔ
19 Ⓐ Ⓑ Ⓒ Ⓓ Ⓔ 44 Ⓐ Ⓑ Ⓒ Ⓓ Ⓔ 69 Ⓐ Ⓑ Ⓒ Ⓓ Ⓔ 94 Ⓐ Ⓑ Ⓒ Ⓓ Ⓔ
20 Ⓐ Ⓑ Ⓒ Ⓓ Ⓔ 45 Ⓐ Ⓑ Ⓒ Ⓓ Ⓔ 70 Ⓐ Ⓑ Ⓒ Ⓓ Ⓔ 95 Ⓐ Ⓑ Ⓒ Ⓓ Ⓔ
21 Ⓐ Ⓑ Ⓒ Ⓓ Ⓔ 46 Ⓐ Ⓑ Ⓒ Ⓓ Ⓔ 71 Ⓐ Ⓑ Ⓒ Ⓓ Ⓔ 96 Ⓐ Ⓑ Ⓒ Ⓓ Ⓔ
22 Ⓐ Ⓑ Ⓒ Ⓓ Ⓔ 47 Ⓐ Ⓑ Ⓒ Ⓓ Ⓔ 72 Ⓐ Ⓑ Ⓒ Ⓓ Ⓔ 97 Ⓐ Ⓑ Ⓒ Ⓓ Ⓔ
23 Ⓐ Ⓑ Ⓒ Ⓓ Ⓔ 48 Ⓐ Ⓑ Ⓒ Ⓓ Ⓔ 73 Ⓐ Ⓑ Ⓒ Ⓓ Ⓔ 98 Ⓐ Ⓑ Ⓒ Ⓓ Ⓔ
24 Ⓐ Ⓑ Ⓒ Ⓓ Ⓔ 49 Ⓐ Ⓑ Ⓒ Ⓓ Ⓔ 74 Ⓐ Ⓑ Ⓒ Ⓓ Ⓔ 99 Ⓐ Ⓑ Ⓒ Ⓓ Ⓔ
25 Ⓐ Ⓑ Ⓒ Ⓓ Ⓔ 50 Ⓐ Ⓑ Ⓒ Ⓓ Ⓔ 75 Ⓐ Ⓑ Ⓒ Ⓓ Ⓔ 100 Ⓐ Ⓑ Ⓒ Ⓓ Ⓔ

PLEASE MAKE SURE to fill in these fields completely and correctly. If they are not correct, we won't be able to score your test(s)!

7 TEST BOOK SERIAL NUMBER
(Copy from front of test book.)

0 0 0 0 0 0 0
1 1 1 1 1 1 1
2 2 2 2 2 2 2
3 3 3 3 3 3 3
4 4 4 4 4 4 4
5 5 5 5 5 5 5
6 6 6 6 6 6 6
7 7 7 7 7 7 7
8 8 8 8 8 8 8
9 9 9 9 9 9 9

8 BOOK CODE
(Copy and grid as on back of test book.)

0 Ⓐ 0
1 Ⓑ 1
2 Ⓒ 2
3 Ⓓ 3
4 Ⓔ 4
5 Ⓕ 5
6 Ⓖ 6
7 Ⓗ 7
8 Ⓘ 8
9 Ⓙ 9
Ⓚ
Ⓛ
Ⓜ
Ⓝ
Ⓞ
Ⓟ
Ⓠ
Ⓡ
Ⓢ
Ⓣ
Ⓤ
Ⓥ
Ⓦ
Ⓧ
Ⓨ
Ⓩ

9 BOOK ID
(Copy from back of test book.)

Quality Assurance Mark ●

Chemistry *Fill in circle CE only if II is correct explanation of I.

	I	II	CE*		I	II	CE*
101	Ⓣ Ⓕ	Ⓣ Ⓕ	○	109	Ⓣ Ⓕ	Ⓣ Ⓕ	○
102	Ⓣ Ⓕ	Ⓣ Ⓕ	○	110	Ⓣ Ⓕ	Ⓣ Ⓕ	○
103	Ⓣ Ⓕ	Ⓣ Ⓕ	○	111	Ⓣ Ⓕ	Ⓣ Ⓕ	○
104	Ⓣ Ⓕ	Ⓣ Ⓕ	○	112	Ⓣ Ⓕ	Ⓣ Ⓕ	○
105	Ⓣ Ⓕ	Ⓣ Ⓕ	○	113	Ⓣ Ⓕ	Ⓣ Ⓕ	○
106	Ⓣ Ⓕ	Ⓣ Ⓕ	○	114	Ⓣ Ⓕ	Ⓣ Ⓕ	○
107	Ⓣ Ⓕ	Ⓣ Ⓕ	○	115	Ⓣ Ⓕ	Ⓣ Ⓕ	○
108	Ⓣ Ⓕ	Ⓣ Ⓕ	○				

FOR OFFICIAL USE ONLY

R/C	W/S1	FS/S2	CS/S3	WS

CERTIFICATION STATEMENT
Copy the statement below and sign your name as you would an official document.

I hereby agree to the conditions set forth online at sat.collegeboard.org and in any paper registration materials given to me and certify that I am the person whose name, address and signature appear on this answer sheet.

_____

_____

_____

_____

Signature _____   Date _____

- ○ Literature
- ○ Biology E
- ○ Biology M
- ○ Chemistry
- ○ Physics

- ○ Mathematics Level 1
- ○ Mathematics Level 2
- ○ U.S. History
- ○ World History
- ○ French

- ○ German
- ○ Italian
- ○ Latin
- ○ Modern Hebrew
- ○ Spanish

- ○ Chinese Listening
- ○ French Listening
- ○ German Listening

- ○ Japanese Listening
- ○ Korean Listening
- ○ Spanish Listening

Background Questions: ① ② ③ ④ ⑤ ⑥ ⑦ ⑧ ⑨

PLEASE MAKE SURE to fill in these fields completely and correctly. If they are not correct, we won't be able to score your test(s)!

1 ⒶⒷⒸⒹⒺ 26 ⒶⒷⒸⒹⒺ 51 ⒶⒷⒸⒹⒺ 76 ⒶⒷⒸⒹⒺ
2 ⒶⒷⒸⒹⒺ 27 ⒶⒷⒸⒹⒺ 52 ⒶⒷⒸⒹⒺ 77 ⒶⒷⒸⒹⒺ
3 ⒶⒷⒸⒹⒺ 28 ⒶⒷⒸⒹⒺ 53 ⒶⒷⒸⒹⒺ 78 ⒶⒷⒸⒹⒺ
4 ⒶⒷⒸⒹⒺ 29 ⒶⒷⒸⒹⒺ 54 ⒶⒷⒸⒹⒺ 79 ⒶⒷⒸⒹⒺ
5 ⒶⒷⒸⒹⒺ 30 ⒶⒷⒸⒹⒺ 55 ⒶⒷⒸⒹⒺ 80 ⒶⒷⒸⒹⒺ
6 ⒶⒷⒸⒹⒺ 31 ⒶⒷⒸⒹⒺ 56 ⒶⒷⒸⒹⒺ 81 ⒶⒷⒸⒹⒺ
7 ⒶⒷⒸⒹⒺ 32 ⒶⒷⒸⒹⒺ 57 ⒶⒷⒸⒹⒺ 82 ⒶⒷⒸⒹⒺ
8 ⒶⒷⒸⒹⒺ 33 ⒶⒷⒸⒹⒺ 58 ⒶⒷⒸⒹⒺ 83 ⒶⒷⒸⒹⒺ
9 ⒶⒷⒸⒹⒺ 34 ⒶⒷⒸⒹⒺ 59 ⒶⒷⒸⒹⒺ 84 ⒶⒷⒸⒹⒺ
10 ⒶⒷⒸⒹⒺ 35 ⒶⒷⒸⒹⒺ 60 ⒶⒷⒸⒹⒺ 85 ⒶⒷⒸⒹⒺ
11 ⒶⒷⒸⒹⒺ 36 ⒶⒷⒸⒹⒺ 61 ⒶⒷⒸⒹⒺ 86 ⒶⒷⒸⒹⒺ
12 ⒶⒷⒸⒹⒺ 37 ⒶⒷⒸⒹⒺ 62 ⒶⒷⒸⒹⒺ 87 ⒶⒷⒸⒹⒺ
13 ⒶⒷⒸⒹⒺ 38 ⒶⒷⒸⒹⒺ 63 ⒶⒷⒸⒹⒺ 88 ⒶⒷⒸⒹⒺ
14 ⒶⒷⒸⒹⒺ 39 ⒶⒷⒸⒹⒺ 64 ⒶⒷⒸⒹⒺ 89 ⒶⒷⒸⒹⒺ
15 ⒶⒷⒸⒹⒺ 40 ⒶⒷⒸⒹⒺ 65 ⒶⒷⒸⒹⒺ 90 ⒶⒷⒸⒹⒺ
16 ⒶⒷⒸⒹⒺ 41 ⒶⒷⒸⒹⒺ 66 ⒶⒷⒸⒹⒺ 91 ⒶⒷⒸⒹⒺ
17 ⒶⒷⒸⒹⒺ 42 ⒶⒷⒸⒹⒺ 67 ⒶⒷⒸⒹⒺ 92 ⒶⒷⒸⒹⒺ
18 ⒶⒷⒸⒹⒺ 43 ⒶⒷⒸⒹⒺ 68 ⒶⒷⒸⒹⒺ 93 ⒶⒷⒸⒹⒺ
19 ⒶⒷⒸⒹⒺ 44 ⒶⒷⒸⒹⒺ 69 ⒶⒷⒸⒹⒺ 94 ⒶⒷⒸⒹⒺ
20 ⒶⒷⒸⒹⒺ 45 ⒶⒷⒸⒹⒺ 70 ⒶⒷⒸⒹⒺ 95 ⒶⒷⒸⒹⒺ
21 ⒶⒷⒸⒹⒺ 46 ⒶⒷⒸⒹⒺ 71 ⒶⒷⒸⒹⒺ 96 ⒶⒷⒸⒹⒺ
22 ⒶⒷⒸⒹⒺ 47 ⒶⒷⒸⒹⒺ 72 ⒶⒷⒸⒹⒺ 97 ⒶⒷⒸⒹⒺ
23 ⒶⒷⒸⒹⒺ 48 ⒶⒷⒸⒹⒺ 73 ⒶⒷⒸⒹⒺ 98 ⒶⒷⒸⒹⒺ
24 ⒶⒷⒸⒹⒺ 49 ⒶⒷⒸⒹⒺ 74 ⒶⒷⒸⒹⒺ 99 ⒶⒷⒸⒹⒺ
25 ⒶⒷⒸⒹⒺ 50 ⒶⒷⒸⒹⒺ 75 ⒶⒷⒸⒹⒺ 100 ⒶⒷⒸⒹⒺ

Quality Assurance Mark ●

7 TEST BOOK SERIAL NUMBER
(Copy from front of test book.)

8 BOOK CODE
(Copy and grid as on back of test book.)

Book Code grid columns: 0 / A–Z letters / 0, with number columns 0–9.

9 BOOK ID
(Copy from back of test book.)

Chemistry *Fill in circle CE only if II is correct explanation of I.

	I	II	CE*		I	II	CE*
101	ⓉⒻ	ⓉⒻ	○	109	ⓉⒻ	ⓉⒻ	○
102	ⓉⒻ	ⓉⒻ	○	110	ⓉⒻ	ⓉⒻ	○
103	ⓉⒻ	ⓉⒻ	○	111	ⓉⒻ	ⓉⒻ	○
104	ⓉⒻ	ⓉⒻ	○	112	ⓉⒻ	ⓉⒻ	○
105	ⓉⒻ	ⓉⒻ	○	113	ⓉⒻ	ⓉⒻ	○
106	ⓉⒻ	ⓉⒻ	○	114	ⓉⒻ	ⓉⒻ	○
107	ⓉⒻ	ⓉⒻ	○	115	ⓉⒻ	ⓉⒻ	○
108	ⓉⒻ	ⓉⒻ	○				

- ○ Literature
- ○ Biology E
- ○ Biology M
- ○ Chemistry
- ○ Physics

- ○ Mathematics Level 1
- ○ Mathematics Level 2
- ○ U.S. History
- ○ World History
- ○ French

- ○ German
- ○ Italian
- ○ Latin
- ○ Modern Hebrew
- ○ Spanish

- ○ Chinese Listening
- ○ French Listening
- ○ German Listening

- ○ Japanese Listening
- ○ Korean Listening
- ○ Spanish Listening

Background Questions: ① ② ③ ④ ⑤ ⑥ ⑦ ⑧ ⑨

PLEASE MAKE SURE to fill in these fields completely and correctly. If they are not correct, we won't be able to score your test(s)!

1–100: (A) (B) (C) (D) (E) answer bubbles for questions 1 through 100

7 TEST BOOK SERIAL NUMBER (Copy from front of test book.)

8 BOOK CODE (Copy and grid as on back of test book.)

9 BOOK ID (Copy from back of test book.)

Quality Assurance Mark ●

Chemistry *Fill in circle CE only if II is correct explanation of I.

	I	II	CE*		I	II	CE*
101	T F	T F	○	109	T F	T F	○
102	T F	T F	○	110	T F	T F	○
103	T F	T F	○	111	T F	T F	○
104	T F	T F	○	112	T F	T F	○
105	T F	T F	○	113	T F	T F	○
106	T F	T F	○	114	T F	T F	○
107	T F	T F	○	115	T F	T F	○
108	T F	T F	○				

FOR OFFICIAL USE ONLY

R/C	W/S1	FS/S2	CS/S3	WS

Page 4

SAT Subject Tests™

COMPLETE MARK ● **EXAMPLES OF INCOMPLETE MARKS** ⊘ ⊗ ⊙ ⊕ ⊖ ⊘ ⊗ ⊙

You must use a No. 2 pencil and marks must be complete. Do not use a mechanical pencil. It is very important that you fill in the entire circle darkly and completely. If you change your response, erase as completely as possible. Incomplete marks or erasures may affect your score.

1 **Your Name:**
(Print)

Last _____ First _____ M.I. _____

I agree to the conditions on the front and back of the SAT Subject Tests™ book. I also agree with the SAT Test Security and Fairness policies and understand that any violation of these policies will result in score cancellation and may result in reporting of certain violations to law enforcement.

Signature: _____ Today's Date: ___ / ___ / ___
MM DD YY

Home Address: _____
(Print) Number and Street   City   State/Country   Zip Code

Phone: ( ) _____ **Test Center:** _____
(Print)   City   State/Country

2 YOUR NAME

Last Name (First 6 Letters)   First Name (First 4 Letters)   Mid. Init.

3 DATE OF BIRTH

MONTH DAY YEAR

○ Jan ○ Feb ○ Mar ○ Apr ○ May ○ Jun ○ Jul ○ Aug ○ Sep ○ Oct ○ Nov ○ Dec

4 REGISTRATION NUMBER
(Copy from Admission Ticket.)

Important: Fill in items 8 and 9 exactly as shown on the back of test book.

7 TEST BOOK SERIAL NUMBER
(Copy from front of test book.)

8 BOOK CODE
(Copy and grid as on back of test book.)

9 BOOK ID
(Copy from back of test book.)

PLEASE MAKE SURE to fill in these fields completely and correctly. If they are not correct, we won't be able to score your test(s)!

5 ZIP CODE

6 TEST CENTER
(Supplied by Test Center Supervisor.)

FOR OFFICIAL USE ONLY
⓪①②③④⑤⑥
⓪①②③④⑤⑥
⓪①②③④⑤⑥

103648-77191 • NS1114C1085 • Printed in U.S.A.

© 2015 The College Board. College Board, SAT, and the acorn logo are registered trademarks of the College Board. SAT Subject Tests is a trademark owned by the College Board.

194415-001   1 2 3 4 5 A B C D E   Printed in the USA   ISD11312

783175

PLEASE DO NOT WRITE IN THIS AREA

SERIAL #

| COMPLETE MARK ● | EXAMPLES OF INCOMPLETE MARKS | Ⓐ ⓧ ⊖ ⓓ / ⊘ ⓐ | You must use a No. 2 pencil and marks must be complete. Do not use a mechanical pencil. It is very important that you fill in the entire circle darkly and completely. If you change your response, erase as completely as possible. Incomplete marks or erasures may affect your score. |

○ Literature
○ Biology E
○ Biology M
○ Chemistry
○ Physics

○ Mathematics Level 1
○ Mathematics Level 2
○ U.S. History
○ World History
○ French

○ German
○ Italian
○ Latin
○ Modern Hebrew
○ Spanish

○ Chinese Listening
○ French Listening
○ German Listening

○ Japanese Listening
○ Korean Listening
○ Spanish Listening

Background Questions: ① ② ③ ④ ⑤ ⑥ ⑦ ⑧ ⑨

1 Ⓐ Ⓑ Ⓒ Ⓓ Ⓔ 26 Ⓐ Ⓑ Ⓒ Ⓓ Ⓔ 51 Ⓐ Ⓑ Ⓒ Ⓓ Ⓔ 76 Ⓐ Ⓑ Ⓒ Ⓓ Ⓔ
2 Ⓐ Ⓑ Ⓒ Ⓓ Ⓔ 27 Ⓐ Ⓑ Ⓒ Ⓓ Ⓔ 52 Ⓐ Ⓑ Ⓒ Ⓓ Ⓔ 77 Ⓐ Ⓑ Ⓒ Ⓓ Ⓔ
3 Ⓐ Ⓑ Ⓒ Ⓓ Ⓔ 28 Ⓐ Ⓑ Ⓒ Ⓓ Ⓔ 53 Ⓐ Ⓑ Ⓒ Ⓓ Ⓔ 78 Ⓐ Ⓑ Ⓒ Ⓓ Ⓔ
4 Ⓐ Ⓑ Ⓒ Ⓓ Ⓔ 29 Ⓐ Ⓑ Ⓒ Ⓓ Ⓔ 54 Ⓐ Ⓑ Ⓒ Ⓓ Ⓔ 79 Ⓐ Ⓑ Ⓒ Ⓓ Ⓔ
5 Ⓐ Ⓑ Ⓒ Ⓓ Ⓔ 30 Ⓐ Ⓑ Ⓒ Ⓓ Ⓔ 55 Ⓐ Ⓑ Ⓒ Ⓓ Ⓔ 80 Ⓐ Ⓑ Ⓒ Ⓓ Ⓔ
6 Ⓐ Ⓑ Ⓒ Ⓓ Ⓔ 31 Ⓐ Ⓑ Ⓒ Ⓓ Ⓔ 56 Ⓐ Ⓑ Ⓒ Ⓓ Ⓔ 81 Ⓐ Ⓑ Ⓒ Ⓓ Ⓔ
7 Ⓐ Ⓑ Ⓒ Ⓓ Ⓔ 32 Ⓐ Ⓑ Ⓒ Ⓓ Ⓔ 57 Ⓐ Ⓑ Ⓒ Ⓓ Ⓔ 82 Ⓐ Ⓑ Ⓒ Ⓓ Ⓔ
8 Ⓐ Ⓑ Ⓒ Ⓓ Ⓔ 33 Ⓐ Ⓑ Ⓒ Ⓓ Ⓔ 58 Ⓐ Ⓑ Ⓒ Ⓓ Ⓔ 83 Ⓐ Ⓑ Ⓒ Ⓓ Ⓔ
9 Ⓐ Ⓑ Ⓒ Ⓓ Ⓔ 34 Ⓐ Ⓑ Ⓒ Ⓓ Ⓔ 59 Ⓐ Ⓑ Ⓒ Ⓓ Ⓔ 84 Ⓐ Ⓑ Ⓒ Ⓓ Ⓔ
10 Ⓐ Ⓑ Ⓒ Ⓓ Ⓔ 35 Ⓐ Ⓑ Ⓒ Ⓓ Ⓔ 60 Ⓐ Ⓑ Ⓒ Ⓓ Ⓔ 85 Ⓐ Ⓑ Ⓒ Ⓓ Ⓔ
11 Ⓐ Ⓑ Ⓒ Ⓓ Ⓔ 36 Ⓐ Ⓑ Ⓒ Ⓓ Ⓔ 61 Ⓐ Ⓑ Ⓒ Ⓓ Ⓔ 86 Ⓐ Ⓑ Ⓒ Ⓓ Ⓔ
12 Ⓐ Ⓑ Ⓒ Ⓓ Ⓔ 37 Ⓐ Ⓑ Ⓒ Ⓓ Ⓔ 62 Ⓐ Ⓑ Ⓒ Ⓓ Ⓔ 87 Ⓐ Ⓑ Ⓒ Ⓓ Ⓔ
13 Ⓐ Ⓑ Ⓒ Ⓓ Ⓔ 38 Ⓐ Ⓑ Ⓒ Ⓓ Ⓔ 63 Ⓐ Ⓑ Ⓒ Ⓓ Ⓔ 88 Ⓐ Ⓑ Ⓒ Ⓓ Ⓔ
14 Ⓐ Ⓑ Ⓒ Ⓓ Ⓔ 39 Ⓐ Ⓑ Ⓒ Ⓓ Ⓔ 64 Ⓐ Ⓑ Ⓒ Ⓓ Ⓔ 89 Ⓐ Ⓑ Ⓒ Ⓓ Ⓔ
15 Ⓐ Ⓑ Ⓒ Ⓓ Ⓔ 40 Ⓐ Ⓑ Ⓒ Ⓓ Ⓔ 65 Ⓐ Ⓑ Ⓒ Ⓓ Ⓔ 90 Ⓐ Ⓑ Ⓒ Ⓓ Ⓔ
16 Ⓐ Ⓑ Ⓒ Ⓓ Ⓔ 41 Ⓐ Ⓑ Ⓒ Ⓓ Ⓔ 66 Ⓐ Ⓑ Ⓒ Ⓓ Ⓔ 91 Ⓐ Ⓑ Ⓒ Ⓓ Ⓔ
17 Ⓐ Ⓑ Ⓒ Ⓓ Ⓔ 42 Ⓐ Ⓑ Ⓒ Ⓓ Ⓔ 67 Ⓐ Ⓑ Ⓒ Ⓓ Ⓔ 92 Ⓐ Ⓑ Ⓒ Ⓓ Ⓔ
18 Ⓐ Ⓑ Ⓒ Ⓓ Ⓔ 43 Ⓐ Ⓑ Ⓒ Ⓓ Ⓔ 68 Ⓐ Ⓑ Ⓒ Ⓓ Ⓔ 93 Ⓐ Ⓑ Ⓒ Ⓓ Ⓔ
19 Ⓐ Ⓑ Ⓒ Ⓓ Ⓔ 44 Ⓐ Ⓑ Ⓒ Ⓓ Ⓔ 69 Ⓐ Ⓑ Ⓒ Ⓓ Ⓔ 94 Ⓐ Ⓑ Ⓒ Ⓓ Ⓔ
20 Ⓐ Ⓑ Ⓒ Ⓓ Ⓔ 45 Ⓐ Ⓑ Ⓒ Ⓓ Ⓔ 70 Ⓐ Ⓑ Ⓒ Ⓓ Ⓔ 95 Ⓐ Ⓑ Ⓒ Ⓓ Ⓔ
21 Ⓐ Ⓑ Ⓒ Ⓓ Ⓔ 46 Ⓐ Ⓑ Ⓒ Ⓓ Ⓔ 71 Ⓐ Ⓑ Ⓒ Ⓓ Ⓔ 96 Ⓐ Ⓑ Ⓒ Ⓓ Ⓔ
22 Ⓐ Ⓑ Ⓒ Ⓓ Ⓔ 47 Ⓐ Ⓑ Ⓒ Ⓓ Ⓔ 72 Ⓐ Ⓑ Ⓒ Ⓓ Ⓔ 97 Ⓐ Ⓑ Ⓒ Ⓓ Ⓔ
23 Ⓐ Ⓑ Ⓒ Ⓓ Ⓔ 48 Ⓐ Ⓑ Ⓒ Ⓓ Ⓔ 73 Ⓐ Ⓑ Ⓒ Ⓓ Ⓔ 98 Ⓐ Ⓑ Ⓒ Ⓓ Ⓔ
24 Ⓐ Ⓑ Ⓒ Ⓓ Ⓔ 49 Ⓐ Ⓑ Ⓒ Ⓓ Ⓔ 74 Ⓐ Ⓑ Ⓒ Ⓓ Ⓔ 99 Ⓐ Ⓑ Ⓒ Ⓓ Ⓔ
25 Ⓐ Ⓑ Ⓒ Ⓓ Ⓔ 50 Ⓐ Ⓑ Ⓒ Ⓓ Ⓔ 75 Ⓐ Ⓑ Ⓒ Ⓓ Ⓔ 100 Ⓐ Ⓑ Ⓒ Ⓓ Ⓔ

PLEASE MAKE SURE to fill in these fields completely and correctly. If they are not correct, we won't be able to score your test(s)!

7 TEST BOOK SERIAL NUMBER
(Copy from front of test book.)

0 0 0 0 0 0
1 1 1 1 1 1
2 2 2 2 2 2
3 3 3 3 3 3
4 4 4 4 4 4
5 5 5 5 5 5
6 6 6 6 6 6
7 7 7 7 7 7
8 8 8 8 8 8
9 9 9 9 9 9

8 BOOK CODE
(Copy and grid as on back of test book.)

0 Ⓐ 0
1 Ⓑ 1
2 Ⓒ 2
3 Ⓓ 3
4 Ⓔ 4
5 Ⓕ 5
6 Ⓖ 6
7 Ⓗ 7
8 Ⓘ 8
9 Ⓙ 9
Ⓚ
Ⓛ
Ⓜ
Ⓝ
Ⓞ
Ⓟ
Ⓠ
Ⓡ
Ⓢ
Ⓣ
Ⓤ
Ⓥ
Ⓦ
Ⓧ
Ⓨ
Ⓩ

9 BOOK ID
(Copy from back of test book.)

● Quality Assurance Mark

Chemistry *Fill in circle CE only if II is correct explanation of I.

	I	II	CE*		I	II	CE*
101	Ⓣ Ⓕ	Ⓣ Ⓕ	○	109	Ⓣ Ⓕ	Ⓣ Ⓕ	○
102	Ⓣ Ⓕ	Ⓣ Ⓕ	○	110	Ⓣ Ⓕ	Ⓣ Ⓕ	○
103	Ⓣ Ⓕ	Ⓣ Ⓕ	○	111	Ⓣ Ⓕ	Ⓣ Ⓕ	○
104	Ⓣ Ⓕ	Ⓣ Ⓕ	○	112	Ⓣ Ⓕ	Ⓣ Ⓕ	○
105	Ⓣ Ⓕ	Ⓣ Ⓕ	○	113	Ⓣ Ⓕ	Ⓣ Ⓕ	○
106	Ⓣ Ⓕ	Ⓣ Ⓕ	○	114	Ⓣ Ⓕ	Ⓣ Ⓕ	○
107	Ⓣ Ⓕ	Ⓣ Ⓕ	○	115	Ⓣ Ⓕ	Ⓣ Ⓕ	○
108	Ⓣ Ⓕ	Ⓣ Ⓕ	○				

FOR OFFICIAL USE ONLY				
R/C	W/S1	FS/S2	CS/S3	WS

CERTIFICATION STATEMENT
Copy the statement below and sign your name as you would an official document.

I hereby agree to the conditions set forth online at sat.collegeboard.org and in any paper registration materials given to me and certify that I am the person whose name, address and signature appear on this answer sheet.

_____

_____

_____

_____

Signature _____   Date _____

- ◯ Literature
- ◯ Biology E
- ◯ Biology M
- ◯ Chemistry
- ◯ Physics

- ◯ Mathematics Level 1
- ◯ Mathematics Level 2
- ◯ U.S. History
- ◯ World History
- ◯ French

- ◯ German
- ◯ Italian
- ◯ Latin
- ◯ Modern Hebrew
- ◯ Spanish

- ◯ Chinese Listening
- ◯ French Listening
- ◯ German Listening

- ◯ Japanese Listening
- ◯ Korean Listening
- ◯ Spanish Listening

Background Questions: ① ② ③ ④ ⑤ ⑥ ⑦ ⑧ ⑨

PLEASE MAKE SURE to fill in these fields completely and correctly. If they are not correct, we won't be able to score your test(s)!

Quality Assurance Mark

1 Ⓐ Ⓑ Ⓒ Ⓓ Ⓔ   26 Ⓐ Ⓑ Ⓒ Ⓓ Ⓔ   51 Ⓐ Ⓑ Ⓒ Ⓓ Ⓔ   76 Ⓐ Ⓑ Ⓒ Ⓓ Ⓔ
2 Ⓐ Ⓑ Ⓒ Ⓓ Ⓔ   27 Ⓐ Ⓑ Ⓒ Ⓓ Ⓔ   52 Ⓐ Ⓑ Ⓒ Ⓓ Ⓔ   77 Ⓐ Ⓑ Ⓒ Ⓓ Ⓔ
3 Ⓐ Ⓑ Ⓒ Ⓓ Ⓔ   28 Ⓐ Ⓑ Ⓒ Ⓓ Ⓔ   53 Ⓐ Ⓑ Ⓒ Ⓓ Ⓔ   78 Ⓐ Ⓑ Ⓒ Ⓓ Ⓔ
4 Ⓐ Ⓑ Ⓒ Ⓓ Ⓔ   29 Ⓐ Ⓑ Ⓒ Ⓓ Ⓔ   54 Ⓐ Ⓑ Ⓒ Ⓓ Ⓔ   79 Ⓐ Ⓑ Ⓒ Ⓓ Ⓔ
5 Ⓐ Ⓑ Ⓒ Ⓓ Ⓔ   30 Ⓐ Ⓑ Ⓒ Ⓓ Ⓔ   55 Ⓐ Ⓑ Ⓒ Ⓓ Ⓔ   80 Ⓐ Ⓑ Ⓒ Ⓓ Ⓔ
6 Ⓐ Ⓑ Ⓒ Ⓓ Ⓔ   31 Ⓐ Ⓑ Ⓒ Ⓓ Ⓔ   56 Ⓐ Ⓑ Ⓒ Ⓓ Ⓔ   81 Ⓐ Ⓑ Ⓒ Ⓓ Ⓔ
7 Ⓐ Ⓑ Ⓒ Ⓓ Ⓔ   32 Ⓐ Ⓑ Ⓒ Ⓓ Ⓔ   57 Ⓐ Ⓑ Ⓒ Ⓓ Ⓔ   82 Ⓐ Ⓑ Ⓒ Ⓓ Ⓔ
8 Ⓐ Ⓑ Ⓒ Ⓓ Ⓔ   33 Ⓐ Ⓑ Ⓒ Ⓓ Ⓔ   58 Ⓐ Ⓑ Ⓒ Ⓓ Ⓔ   83 Ⓐ Ⓑ Ⓒ Ⓓ Ⓔ
9 Ⓐ Ⓑ Ⓒ Ⓓ Ⓔ   34 Ⓐ Ⓑ Ⓒ Ⓓ Ⓔ   59 Ⓐ Ⓑ Ⓒ Ⓓ Ⓔ   84 Ⓐ Ⓑ Ⓒ Ⓓ Ⓔ
10 Ⓐ Ⓑ Ⓒ Ⓓ Ⓔ   35 Ⓐ Ⓑ Ⓒ Ⓓ Ⓔ   60 Ⓐ Ⓑ Ⓒ Ⓓ Ⓔ   85 Ⓐ Ⓑ Ⓒ Ⓓ Ⓔ
11 Ⓐ Ⓑ Ⓒ Ⓓ Ⓔ   36 Ⓐ Ⓑ Ⓒ Ⓓ Ⓔ   61 Ⓐ Ⓑ Ⓒ Ⓓ Ⓔ   86 Ⓐ Ⓑ Ⓒ Ⓓ Ⓔ
12 Ⓐ Ⓑ Ⓒ Ⓓ Ⓔ   37 Ⓐ Ⓑ Ⓒ Ⓓ Ⓔ   62 Ⓐ Ⓑ Ⓒ Ⓓ Ⓔ   87 Ⓐ Ⓑ Ⓒ Ⓓ Ⓔ
13 Ⓐ Ⓑ Ⓒ Ⓓ Ⓔ   38 Ⓐ Ⓑ Ⓒ Ⓓ Ⓔ   63 Ⓐ Ⓑ Ⓒ Ⓓ Ⓔ   88 Ⓐ Ⓑ Ⓒ Ⓓ Ⓔ
14 Ⓐ Ⓑ Ⓒ Ⓓ Ⓔ   39 Ⓐ Ⓑ Ⓒ Ⓓ Ⓔ   64 Ⓐ Ⓑ Ⓒ Ⓓ Ⓔ   89 Ⓐ Ⓑ Ⓒ Ⓓ Ⓔ
15 Ⓐ Ⓑ Ⓒ Ⓓ Ⓔ   40 Ⓐ Ⓑ Ⓒ Ⓓ Ⓔ   65 Ⓐ Ⓑ Ⓒ Ⓓ Ⓔ   90 Ⓐ Ⓑ Ⓒ Ⓓ Ⓔ
16 Ⓐ Ⓑ Ⓒ Ⓓ Ⓔ   41 Ⓐ Ⓑ Ⓒ Ⓓ Ⓔ   66 Ⓐ Ⓑ Ⓒ Ⓓ Ⓔ   91 Ⓐ Ⓑ Ⓒ Ⓓ Ⓔ
17 Ⓐ Ⓑ Ⓒ Ⓓ Ⓔ   42 Ⓐ Ⓑ Ⓒ Ⓓ Ⓔ   67 Ⓐ Ⓑ Ⓒ Ⓓ Ⓔ   92 Ⓐ Ⓑ Ⓒ Ⓓ Ⓔ
18 Ⓐ Ⓑ Ⓒ Ⓓ Ⓔ   43 Ⓐ Ⓑ Ⓒ Ⓓ Ⓔ   68 Ⓐ Ⓑ Ⓒ Ⓓ Ⓔ   93 Ⓐ Ⓑ Ⓒ Ⓓ Ⓔ
19 Ⓐ Ⓑ Ⓒ Ⓓ Ⓔ   44 Ⓐ Ⓑ Ⓒ Ⓓ Ⓔ   69 Ⓐ Ⓑ Ⓒ Ⓓ Ⓔ   94 Ⓐ Ⓑ Ⓒ Ⓓ Ⓔ
20 Ⓐ Ⓑ Ⓒ Ⓓ Ⓔ   45 Ⓐ Ⓑ Ⓒ Ⓓ Ⓔ   70 Ⓐ Ⓑ Ⓒ Ⓓ Ⓔ   95 Ⓐ Ⓑ Ⓒ Ⓓ Ⓔ
21 Ⓐ Ⓑ Ⓒ Ⓓ Ⓔ   46 Ⓐ Ⓑ Ⓒ Ⓓ Ⓔ   71 Ⓐ Ⓑ Ⓒ Ⓓ Ⓔ   96 Ⓐ Ⓑ Ⓒ Ⓓ Ⓔ
22 Ⓐ Ⓑ Ⓒ Ⓓ Ⓔ   47 Ⓐ Ⓑ Ⓒ Ⓓ Ⓔ   72 Ⓐ Ⓑ Ⓒ Ⓓ Ⓔ   97 Ⓐ Ⓑ Ⓒ Ⓓ Ⓔ
23 Ⓐ Ⓑ Ⓒ Ⓓ Ⓔ   48 Ⓐ Ⓑ Ⓒ Ⓓ Ⓔ   73 Ⓐ Ⓑ Ⓒ Ⓓ Ⓔ   98 Ⓐ Ⓑ Ⓒ Ⓓ Ⓔ
24 Ⓐ Ⓑ Ⓒ Ⓓ Ⓔ   49 Ⓐ Ⓑ Ⓒ Ⓓ Ⓔ   74 Ⓐ Ⓑ Ⓒ Ⓓ Ⓔ   99 Ⓐ Ⓑ Ⓒ Ⓓ Ⓔ
25 Ⓐ Ⓑ Ⓒ Ⓓ Ⓔ   50 Ⓐ Ⓑ Ⓒ Ⓓ Ⓔ   75 Ⓐ Ⓑ Ⓒ Ⓓ Ⓔ   100 Ⓐ Ⓑ Ⓒ Ⓓ Ⓔ

7 TEST BOOK SERIAL NUMBER
(Copy from front of test book.)

0 0 0 0 0 0
1 1 1 1 1 1
2 2 2 2 2 2
3 3 3 3 3 3
4 4 4 4 4 4
5 5 5 5 5 5
6 6 6 6 6 6
7 7 7 7 7 7
8 8 8 8 8 8
9 9 9 9 9 9

8 BOOK CODE
(Copy and grid as on back of test book.)

0 Ⓐ 0
1 Ⓑ 1
2 Ⓒ 2
3 Ⓓ 3
4 Ⓔ 4
5 Ⓕ 5
6 Ⓖ 6
7 Ⓗ 7
8 Ⓘ 8
9 Ⓙ 9
Ⓚ
Ⓛ
Ⓜ
Ⓝ
Ⓞ
Ⓟ
Ⓠ
Ⓡ
Ⓢ
Ⓣ
Ⓤ
Ⓥ
Ⓦ
Ⓧ
Ⓨ
Ⓩ

9 BOOK ID
(Copy from back of test book.)

Chemistry *Fill in circle CE only if II is correct explanation of I.

	I	II	CE*		I	II	CE*
101	Ⓣ Ⓕ	Ⓣ Ⓕ	◯	109	Ⓣ Ⓕ	Ⓣ Ⓕ	◯
102	Ⓣ Ⓕ	Ⓣ Ⓕ	◯	110	Ⓣ Ⓕ	Ⓣ Ⓕ	◯
103	Ⓣ Ⓕ	Ⓣ Ⓕ	◯	111	Ⓣ Ⓕ	Ⓣ Ⓕ	◯
104	Ⓣ Ⓕ	Ⓣ Ⓕ	◯	112	Ⓣ Ⓕ	Ⓣ Ⓕ	◯
105	Ⓣ Ⓕ	Ⓣ Ⓕ	◯	113	Ⓣ Ⓕ	Ⓣ Ⓕ	◯
106	Ⓣ Ⓕ	Ⓣ Ⓕ	◯	114	Ⓣ Ⓕ	Ⓣ Ⓕ	◯
107	Ⓣ Ⓕ	Ⓣ Ⓕ	◯	115	Ⓣ Ⓕ	Ⓣ Ⓕ	◯
108	Ⓣ Ⓕ	Ⓣ Ⓕ	◯				

FOR OFFICIAL USE ONLY				
R/C	W/S1	FS/S2	CS/S3	WS

○ Literature
○ Biology E
○ Biology M
○ Chemistry
○ Physics

○ Mathematics Level 1
○ Mathematics Level 2
○ U.S. History
○ World History
○ French

○ German
○ Italian
○ Latin
○ Modern Hebrew
○ Spanish

○ Chinese Listening
○ French Listening
○ German Listening

○ Japanese Listening
○ Korean Listening
○ Spanish Listening

Background Questions: ① ② ③ ④ ⑤ ⑥ ⑦ ⑧ ⑨

1 Ⓐ Ⓑ Ⓒ Ⓓ Ⓔ   26 Ⓐ Ⓑ Ⓒ Ⓓ Ⓔ   51 Ⓐ Ⓑ Ⓒ Ⓓ Ⓔ   76 Ⓐ Ⓑ Ⓒ Ⓓ Ⓔ
2 Ⓐ Ⓑ Ⓒ Ⓓ Ⓔ   27 Ⓐ Ⓑ Ⓒ Ⓓ Ⓔ   52 Ⓐ Ⓑ Ⓒ Ⓓ Ⓔ   77 Ⓐ Ⓑ Ⓒ Ⓓ Ⓔ
3 Ⓐ Ⓑ Ⓒ Ⓓ Ⓔ   28 Ⓐ Ⓑ Ⓒ Ⓓ Ⓔ   53 Ⓐ Ⓑ Ⓒ Ⓓ Ⓔ   78 Ⓐ Ⓑ Ⓒ Ⓓ Ⓔ
4 Ⓐ Ⓑ Ⓒ Ⓓ Ⓔ   29 Ⓐ Ⓑ Ⓒ Ⓓ Ⓔ   54 Ⓐ Ⓑ Ⓒ Ⓓ Ⓔ   79 Ⓐ Ⓑ Ⓒ Ⓓ Ⓔ
5 Ⓐ Ⓑ Ⓒ Ⓓ Ⓔ   30 Ⓐ Ⓑ Ⓒ Ⓓ Ⓔ   55 Ⓐ Ⓑ Ⓒ Ⓓ Ⓔ   80 Ⓐ Ⓑ Ⓒ Ⓓ Ⓔ
6 Ⓐ Ⓑ Ⓒ Ⓓ Ⓔ   31 Ⓐ Ⓑ Ⓒ Ⓓ Ⓔ   56 Ⓐ Ⓑ Ⓒ Ⓓ Ⓔ   81 Ⓐ Ⓑ Ⓒ Ⓓ Ⓔ
7 Ⓐ Ⓑ Ⓒ Ⓓ Ⓔ   32 Ⓐ Ⓑ Ⓒ Ⓓ Ⓔ   57 Ⓐ Ⓑ Ⓒ Ⓓ Ⓔ   82 Ⓐ Ⓑ Ⓒ Ⓓ Ⓔ
8 Ⓐ Ⓑ Ⓒ Ⓓ Ⓔ   33 Ⓐ Ⓑ Ⓒ Ⓓ Ⓔ   58 Ⓐ Ⓑ Ⓒ Ⓓ Ⓔ   83 Ⓐ Ⓑ Ⓒ Ⓓ Ⓔ
9 Ⓐ Ⓑ Ⓒ Ⓓ Ⓔ   34 Ⓐ Ⓑ Ⓒ Ⓓ Ⓔ   59 Ⓐ Ⓑ Ⓒ Ⓓ Ⓔ   84 Ⓐ Ⓑ Ⓒ Ⓓ Ⓔ
10 Ⓐ Ⓑ Ⓒ Ⓓ Ⓔ   35 Ⓐ Ⓑ Ⓒ Ⓓ Ⓔ   60 Ⓐ Ⓑ Ⓒ Ⓓ Ⓔ   85 Ⓐ Ⓑ Ⓒ Ⓓ Ⓔ
11 Ⓐ Ⓑ Ⓒ Ⓓ Ⓔ   36 Ⓐ Ⓑ Ⓒ Ⓓ Ⓔ   61 Ⓐ Ⓑ Ⓒ Ⓓ Ⓔ   86 Ⓐ Ⓑ Ⓒ Ⓓ Ⓔ
12 Ⓐ Ⓑ Ⓒ Ⓓ Ⓔ   37 Ⓐ Ⓑ Ⓒ Ⓓ Ⓔ   62 Ⓐ Ⓑ Ⓒ Ⓓ Ⓔ   87 Ⓐ Ⓑ Ⓒ Ⓓ Ⓔ
13 Ⓐ Ⓑ Ⓒ Ⓓ Ⓔ   38 Ⓐ Ⓑ Ⓒ Ⓓ Ⓔ   63 Ⓐ Ⓑ Ⓒ Ⓓ Ⓔ   88 Ⓐ Ⓑ Ⓒ Ⓓ Ⓔ
14 Ⓐ Ⓑ Ⓒ Ⓓ Ⓔ   39 Ⓐ Ⓑ Ⓒ Ⓓ Ⓔ   64 Ⓐ Ⓑ Ⓒ Ⓓ Ⓔ   89 Ⓐ Ⓑ Ⓒ Ⓓ Ⓔ
15 Ⓐ Ⓑ Ⓒ Ⓓ Ⓔ   40 Ⓐ Ⓑ Ⓒ Ⓓ Ⓔ   65 Ⓐ Ⓑ Ⓒ Ⓓ Ⓔ   90 Ⓐ Ⓑ Ⓒ Ⓓ Ⓔ
16 Ⓐ Ⓑ Ⓒ Ⓓ Ⓔ   41 Ⓐ Ⓑ Ⓒ Ⓓ Ⓔ   66 Ⓐ Ⓑ Ⓒ Ⓓ Ⓔ   91 Ⓐ Ⓑ Ⓒ Ⓓ Ⓔ
17 Ⓐ Ⓑ Ⓒ Ⓓ Ⓔ   42 Ⓐ Ⓑ Ⓒ Ⓓ Ⓔ   67 Ⓐ Ⓑ Ⓒ Ⓓ Ⓔ   92 Ⓐ Ⓑ Ⓒ Ⓓ Ⓔ
18 Ⓐ Ⓑ Ⓒ Ⓓ Ⓔ   43 Ⓐ Ⓑ Ⓒ Ⓓ Ⓔ   68 Ⓐ Ⓑ Ⓒ Ⓓ Ⓔ   93 Ⓐ Ⓑ Ⓒ Ⓓ Ⓔ
19 Ⓐ Ⓑ Ⓒ Ⓓ Ⓔ   44 Ⓐ Ⓑ Ⓒ Ⓓ Ⓔ   69 Ⓐ Ⓑ Ⓒ Ⓓ Ⓔ   94 Ⓐ Ⓑ Ⓒ Ⓓ Ⓔ
20 Ⓐ Ⓑ Ⓒ Ⓓ Ⓔ   45 Ⓐ Ⓑ Ⓒ Ⓓ Ⓔ   70 Ⓐ Ⓑ Ⓒ Ⓓ Ⓔ   95 Ⓐ Ⓑ Ⓒ Ⓓ Ⓔ
21 Ⓐ Ⓑ Ⓒ Ⓓ Ⓔ   46 Ⓐ Ⓑ Ⓒ Ⓓ Ⓔ   71 Ⓐ Ⓑ Ⓒ Ⓓ Ⓔ   96 Ⓐ Ⓑ Ⓒ Ⓓ Ⓔ
22 Ⓐ Ⓑ Ⓒ Ⓓ Ⓔ   47 Ⓐ Ⓑ Ⓒ Ⓓ Ⓔ   72 Ⓐ Ⓑ Ⓒ Ⓓ Ⓔ   97 Ⓐ Ⓑ Ⓒ Ⓓ Ⓔ
23 Ⓐ Ⓑ Ⓒ Ⓓ Ⓔ   48 Ⓐ Ⓑ Ⓒ Ⓓ Ⓔ   73 Ⓐ Ⓑ Ⓒ Ⓓ Ⓔ   98 Ⓐ Ⓑ Ⓒ Ⓓ Ⓔ
24 Ⓐ Ⓑ Ⓒ Ⓓ Ⓔ   49 Ⓐ Ⓑ Ⓒ Ⓓ Ⓔ   74 Ⓐ Ⓑ Ⓒ Ⓓ Ⓔ   99 Ⓐ Ⓑ Ⓒ Ⓓ Ⓔ
25 Ⓐ Ⓑ Ⓒ Ⓓ Ⓔ   50 Ⓐ Ⓑ Ⓒ Ⓓ Ⓔ   75 Ⓐ Ⓑ Ⓒ Ⓓ Ⓔ   100 Ⓐ Ⓑ Ⓒ Ⓓ Ⓔ

PLEASE MAKE SURE to fill in these fields completely and correctly. If they are not correct, we won't be able to score your test(s)!

7 TEST BOOK SERIAL NUMBER
(Copy from front of test book.)

0 0 0 0 0 0 0
1 1 1 1 1 1 1
2 2 2 2 2 2 2
3 3 3 3 3 3 3
4 4 4 4 4 4 4
5 5 5 5 5 5 5
6 6 6 6 6 6 6
7 7 7 7 7 7 7
8 8 8 8 8 8 8
9 9 9 9 9 9 9

8 BOOK CODE
(Copy and grid as on back of test book.)

0 Ⓐ 0
1 Ⓑ 1
2 Ⓒ 2
3 Ⓓ 3
4 Ⓔ 4
5 Ⓕ 5
6 Ⓖ 6
7 Ⓗ 7
8 Ⓘ 8
9 Ⓙ 9
  Ⓚ
  Ⓛ
  Ⓜ
  Ⓝ
  Ⓞ
  Ⓟ
  Ⓠ
  Ⓡ
  Ⓢ
  Ⓣ
  Ⓤ
  Ⓥ
  Ⓦ
  Ⓧ
  Ⓨ
  Ⓩ

9 BOOK ID
(Copy from back of test book.)

● Quality Assurance Mark

Chemistry *Fill in circle CE only if II is correct explanation of I.

	I	II	CE*		I	II	CE*
101	Ⓣ Ⓕ	Ⓣ Ⓕ	○	109	Ⓣ Ⓕ	Ⓣ Ⓕ	○
102	Ⓣ Ⓕ	Ⓣ Ⓕ	○	110	Ⓣ Ⓕ	Ⓣ Ⓕ	○
103	Ⓣ Ⓕ	Ⓣ Ⓕ	○	111	Ⓣ Ⓕ	Ⓣ Ⓕ	○
104	Ⓣ Ⓕ	Ⓣ Ⓕ	○	112	Ⓣ Ⓕ	Ⓣ Ⓕ	○
105	Ⓣ Ⓕ	Ⓣ Ⓕ	○	113	Ⓣ Ⓕ	Ⓣ Ⓕ	○
106	Ⓣ Ⓕ	Ⓣ Ⓕ	○	114	Ⓣ Ⓕ	Ⓣ Ⓕ	○
107	Ⓣ Ⓕ	Ⓣ Ⓕ	○	115	Ⓣ Ⓕ	Ⓣ Ⓕ	○
108	Ⓣ Ⓕ	Ⓣ Ⓕ	○				

FOR OFFICIAL USE ONLY				
R/C	W/S1	FS/S2	CS/S3	WS

Page 4

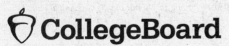
SAT Subject Tests™

COMPLETE MARK ● **EXAMPLES OF INCOMPLETE MARKS**

You must use a No. 2 pencil and marks must be complete. Do not use a mechanical pencil. It is very important that you fill in the entire circle darkly and completely. If you change your response, erase as completely as possible. Incomplete marks or erasures may affect your score.

1 **Your Name:**
(Print)

Last _____ First _____ M.I. _____

I agree to the conditions on the front and back of the SAT Subject Tests™ book. I also agree with the SAT Test Security and Fairness policies and understand that any violation of these policies will result in score cancellation and may result in reporting of certain violations to law enforcement.

Signature: _____ Today's Date: ___/___/___
MM DD YY

Home Address:
(Print) _____ Number and Street _____ City _____ State/Country _____ Zip Code
Phone: (____) _____ **Test Center:**
(Print) _____ City _____ State/Country

2 YOUR NAME

Last Name (First 6 Letters) First Name (First 4 Letters) Mid. Init.

3 DATE OF BIRTH

MONTH | DAY | YEAR
Jan
Feb
Mar
Apr
May
Jun
Jul
Aug
Sep
Oct
Nov
Dec

4 REGISTRATION NUMBER
(Copy from Admission Ticket.)

Important: Fill in items 8 and 9 exactly as shown on the back of test book.

7 TEST BOOK SERIAL NUMBER
(Copy from front of test book.)

8 BOOK CODE
(Copy and grid as on back of test book.)

9 BOOK ID
(Copy from back of test book.)

PLEASE MAKE SURE to fill in these fields completely and correctly. If they are not correct, we won't be able to score your test(s)!

5 ZIP CODE

6 TEST CENTER
(Supplied by Test Center Supervisor.)

FOR OFFICIAL USE ONLY
0 1 2 3 4 5 6
0 1 2 3 4 5 6
0 1 2 3 4 5 6

103648-77191 • NS1114C1085 • Printed in U.S.A.

194415-001 • 1 2 3 4 5 A B C D E   Printed in the USA   ISD11312   783175

PLEASE DO NOT WRITE IN THIS AREA

SERIAL #

○ Literature
○ Biology E
○ Biology M
○ Chemistry
○ Physics

○ Mathematics Level 1
○ Mathematics Level 2
○ U.S. History
○ World History
○ French

○ German
○ Italian
○ Latin
○ Modern Hebrew
○ Spanish

○ Chinese Listening
○ French Listening
○ German Listening

○ Japanese Listening
○ Korean Listening
○ Spanish Listening

Background Questions: ① ② ③ ④ ⑤ ⑥ ⑦ ⑧ ⑨

1 Ⓐ Ⓑ Ⓒ Ⓓ Ⓔ   26 Ⓐ Ⓑ Ⓒ Ⓓ Ⓔ   51 Ⓐ Ⓑ Ⓒ Ⓓ Ⓔ   76 Ⓐ Ⓑ Ⓒ Ⓓ Ⓔ
2 Ⓐ Ⓑ Ⓒ Ⓓ Ⓔ   27 Ⓐ Ⓑ Ⓒ Ⓓ Ⓔ   52 Ⓐ Ⓑ Ⓒ Ⓓ Ⓔ   77 Ⓐ Ⓑ Ⓒ Ⓓ Ⓔ
3 Ⓐ Ⓑ Ⓒ Ⓓ Ⓔ   28 Ⓐ Ⓑ Ⓒ Ⓓ Ⓔ   53 Ⓐ Ⓑ Ⓒ Ⓓ Ⓔ   78 Ⓐ Ⓑ Ⓒ Ⓓ Ⓔ
4 Ⓐ Ⓑ Ⓒ Ⓓ Ⓔ   29 Ⓐ Ⓑ Ⓒ Ⓓ Ⓔ   54 Ⓐ Ⓑ Ⓒ Ⓓ Ⓔ   79 Ⓐ Ⓑ Ⓒ Ⓓ Ⓔ
5 Ⓐ Ⓑ Ⓒ Ⓓ Ⓔ   30 Ⓐ Ⓑ Ⓒ Ⓓ Ⓔ   55 Ⓐ Ⓑ Ⓒ Ⓓ Ⓔ   80 Ⓐ Ⓑ Ⓒ Ⓓ Ⓔ
6 Ⓐ Ⓑ Ⓒ Ⓓ Ⓔ   31 Ⓐ Ⓑ Ⓒ Ⓓ Ⓔ   56 Ⓐ Ⓑ Ⓒ Ⓓ Ⓔ   81 Ⓐ Ⓑ Ⓒ Ⓓ Ⓔ
7 Ⓐ Ⓑ Ⓒ Ⓓ Ⓔ   32 Ⓐ Ⓑ Ⓒ Ⓓ Ⓔ   57 Ⓐ Ⓑ Ⓒ Ⓓ Ⓔ   82 Ⓐ Ⓑ Ⓒ Ⓓ Ⓔ
8 Ⓐ Ⓑ Ⓒ Ⓓ Ⓔ   33 Ⓐ Ⓑ Ⓒ Ⓓ Ⓔ   58 Ⓐ Ⓑ Ⓒ Ⓓ Ⓔ   83 Ⓐ Ⓑ Ⓒ Ⓓ Ⓔ
9 Ⓐ Ⓑ Ⓒ Ⓓ Ⓔ   34 Ⓐ Ⓑ Ⓒ Ⓓ Ⓔ   59 Ⓐ Ⓑ Ⓒ Ⓓ Ⓔ   84 Ⓐ Ⓑ Ⓒ Ⓓ Ⓔ
10 Ⓐ Ⓑ Ⓒ Ⓓ Ⓔ   35 Ⓐ Ⓑ Ⓒ Ⓓ Ⓔ   60 Ⓐ Ⓑ Ⓒ Ⓓ Ⓔ   85 Ⓐ Ⓑ Ⓒ Ⓓ Ⓔ
11 Ⓐ Ⓑ Ⓒ Ⓓ Ⓔ   36 Ⓐ Ⓑ Ⓒ Ⓓ Ⓔ   61 Ⓐ Ⓑ Ⓒ Ⓓ Ⓔ   86 Ⓐ Ⓑ Ⓒ Ⓓ Ⓔ
12 Ⓐ Ⓑ Ⓒ Ⓓ Ⓔ   37 Ⓐ Ⓑ Ⓒ Ⓓ Ⓔ   62 Ⓐ Ⓑ Ⓒ Ⓓ Ⓔ   87 Ⓐ Ⓑ Ⓒ Ⓓ Ⓔ
13 Ⓐ Ⓑ Ⓒ Ⓓ Ⓔ   38 Ⓐ Ⓑ Ⓒ Ⓓ Ⓔ   63 Ⓐ Ⓑ Ⓒ Ⓓ Ⓔ   88 Ⓐ Ⓑ Ⓒ Ⓓ Ⓔ
14 Ⓐ Ⓑ Ⓒ Ⓓ Ⓔ   39 Ⓐ Ⓑ Ⓒ Ⓓ Ⓔ   64 Ⓐ Ⓑ Ⓒ Ⓓ Ⓔ   89 Ⓐ Ⓑ Ⓒ Ⓓ Ⓔ
15 Ⓐ Ⓑ Ⓒ Ⓓ Ⓔ   40 Ⓐ Ⓑ Ⓒ Ⓓ Ⓔ   65 Ⓐ Ⓑ Ⓒ Ⓓ Ⓔ   90 Ⓐ Ⓑ Ⓒ Ⓓ Ⓔ
16 Ⓐ Ⓑ Ⓒ Ⓓ Ⓔ   41 Ⓐ Ⓑ Ⓒ Ⓓ Ⓔ   66 Ⓐ Ⓑ Ⓒ Ⓓ Ⓔ   91 Ⓐ Ⓑ Ⓒ Ⓓ Ⓔ
17 Ⓐ Ⓑ Ⓒ Ⓓ Ⓔ   42 Ⓐ Ⓑ Ⓒ Ⓓ Ⓔ   67 Ⓐ Ⓑ Ⓒ Ⓓ Ⓔ   92 Ⓐ Ⓑ Ⓒ Ⓓ Ⓔ
18 Ⓐ Ⓑ Ⓒ Ⓓ Ⓔ   43 Ⓐ Ⓑ Ⓒ Ⓓ Ⓔ   68 Ⓐ Ⓑ Ⓒ Ⓓ Ⓔ   93 Ⓐ Ⓑ Ⓒ Ⓓ Ⓔ
19 Ⓐ Ⓑ Ⓒ Ⓓ Ⓔ   44 Ⓐ Ⓑ Ⓒ Ⓓ Ⓔ   69 Ⓐ Ⓑ Ⓒ Ⓓ Ⓔ   94 Ⓐ Ⓑ Ⓒ Ⓓ Ⓔ
20 Ⓐ Ⓑ Ⓒ Ⓓ Ⓔ   45 Ⓐ Ⓑ Ⓒ Ⓓ Ⓔ   70 Ⓐ Ⓑ Ⓒ Ⓓ Ⓔ   95 Ⓐ Ⓑ Ⓒ Ⓓ Ⓔ
21 Ⓐ Ⓑ Ⓒ Ⓓ Ⓔ   46 Ⓐ Ⓑ Ⓒ Ⓓ Ⓔ   71 Ⓐ Ⓑ Ⓒ Ⓓ Ⓔ   96 Ⓐ Ⓑ Ⓒ Ⓓ Ⓔ
22 Ⓐ Ⓑ Ⓒ Ⓓ Ⓔ   47 Ⓐ Ⓑ Ⓒ Ⓓ Ⓔ   72 Ⓐ Ⓑ Ⓒ Ⓓ Ⓔ   97 Ⓐ Ⓑ Ⓒ Ⓓ Ⓔ
23 Ⓐ Ⓑ Ⓒ Ⓓ Ⓔ   48 Ⓐ Ⓑ Ⓒ Ⓓ Ⓔ   73 Ⓐ Ⓑ Ⓒ Ⓓ Ⓔ   98 Ⓐ Ⓑ Ⓒ Ⓓ Ⓔ
24 Ⓐ Ⓑ Ⓒ Ⓓ Ⓔ   49 Ⓐ Ⓑ Ⓒ Ⓓ Ⓔ   74 Ⓐ Ⓑ Ⓒ Ⓓ Ⓔ   99 Ⓐ Ⓑ Ⓒ Ⓓ Ⓔ
25 Ⓐ Ⓑ Ⓒ Ⓓ Ⓔ   50 Ⓐ Ⓑ Ⓒ Ⓓ Ⓔ   75 Ⓐ Ⓑ Ⓒ Ⓓ Ⓔ   100 Ⓐ Ⓑ Ⓒ Ⓓ Ⓔ

PLEASE MAKE SURE to fill in these fields completely and correctly. If they are not correct, we won't be able to score your test(s)!

7 TEST BOOK SERIAL NUMBER (Copy from front of test book.)

8 BOOK CODE (Copy and grid as on back of test book.)

9 BOOK ID (Copy from back of test book.)

Quality Assurance Mark ●

Chemistry *Fill in circle CE only if II is correct explanation of I.

	I	II	CE*		I	II	CE*
101	Ⓣ Ⓕ	Ⓣ Ⓕ	○	109	Ⓣ Ⓕ	Ⓣ Ⓕ	○
102	Ⓣ Ⓕ	Ⓣ Ⓕ	○	110	Ⓣ Ⓕ	Ⓣ Ⓕ	○
103	Ⓣ Ⓕ	Ⓣ Ⓕ	○	111	Ⓣ Ⓕ	Ⓣ Ⓕ	○
104	Ⓣ Ⓕ	Ⓣ Ⓕ	○	112	Ⓣ Ⓕ	Ⓣ Ⓕ	○
105	Ⓣ Ⓕ	Ⓣ Ⓕ	○	113	Ⓣ Ⓕ	Ⓣ Ⓕ	○
106	Ⓣ Ⓕ	Ⓣ Ⓕ	○	114	Ⓣ Ⓕ	Ⓣ Ⓕ	○
107	Ⓣ Ⓕ	Ⓣ Ⓕ	○	115	Ⓣ Ⓕ	Ⓣ Ⓕ	○
108	Ⓣ Ⓕ	Ⓣ Ⓕ	○				

FOR OFFICIAL USE ONLY				
R/C	W/S1	FS/S2	CS/S3	WS

CERTIFICATION STATEMENT

Copy the statement below and sign your name as you would an official document.

I hereby agree to the conditions set forth online at sat.collegeboard.org and in any paper registration materials given to me and certify that I am the person whose name, address and signature appear on this answer sheet.

Signature _____   Date _____

- ○ Literature
- ○ Biology E
- ○ Biology M
- ○ Chemistry
- ○ Physics
- ○ Mathematics Level 1
- ○ Mathematics Level 2
- ○ U.S. History
- ○ World History
- ○ French
- ○ German
- ○ Italian
- ○ Latin
- ○ Modern Hebrew
- ○ Spanish
- ○ Chinese Listening
- ○ French Listening
- ○ German Listening
- ○ Japanese Listening
- ○ Korean Listening
- ○ Spanish Listening

Background Questions: ① ② ③ ④ ⑤ ⑥ ⑦ ⑧ ⑨

PLEASE MAKE SURE to fill in these fields completely and correctly. If they are not correct, we won't be able to score your test(s)!

Quality Assurance Mark ●

#		#		#		#	
1	Ⓐ Ⓑ Ⓒ Ⓓ Ⓔ	26	Ⓐ Ⓑ Ⓒ Ⓓ Ⓔ	51	Ⓐ Ⓑ Ⓒ Ⓓ Ⓔ	76	Ⓐ Ⓑ Ⓒ Ⓓ Ⓔ
2	Ⓐ Ⓑ Ⓒ Ⓓ Ⓔ	27	Ⓐ Ⓑ Ⓒ Ⓓ Ⓔ	52	Ⓐ Ⓑ Ⓒ Ⓓ Ⓔ	77	Ⓐ Ⓑ Ⓒ Ⓓ Ⓔ
3	Ⓐ Ⓑ Ⓒ Ⓓ Ⓔ	28	Ⓐ Ⓑ Ⓒ Ⓓ Ⓔ	53	Ⓐ Ⓑ Ⓒ Ⓓ Ⓔ	78	Ⓐ Ⓑ Ⓒ Ⓓ Ⓔ
4	Ⓐ Ⓑ Ⓒ Ⓓ Ⓔ	29	Ⓐ Ⓑ Ⓒ Ⓓ Ⓔ	54	Ⓐ Ⓑ Ⓒ Ⓓ Ⓔ	79	Ⓐ Ⓑ Ⓒ Ⓓ Ⓔ
5	Ⓐ Ⓑ Ⓒ Ⓓ Ⓔ	30	Ⓐ Ⓑ Ⓒ Ⓓ Ⓔ	55	Ⓐ Ⓑ Ⓒ Ⓓ Ⓔ	80	Ⓐ Ⓑ Ⓒ Ⓓ Ⓔ
6	Ⓐ Ⓑ Ⓒ Ⓓ Ⓔ	31	Ⓐ Ⓑ Ⓒ Ⓓ Ⓔ	56	Ⓐ Ⓑ Ⓒ Ⓓ Ⓔ	81	Ⓐ Ⓑ Ⓒ Ⓓ Ⓔ
7	Ⓐ Ⓑ Ⓒ Ⓓ Ⓔ	32	Ⓐ Ⓑ Ⓒ Ⓓ Ⓔ	57	Ⓐ Ⓑ Ⓒ Ⓓ Ⓔ	82	Ⓐ Ⓑ Ⓒ Ⓓ Ⓔ
8	Ⓐ Ⓑ Ⓒ Ⓓ Ⓔ	33	Ⓐ Ⓑ Ⓒ Ⓓ Ⓔ	58	Ⓐ Ⓑ Ⓒ Ⓓ Ⓔ	83	Ⓐ Ⓑ Ⓒ Ⓓ Ⓔ
9	Ⓐ Ⓑ Ⓒ Ⓓ Ⓔ	34	Ⓐ Ⓑ Ⓒ Ⓓ Ⓔ	59	Ⓐ Ⓑ Ⓒ Ⓓ Ⓔ	84	Ⓐ Ⓑ Ⓒ Ⓓ Ⓔ
10	Ⓐ Ⓑ Ⓒ Ⓓ Ⓔ	35	Ⓐ Ⓑ Ⓒ Ⓓ Ⓔ	60	Ⓐ Ⓑ Ⓒ Ⓓ Ⓔ	85	Ⓐ Ⓑ Ⓒ Ⓓ Ⓔ
11	Ⓐ Ⓑ Ⓒ Ⓓ Ⓔ	36	Ⓐ Ⓑ Ⓒ Ⓓ Ⓔ	61	Ⓐ Ⓑ Ⓒ Ⓓ Ⓔ	86	Ⓐ Ⓑ Ⓒ Ⓓ Ⓔ
12	Ⓐ Ⓑ Ⓒ Ⓓ Ⓔ	37	Ⓐ Ⓑ Ⓒ Ⓓ Ⓔ	62	Ⓐ Ⓑ Ⓒ Ⓓ Ⓔ	87	Ⓐ Ⓑ Ⓒ Ⓓ Ⓔ
13	Ⓐ Ⓑ Ⓒ Ⓓ Ⓔ	38	Ⓐ Ⓑ Ⓒ Ⓓ Ⓔ	63	Ⓐ Ⓑ Ⓒ Ⓓ Ⓔ	88	Ⓐ Ⓑ Ⓒ Ⓓ Ⓔ
14	Ⓐ Ⓑ Ⓒ Ⓓ Ⓔ	39	Ⓐ Ⓑ Ⓒ Ⓓ Ⓔ	64	Ⓐ Ⓑ Ⓒ Ⓓ Ⓔ	89	Ⓐ Ⓑ Ⓒ Ⓓ Ⓔ
15	Ⓐ Ⓑ Ⓒ Ⓓ Ⓔ	40	Ⓐ Ⓑ Ⓒ Ⓓ Ⓔ	65	Ⓐ Ⓑ Ⓒ Ⓓ Ⓔ	90	Ⓐ Ⓑ Ⓒ Ⓓ Ⓔ
16	Ⓐ Ⓑ Ⓒ Ⓓ Ⓔ	41	Ⓐ Ⓑ Ⓒ Ⓓ Ⓔ	66	Ⓐ Ⓑ Ⓒ Ⓓ Ⓔ	91	Ⓐ Ⓑ Ⓒ Ⓓ Ⓔ
17	Ⓐ Ⓑ Ⓒ Ⓓ Ⓔ	42	Ⓐ Ⓑ Ⓒ Ⓓ Ⓔ	67	Ⓐ Ⓑ Ⓒ Ⓓ Ⓔ	92	Ⓐ Ⓑ Ⓒ Ⓓ Ⓔ
18	Ⓐ Ⓑ Ⓒ Ⓓ Ⓔ	43	Ⓐ Ⓑ Ⓒ Ⓓ Ⓔ	68	Ⓐ Ⓑ Ⓒ Ⓓ Ⓔ	93	Ⓐ Ⓑ Ⓒ Ⓓ Ⓔ
19	Ⓐ Ⓑ Ⓒ Ⓓ Ⓔ	44	Ⓐ Ⓑ Ⓒ Ⓓ Ⓔ	69	Ⓐ Ⓑ Ⓒ Ⓓ Ⓔ	94	Ⓐ Ⓑ Ⓒ Ⓓ Ⓔ
20	Ⓐ Ⓑ Ⓒ Ⓓ Ⓔ	45	Ⓐ Ⓑ Ⓒ Ⓓ Ⓔ	70	Ⓐ Ⓑ Ⓒ Ⓓ Ⓔ	95	Ⓐ Ⓑ Ⓒ Ⓓ Ⓔ
21	Ⓐ Ⓑ Ⓒ Ⓓ Ⓔ	46	Ⓐ Ⓑ Ⓒ Ⓓ Ⓔ	71	Ⓐ Ⓑ Ⓒ Ⓓ Ⓔ	96	Ⓐ Ⓑ Ⓒ Ⓓ Ⓔ
22	Ⓐ Ⓑ Ⓒ Ⓓ Ⓔ	47	Ⓐ Ⓑ Ⓒ Ⓓ Ⓔ	72	Ⓐ Ⓑ Ⓒ Ⓓ Ⓔ	97	Ⓐ Ⓑ Ⓒ Ⓓ Ⓔ
23	Ⓐ Ⓑ Ⓒ Ⓓ Ⓔ	48	Ⓐ Ⓑ Ⓒ Ⓓ Ⓔ	73	Ⓐ Ⓑ Ⓒ Ⓓ Ⓔ	98	Ⓐ Ⓑ Ⓒ Ⓓ Ⓔ
24	Ⓐ Ⓑ Ⓒ Ⓓ Ⓔ	49	Ⓐ Ⓑ Ⓒ Ⓓ Ⓔ	74	Ⓐ Ⓑ Ⓒ Ⓓ Ⓔ	99	Ⓐ Ⓑ Ⓒ Ⓓ Ⓔ
25	Ⓐ Ⓑ Ⓒ Ⓓ Ⓔ	50	Ⓐ Ⓑ Ⓒ Ⓓ Ⓔ	75	Ⓐ Ⓑ Ⓒ Ⓓ Ⓔ	100	Ⓐ Ⓑ Ⓒ Ⓓ Ⓔ

Chemistry *Fill in circle CE only if II is correct explanation of I.

	I	II	CE*		I	II	CE*
101	Ⓣ Ⓕ	Ⓣ Ⓕ	○	109	Ⓣ Ⓕ	Ⓣ Ⓕ	○
102	Ⓣ Ⓕ	Ⓣ Ⓕ	○	110	Ⓣ Ⓕ	Ⓣ Ⓕ	○
103	Ⓣ Ⓕ	Ⓣ Ⓕ	○	111	Ⓣ Ⓕ	Ⓣ Ⓕ	○
104	Ⓣ Ⓕ	Ⓣ Ⓕ	○	112	Ⓣ Ⓕ	Ⓣ Ⓕ	○
105	Ⓣ Ⓕ	Ⓣ Ⓕ	○	113	Ⓣ Ⓕ	Ⓣ Ⓕ	○
106	Ⓣ Ⓕ	Ⓣ Ⓕ	○	114	Ⓣ Ⓕ	Ⓣ Ⓕ	○
107	Ⓣ Ⓕ	Ⓣ Ⓕ	○	115	Ⓣ Ⓕ	Ⓣ Ⓕ	○
108	Ⓣ Ⓕ	Ⓣ Ⓕ	○				

8 BOOK CODE (Copy and grid as on back of test book.)

⓪	Ⓐ	⓪
①	Ⓑ	①
②	Ⓒ	②
③	Ⓓ	③
④	Ⓔ	④
⑤	Ⓕ	⑤
⑥	Ⓖ	⑥
⑦	Ⓗ	⑦
⑧	Ⓘ	⑧
⑨	Ⓙ	⑨
	Ⓚ	
	Ⓛ	
	Ⓜ	
	Ⓝ	
	Ⓞ	
	Ⓟ	
	Ⓠ	
	Ⓡ	
	Ⓢ	
	Ⓣ	
	Ⓤ	
	Ⓥ	
	Ⓦ	
	Ⓧ	
	Ⓨ	
	Ⓩ	

7 TEST BOOK SERIAL NUMBER (Copy from front of test book.)

0	0	0	0	0	0
1	1	1	1	1	1
2	2	2	2	2	2
3	3	3	3	3	3
4	4	4	4	4	4
5	5	5	5	5	5
6	6	6	6	6	6
7	7	7	7	7	7
8	8	8	8	8	8
9	9	9	9	9	9

9 BOOK ID (Copy from back of test book.)

FOR OFFICIAL USE ONLY				
R/C	W/S1	FS/S2	CS/S3	WS

○ Literature
○ Biology E
○ Biology M
○ Chemistry
○ Physics

○ Mathematics Level 1
○ Mathematics Level 2
○ U.S. History
○ World History
○ French

○ German
○ Italian
○ Latin
○ Modern Hebrew
○ Spanish

○ Chinese Listening
○ French Listening
○ German Listening

○ Japanese Listening
○ Korean Listening
○ Spanish Listening

Background Questions: ① ② ③ ④ ⑤ ⑥ ⑦ ⑧ ⑨

1–100: (A) (B) (C) (D) (E)

PLEASE MAKE SURE to fill in these fields completely and correctly. If they are not correct, we won't be able to score your test(s)!

7 TEST BOOK SERIAL NUMBER
(Copy from front of test book.)
0 1 2 3 4 5 6 7 8 9 (per column)

8 BOOK CODE
(Copy and grid as on back of test book.)
0–9, A–Z

9 BOOK ID
(Copy from back of test book.)

Quality Assurance Mark ●

Chemistry *Fill in circle CE only if II is correct explanation of I.

	I	II	CE*		I	II	CE*
101	(T)(F)	(T)(F)	○	109	(T)(F)	(T)(F)	○
102	(T)(F)	(T)(F)	○	110	(T)(F)	(T)(F)	○
103	(T)(F)	(T)(F)	○	111	(T)(F)	(T)(F)	○
104	(T)(F)	(T)(F)	○	112	(T)(F)	(T)(F)	○
105	(T)(F)	(T)(F)	○	113	(T)(F)	(T)(F)	○
106	(T)(F)	(T)(F)	○	114	(T)(F)	(T)(F)	○
107	(T)(F)	(T)(F)	○	115	(T)(F)	(T)(F)	○
108	(T)(F)	(T)(F)	○				

FOR OFFICIAL USE ONLY				
R/C	W/S1	FS/S2	CS/S3	WS

Page 4

PLEASE DO NOT WRITE IN THIS AREA

SERIAL #

SAT Subject Tests™

COMPLETE MARK ● **EXAMPLES OF INCOMPLETE MARKS** Ⓐ Ⓧ Ⓒ Ⓓ Ⓔ Ⓕ

You must use a No. 2 pencil and marks must be complete. Do not use a mechanical pencil. It is very important that you fill in the entire circle darkly and completely. If you change your response, erase as completely as possible. Incomplete marks or erasures may affect your score.

1 **Your Name:**
(Print)

Last _____ First _____ M.I. ____

I agree to the conditions on the front and back of the SAT Subject Tests™ book. I also agree with the SAT Test Security and Fairness policies and understand that any violation of these policies will result in score cancellation and may result in reporting of certain violations to law enforcement.

Signature: _____ Today's Date: ___/___/___
                                              MM DD YY

Home Address: _____
(Print)   Number and Street   City   State/Country   Zip Code

Phone: (   ) _____ **Test Center:** _____
                              (Print)   City   State/Country

2 **YOUR NAME**

Last Name (First 6 Letters) / First Name (First 4 Letters) / Mid. Init.

3 **DATE OF BIRTH**

MONTH	DAY	YEAR
Jan Feb Mar Apr May Jun Jul Aug Sep Oct Nov Dec		

4 **REGISTRATION NUMBER**
(Copy from Admission Ticket.)

Important: Fill in items 8 and 9 exactly as shown on the back of test book.

7 **TEST BOOK SERIAL NUMBER**
(Copy from front of test book.)

8 **BOOK CODE**
(Copy and grid as on back of test book.)

9 **BOOK ID**
(Copy from back of test book.)

PLEASE MAKE SURE to fill in these fields completely and correctly. If they are not correct, we won't be able to score your test(s)!

5 **ZIP CODE**

6 **TEST CENTER**
(Supplied by Test Center Supervisor.)

FOR OFFICIAL USE ONLY

103648-77191 • NS1114C1085 • Printed in U.S.A.

194415-001   1 2 3 4 5 A B C D E   Printed in the USA   ISD11312

783175

PLEASE DO NOT WRITE IN THIS AREA

SERIAL #

COMPLETE MARK ● EXAMPLES OF INCOMPLETE MARKS Ⓐ Ⓧ Ⓔ Ⓓ / Ⓒ

You must use a No. 2 pencil and marks must be complete. Do not use a mechanical pencil. *It is very important that you fill in the entire circle darkly and completely. If you change your response, erase as completely as possible. Incomplete marks or erasures may affect your score.*

- ○ Literature
- ○ Biology E
- ○ Biology M
- ○ Chemistry
- ○ Physics
- ○ Mathematics Level 1
- ○ Mathematics Level 2
- ○ U.S. History
- ○ World History
- ○ French
- ○ German
- ○ Italian
- ○ Latin
- ○ Modern Hebrew
- ○ Spanish
- ○ Chinese Listening
- ○ French Listening
- ○ German Listening
- ○ Japanese Listening
- ○ Korean Listening
- ○ Spanish Listening

Background Questions: ① ② ③ ④ ⑤ ⑥ ⑦ ⑧ ⑨

PLEASE MAKE SURE to fill in these fields completely and correctly. If they are not correct, we won't be able to score your test(s)!

Questions 1–100: A B C D E

7 TEST BOOK SERIAL NUMBER (Copy from front of test book.)

8 BOOK CODE (Copy and grid as on back of test book.)

9 BOOK ID (Copy from back of test book.)

Quality Assurance Mark

Chemistry *Fill in circle CE only if II is correct explanation of I.

Questions 101–115: I (T F) II (T F) CE*

FOR OFFICIAL USE ONLY
R/C W/S1 FS/S2 CS/S3 WS

CERTIFICATION STATEMENT Copy the statement below and sign your name as you would an official document.

I hereby agree to the conditions set forth online at sat.collegeboard.org and in any paper registration materials given to me and certify that I am the person whose name, address and signature appear on this answer sheet.

Signature _____ Date _____

Page 2

You must use a No. 2 pencil and marks must be complete. Do not use a mechanical pencil. *It is very important that you fill in the entire circle darkly and completely. If you change your response, erase as completely as possible. Incomplete marks or erasures may affect your score.*

- ○ Literature
- ○ Biology E
- ○ Biology M
- ○ Chemistry
- ○ Physics
- ○ Mathematics Level 1
- ○ Mathematics Level 2
- ○ U.S. History
- ○ World History
- ○ French
- ○ German
- ○ Italian
- ○ Latin
- ○ Modern Hebrew
- ○ Spanish
- ○ Chinese Listening
- ○ French Listening
- ○ German Listening
- ○ Japanese Listening
- ○ Korean Listening
- ○ Spanish Listening

Background Questions: ① ② ③ ④ ⑤ ⑥ ⑦ ⑧ ⑨

PLEASE MAKE SURE to fill in these fields completely and correctly. If they are not correct, we won't be able to score your test(s)!

Quality Assurance Mark ●

(Answer grid, questions 1–100, each with options A B C D E)

7 TEST BOOK SERIAL NUMBER (Copy from front of test book.)

8 BOOK CODE (Copy and grid as on back of test book.)

9 BOOK ID (Copy from back of test book.)

Chemistry *Fill in circle CE only if II is correct explanation of I.

	I	II	CE*		I	II	CE*
101	T F	T F	○	109	T F	T F	○
102	T F	T F	○	110	T F	T F	○
103	T F	T F	○	111	T F	T F	○
104	T F	T F	○	112	T F	T F	○
105	T F	T F	○	113	T F	T F	○
106	T F	T F	○	114	T F	T F	○
107	T F	T F	○	115	T F	T F	○
108	T F	T F	○				

FOR OFFICIAL USE ONLY				
R/C	W/S1	FS/S2	CS/S3	WS

- ○ Literature
- ○ Biology E
- ○ Biology M
- ○ Chemistry
- ○ Physics
- ○ Mathematics Level 1
- ○ Mathematics Level 2
- ○ U.S. History
- ○ World History
- ○ French
- ○ German
- ○ Italian
- ○ Latin
- ○ Modern Hebrew
- ○ Spanish
- ○ Chinese Listening
- ○ French Listening
- ○ German Listening
- ○ Japanese Listening
- ○ Korean Listening
- ○ Spanish Listening

Background Questions: ① ② ③ ④ ⑤ ⑥ ⑦ ⑧ ⑨

PLEASE MAKE SURE to fill in these fields completely and correctly. If they are not correct, we won't be able to score your test(s)!

1–100: Answer grid with options Ⓐ Ⓑ Ⓒ Ⓓ Ⓔ for each numbered question.

7 TEST BOOK SERIAL NUMBER (Copy from front of test book.)

8 BOOK CODE (Copy and grid as on back of test book.)

9 BOOK ID (Copy from back of test book.)

Quality Assurance Mark

Chemistry *Fill in circle CE only if II is correct explanation of I.

	I	II	CE*		I	II	CE*
101	T F	T F	○	109	T F	T F	○
102	T F	T F	○	110	T F	T F	○
103	T F	T F	○	111	T F	T F	○
104	T F	T F	○	112	T F	T F	○
105	T F	T F	○	113	T F	T F	○
106	T F	T F	○	114	T F	T F	○
107	T F	T F	○	115	T F	T F	○
108	T F	T F	○				

FOR OFFICIAL USE ONLY

R/C	W/S1	FS/S2	CS/S3	WS

Page 4

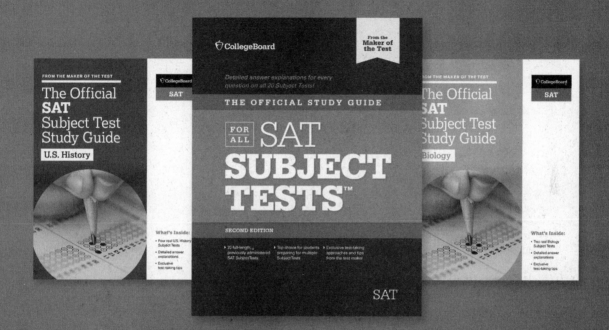

Show up ready on test day.

Watch **free** online lessons
for science from Khan Academy®.

satsubjecttests.org/biology
satsubjecttests.org/chemistry
satsubjecttests.org/physics

There are over 100 videos to watch covering
a variety of science topics. These lessons are
great refreshers to help you get ready for the
science Subject Tests in Biology, Chemistry,
and Physics.

Disclaimer: Playlists were created based on videos available on Khan Academy.
Content is subject to change in the future.

 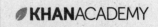